ONCE UPON
A TIME IN ITALY

ONCE UPON A TIME IN ITALY

THE WESTERNS OF SERGIO LEONE

BY CHRISTOPHER FRAYLING

Harry N. Abrams, Inc., Publishers,
in association with the Autry National Center

EDITOR: Holly George-Warren
PROJECT MANAGER: Deborah Aaronson
DESIGN: Project Projects
PRODUCTION MANAGER: Maria Pia Gramaglia

LIBRARY OF CONGRESS CATALOGING-IN-PUBLICATION DATA:
Frayling, Christopher.
   Once upon a time in Italy : the westerns of Sergio Leone / by Christopher
   Frayling ; edited by Holly George-Warren.
      p. cm.
Accompanies an exhibition to be held July 31, 2005-January 22, 2006 at the
   Institute for the Study of the American West, Autry National Center,
   Los Angeles.
Includes an index.
ISBN 0-8109-5884-8 (alk. paper)
1. Leone, Sergio, 1929—Criticism and interpretation. 2. Western films—Italy—
   History and criticism. I. George-Warren, Holly. II. Autry National Center.
   Institute for the Study of the American West. III. Title.
PN1998.3.L463F68 2005
791.4302'33'092—dc22

                                        2004026343

Printed and bound in China
10 9 8 7 6 5 4 3 2 1

Harry N. Abrams, Inc.
100 Fifth Avenue
New York, N.Y. 10011
www.abramsbooks.com

Abrams is a subsidiary of LA MARTINIÈRE

INTRODUCTION

F. FIORENZI
CLINT
EASTWOOD
SERGIO LEONE
PRODUZIONE e DISTRIBUZIONE
PEA
PER QUALCHE DOLLARO IN PIÙ
LEE VAN CLEEF · GIAN MARIA VOLONTÈ
MARA KRUP LUIGI PISTILLI KLAUS KINSKI JOSEF EGGER PANOS PAPADOPULOS BENITO STEFANELLI ROBERT CAMARDIEL ALDO SAMBRELL LUIS RODRIGUEZ e MARIO BREGA
TECHNICOLOR · TECHNISCOPE
MUSICHE DI ENNIO MORRICONE
SCENEGGIATURA E DIALOGHI DI LUCIANO VINCENZONI

LEONE'S WEST: FINDING THE FAIRY TALE

ESTELLA CHUNG

Long-time Sergio Leone fans, the ones who got their start in the 1960s, passionately recount their recent home viewing of Leone DVDs with as much enthusiasm and thoughtfulness as perhaps the very first time they saw Clint Eastwood as the Man With No Name. New fans learn of Leone at film-school screenings, through words of admiration from directors of today's art films and summer blockbusters, or by channel surfing onto *The Good, the Bad and the Ugly*, only to stay glued to the television for more than two-and-a-half hours. This publication and the exhibition it accompanies, *Once Upon a Time in Italy: The Westerns of Sergio Leone,* examines Leone's Westerns – *A Fistful of Dollars*; *For a Few Dollars More*; *The Good, the Bad and the Ugly*; *Once Upon a Time in the West*; *Duck, You Sucker*; *My Name Is Nobody* (the one he produced) – and their cinematic legacy. In organizing *Once Upon a Time in Italy*, we talked with these fans (both old and new). They wanted to know what documentation of Leone's West remains more than forty years after the release of *A Fistful of Dollars*.

Too often, oral histories and materials from film productions are lost. Fortunately, this was not the case with Leone's work. To mount *Once Upon a Time in Italy*, one of the largest exhibitions ever on a single director, the Autry National Center's Museum of the American West sought out the late Sergio Leone's associates and their families. Mrs. Carla Leone, Sergio's widow, remembers author and professor Sir Christopher Frayling as the first film historian to knock on the door. More than two decades after his 1982 visit with Sergio Leone, Professor Frayling, the guest scholar and co-curator of *Once Upon a Time in Italy*, provided this volume with not only Leone's words but also those of his colleagues, some of whom are – like Leone – no longer with us. Professor Frayling's essays and interviews give diverse points of view on the ideas and collaborations that created the films and the objects presented in the exhibition – artifacts from Leone's "fairy tales for grown-ups."

Where are the pieces of Leone's fairy tales – the treasures of cinematic history that helped create El Paso, Sweetwater, Tuco, and Jill McBain? We uncovered artifacts of Leone's West from private and institutional collections stretching from small Italian towns to urban Los Angeles neighborhoods. Film professionals who worked with Sergio held on to props, costumes, sketches, and scripts. In seeking out these artifacts, we crisscrossed metropolitan Rome, passing the Colosseum and a graveyard of chariots from the "sword and sandal" productions, to reach the private homes and businesses of those who own the objects reviewed or touched by Leone. In Italy, whether in Rome or the outskirts of Milan, our meetings usually began with an espresso in a sitting room. As soon as we explained the scope of our project, our hosts were on their

Opposite: **A brutal-looking Clint Eastwood in the Italian poster for Sergio Leone's second Western,** *For a Few Dollars More*

feet. We were given privileged tours of private collections interpreted by first-hand experience or recalled from cherished family oral histories.

The personal and career mementos in *Once Upon a Time in Italy* have come from bedroom walls, stacks of carefully labeled binders, corners of home offices, warehouses of filmmaking supplies, locked boxes, special shelves of prized family heirlooms, and other, less glamorous, storage facilities for precious objects too cumbersome for an Italian closet. Other lenders, inspired by the idea of a museum exhibition on Leone and his work, initiated impromptu excavations of infrequently visited storage spaces.

The unearthing of artifacts continued into the realm of collectors. With pride and delight, these Leone aficionados deinstalled stunning Italian *fotobustas, foglios,* and oversized posters from living room and hallway exhibitions. A sneering Clint Eastwood, a neon Charles Bronson, and multiple Claudia Cardinales remind us of film distributors' early efforts to woo audiences around the world. Courted and committed, members of those first audiences became die-hard fans who preserved the posters, ensuring that enjoyment of Leone's West would not be ephemeral.

And yet, originally, none of the materials in our exhibition were meant to last. The production sketches were drawn to work out the visual environments, the costumes were designed to fit and help create complex characters, and the props were utilized by actors to move the story forward. The fortunate survival of these artifacts permits us to see the behind-the-scenes and onscreen construction of Sergio Leone's fairy tales.

Fans describe favorite elements of Leone's West with vigor and excitement. And it is the appreciation of those elements comprising the whole that fueled the concept behind *Once Upon a Time in Italy*: to furnish an opportunity to experience Leone's fairy tales in a new way, detail by detail. To accomplish this, we provide listening stations to isolate composer Ennio Morricone's musical themes and leitmotifs. We display production designer Carlo Simi's pencil sketch for the Langstone Bridge from *The Good, the Bad and the Ugly* so that his line quality can be seen up-close. On large video screens, we compare clips of 1940s and 1950s Westerns with scenes from *Once Upon a Time in the West,* revealing Leone's filmic references to earlier celluloid Wests.

When we visited those who worked with Leone, they often commented that Leone's Westerns were made much earlier in their careers – for them, a distant but highly prized past. They wondered about the place organizing such an exhibition. We explained that the Museum of the American West is interested in the intersection between history, culture, and myth: With our permanent collection representing the West in film, television, live performance, radio, and fiction, we felt it was time that the museum seek out Sergio Leone,

EURO INTERNATIONAL FILMS presenta
CLAUDIA CARDINALE
HENRY FONDA in JASON ROBARDS
"C'ERA UNA VOLTA IL WEST"

C'ERA UNA VOLTA IL WEST

con CHARLES BRONSON nel ruolo di "Armonica"
GABRIELE FERZETTI · PAOLO STOPPA
JACK ELAM · LIONEL STANDER
WOODY STRODE · FRANK WOLFF
KEENAN WYNN
regia di
SERGIO LEONE
prodotto da
BINO CICOGNA
produttore esecutivo
FULVIO MORSELLA
una produzione RAFRAN · S. MARCO
TECHNICOLOR · TECHNI

to explore this Italian filmmaker's interpretation of the American West and to examine how the films Leone loved culminated in his "cinema cinema" Westerns.

After this explanation of our objectives, those who knew Leone smiled, exclaiming that they would have never suspected, so many years ago, that a Los Angeles–based museum would come looking for objects associated with their work in Leone's Westerns – and that so many years later they would have something to offer.

ESTELLA CHUNG
LOS ANGELES, AUGUST 2004

Estella Chung is associate curator of popular culture at the Autry National Center's Museum of the American West, in Los Angeles, and co-curator of the exhibition Once Upon a Time in Italy: The Westerns of Sergio Leone.

This page: **A radiant Claudia Cardinale as Jill McBain in an Italian poster for *Once Upon a Time in the West***

SERGIO LEONE AND THE WESTERN

SERGIO LEONE
AND THE WESTERN

Sergio Leone once said, "I grew up in the cinema, almost. Both my parents worked there. My life, my reading, everything about me revolves around the cinema. So for me, cinema is life, and vice versa." Born in Rome on January 3, 1929, he spent most of his childhood in that city's Trastevere district. He first wandered onto a soundstage at Cinecittà studios in 1941, at the age of twelve, to watch his father, Vincenzo Leone, shooting a film. Vincenzo, who had adopted the stage name of Roberto Roberti, had been the artistic director of numerous silent films – including a Maciste muscleman thriller in 1918 and a series of melodramas with diva Francesca Bertini. After falling out with Mussolini's Institute of Enlightenment, Vincenzo (a lifelong socialist) was out of work throughout the 1930s when young Sergio was growing up. Leone's mother, Edvige, who had adopted the stage name of Bice Walerian, was an actress who appeared as a Native American princess in the first Italian Western film of note – *La Vampira Indiana* (1913), which opened three years after the premiere of Puccini's opera *The Girl of the Golden West* at the New York Metropolitan Opera. She retired from acting shortly before Sergio, her only child, was born.

Sixty years later, on April 30, 1989, Sergio Leone died of heart failure while watching a film on television in his villa in the EUR district of Rome: The film was Robert Wise's *I Want to Live!* As a child growing up during a time of fascist repression, he had – like many interwar Italians – viewed America as a model of freedom, a glimpse of modernity and promise. All his mature films are about the peculiar strength of American cinematic myths, and how they are at odds with the reality of adult experience. He called his work "fairy tales for grown-ups"; the films offered a way of recapturing the sense of awe he felt when he first went to the cinema in Trastevere to watch Hollywood movies – dubbed into Italian as was the law. Leone's first encounter with real-life Americans, on the other hand, was in the form of GIs advancing north from Salerno by jeep in 1943–45, when he was fourteen years old: "They had come to liberate me! I found them very energetic, but also very deceptive. They were no longer the Americans of the West." He never forgot the experience. "They were soldiers like any others," he later recalled, "with the sole difference that they were *victorious* soldiers . . . In the GIs who chased after our women and sold their cigarettes on the black market, I could see . . . nothing – or almost nothing – of the great prairies and the demigods of my childhood."

In 1946, Leone entered the film industry, against his father's advice but with help from his extensive network of contacts. Having made brief appearances in a couple of Vincenzo's films, Sergio became an unpaid assistant on Vittorio De Sica's 1946 film, *The Bicycle Thief*, in which he also played the nonspeaking role of a priest. Between *La Traviata* (1947) and *The Last Days*

Opposite: **Little Sergio with his father, Vincenzo Leone, mid-1930s**

Above: **Sergio Leone in his early twenties**

Top: **Leone (center) on the set of *The Colossus of Rhodes*, the "sword and sandal" picture, with star Rory Calhoun as Dario (at right).**

Middle: **Leone directs Calhoun in the earthquake sequence of *The Colossus of Rhodes*, 1960.**

Bottom: **Leone was known for miming the action to his players; here, he demonstrates the effects of a spear in the back, for the arena sequence of *The Colossus of Rhodes*, 1960.**

of Pompeii and *Gastone* (1959), Leone served a long apprenticeship, mainly in Rome, as an assistant director on about thirty-five feature films. Most of these were Italian or French productions – one of them directed by his godfather, Mario Camerini, six by Carmine Gallone, nine by his patron Mario Bonnard. Some of them – *Quo Vadis, Helen of Troy, The Nun's Story, Ben-Hur* – were American blockbusters financed by frozen dollars during the era of "Hollywood on the Tiber" (as styled by Federico Fellini), the era of economic miracles. Leone said that he gleaned from this lengthy experience an obsession with the documentary surface of Italian neorealism (which made films believable), a fascination with the logistics of big-budget action sequences, a repertoire of techniques, and a determination to avoid the waste of Hollywood superproductions. The efficiency of the Italian medium – budget filmmaking – strongly appealed to him.

During this apprenticeship period, Leone first worked with some members of what was to become his own creative team: director of photography Tonino Delli Colli, editor Nino Baragli, writer Luciano Vincenzoni. Critics of his work, and of the Italian Western in general, would later claim that Leone and other key directors' experiences of Hollywood second-unit work – or its equivalent – led them to focus on action sequences to the point where dialogue scarcely mattered anymore.

Leone's debut opportunity to direct came with *The Last Days of Pompeii* and *Gastone* – in both cases standing in for the veteran Mario Bonnard. His first full-fledged film was *The Colossus of Rhodes*, in which he pitted a laconic American hero (Rory Calhoun) against the theatrical performances of flamboyant Italian and Spanish actors and lifted the action climax from the Mount Rushmore sequences of *North by Northwest*. The Rory Calhoun character, like Cary Grant's character in the Hitchcock film, finds himself in someone else's adventure story; the Colossus, one of the seven wonders of the ancient world, becomes in this version a political prison. The film was released in 1961, toward the end of the Italian craze for "sword and sandal" movies, which usually featured a bodybuilder as hero (but in this case did not).

After an unfortunate backward career step, directing the second unit of Robert Aldrich's *Sodom and Gomorrah* – Leone was in charge of the large-scale sequences, filmed south of Marrakech, that involved the charging cavalry of the fierce and nomadic Helamite tribe – there was a fallow period in Leone's career, as there was between 1962 and 1964 among most Italian film people. Then in 1964, having been very impressed by Akira Kurosawa's *Yojimbo*, Leone directed *A Fistful of Dollars*. It was shot in Rome, near Madrid, and in Almería, under very difficult circumstances – with secondhand sets, the budget of a C movie, and money crossing borders in suitcases. But the unexpected

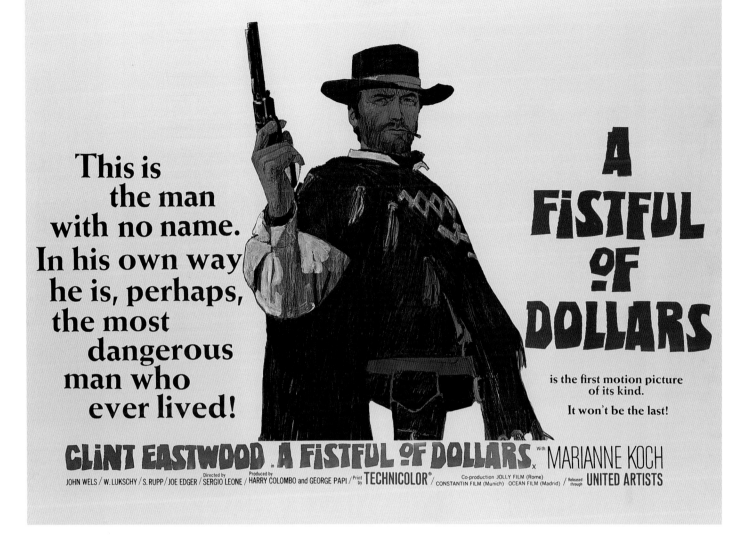

This is
the man
with no name.
In his own way
he is, perhaps,
the most
dangerous
man who
ever lived!

A
FISTFUL
OF
DOLLARS

is the first motion picture
of its kind.

It won't be the last!

CLINT EASTWOOD in A FISTFUL OF DOLLARS x with MARIANNE KOCH

JOHN WELS / W. LUKSCHY / S. RUPP / JOE EDGER / Directed by SERGIO LEONE / Produced by HARRY COLOMBO and GEORGE PAPI / Print by TECHNICOLOR® / Co-production JOLLY FILM (Rome) CONSTANTIN FILM (Munich) OCEAN FILM (Madrid) / Released through UNITED ARTISTS

Above: The poster
that alerted U.S.
moviegoers that a
new type of Western
was on the horizon

box-office success of *A Fistful of Dollars* turned the Western into a new kind of fairy tale: brutal and realistic on the surface but mythic at the core, with a distinctive blend of grungy close-ups and exaggerated spectacle. It also launched Leone's fruitful creative partnership with composer Ennio Morricone (who turned out to have been in elementary school with Leone) and production designer Carlo Simi, and made Clint Eastwood into a superstar in Europe. With Leone's subsequent films and their steeply rising budgets, the director's earthy sense of humor, elliptical way of telling stories, and celebration/deconstruction of Hollywood codes were to become more and more sophisticated. In European cinema of the early 1960s, it had become fashionable to make "films about films," but the results tended to be restricted to the art-house circuit and international festivals. Leone was the first modern *cinéaste* to make seriously popular films – films that remained to a surprising extent personal, incorporating his childhood and wartime memories as well as citations of moments in his favorite films. He called this approach "cinema cinema." In the words of the social philosopher Jean Baudrillard, Sergio Leone was "the first postmodernist film director."

When they were released, from 1967 onward, Leone's three *Dollars* films proved to be just as popular in America as they had been in Italy and

**THE MAN WITH NO NAME IS BACK!
THE MAN IN BLACK IS WAITING...**

It's the second
motion picture of its kind!
It won't be the last!

Western Europe. The delay was due to copyright problems over *Yojimbo*. With *For a Few Dollars More* (1965) and *The Good, the Bad and the Ugly* (1966), Leone kept ahead of what he called the "crazy gold rush" of Italian Westerns by at last getting into his stylistic stride. At the time, most critics of Leone's films complained that they "lacked the true spirit of the Western," which, of course, was their purpose. Italian novelist Alberto Moravia, in an influential review, more accurately wrote that "the Italianization of the Western is complete." Part of this "Italianization" was supplied by scriptwriters Luciano Vincenzoni and Sergio Donati. There was a Mediterranean, carnival atmosphere to Leone's films, with, as the cycle progressed, more humor *and* more historical detail. Such Hollywood actors as Clint Eastwood, Lee Van Cleef, and Eli Wallach shared the credits with Italian and Spanish performers.

Then, in 1968, Leone changed direction with *Once Upon a Time in the West*, a brilliantly choreographed elegy (all the main musical themes on the soundtrack were written in advance) for the golden age of American fairy tales – destroyed by historical reality. It was a labor of love. A pair from a younger generation of cinéastes, Bernardo Bertolucci and Dario Argento, helped Leone with the original treatment, which was turned into a detailed, lengthy script by Sergio Donati. At last, Leone was able to cast Henry Fonda – he'd been trying to achieve this since *A Fistful of Dollars* – as well as Charles Bronson. Unusually, the central character was a woman, played by Claudia Cardinale. *Once Upon a Time in the West* was successful in much of Europe, but a disaster in the United States until it was reappraised in the 1970s by up-and-coming critics and filmmakers.

Duck, You Sucker/A Fistful of Dynamite (1971) was a late reaction against idealistic Italian "political" Westerns set in the Mexican Revolution, as well as Leone's statement of his own disillusionment with politics. It included a more subtle human relationship than before, between the bandit Juan (Rod Steiger) and the cynical revolutionary Sean (James Coburn), which develops throughout the course of the story. Leone, however, was not entirely happy with the result: He had hoped to produce *Duck, You Sucker* while supervising an American director.

There followed a ten-year period of working as a producer (starting with Tonino Valerii's *My Name Is Nobody*), making television commercials, helping the comedian Carlo Verdone launch his film career, and preparing the gangster epic *Once Upon a Time in America* (1984). Upon its completion, it did for the gangster film what *Once Upon a Time in the West* had done for the Western: Its gangsters are Jewish (of Eastern European descent), not Hollywood's Italians; the historical periods shift cleverly from the 1920s to the 1960s; and it is a much darker, more melancholy film than *West*. But the difficulties in releasing

Opposite: **The follow-up to *Fistful* quickly arrived in the states, as the advertising emphasized.**

Above: **A studio
portrait of Sergio
Leone taken to
commemorate his
first communion**

Opposite: **The earliest
Italian poster for the
brilliantly titled third
Leone Western**

Once Upon a Time in America hastened Leone's final illness. When he died,
he was planning an even bigger film – about the 1941–44 siege of Leningrad
by the Nazis – with the inspiration of Shostakovich's Seventh Symphony
and the assistance of the Soviet army. The opening sequence alone would have
involved rebuilding Leningrad (now St. Petersburg), filling the city with 1941
artifacts, and having a Panzer tank division opening fire from the opposite
bank of a sizable river – all to the accompaniment of Shostakovich.

Leone's influence on contemporary cinema – on the modern action
hero, films about films, ironic fairy tales, the interplay of music and image,
and on sound design – has been profound, even though he only directed
six "personal" films. And yet he has always proved difficult for critics
to categorize: art films/popular films; personal films/genre films; tragedies/
comedies; American myths/Italian stories; Hollywood/Cinecittà. Because
of this confusion, he has been seriously underrated. He is one of the finest
storytellers the cinema has ever produced.

Leone once said his first experience of American film was "around 1939,
when I was nine or ten," when he and his friends would go to the Trastevere
cinema where "we would model ourselves on the heroes of the films we'd seen.
We were madly in love with American cinema, always imitating Errol Flynn
and Gary Cooper."

Italian films, especially propaganda films released by Mussolini's Institute
of Enlightenment and glossy "white telephone" comedies, were not nearly
so attractive to Leone and his gang. Hollywood films – and bootleg comics –
represented something of an escape from the straitjacket of reality in fascist
Rome. The philosopher Umberto Eco theorizes that the special fascination held
by Italians – especially in artistic and intellectual circles – for American pop
culture of the 1950s and 1960s had a great deal to do with their experience of
films, comics, and popular music during the fascist era, and of the huge backlog
of Hollywood cinema disgorged shortly afterward. These cultural products
represented forbidden fruit, the "other world"; and this made the ideology they
represented seem doubly attractive. They were a rejection of official culture,
which seemed to have had most of the life squeezed out of it.

The young Leone's love affair with Hollywood films and American
comics – he couldn't read English, but the graphics looked so much more
stylish – occurred within this kind of atmosphere: the projection onto another
world of all that was positive about modernity. Some of the earliest films he
remembered seeing were John Ford's *Stagecoach*, Michael Curtiz's *Angels
With Dirty Faces* starring James Cagney, and Charlie Chaplin's *Modern Times*.
Amazingly, the latter made it through the censor's office because it was
thought to be "a ferocious satire on socialism and communism." Immediately

F. FIORENZI

PRESENTA UN FILM DI
SERGIO LEONE

**CLINT EASTWOOD
ELI WALLACH
LEE VAN CLEEF**
in
**IL BUONO
IL BRUTTO IL CATTIVO**

**TECHNICOLOR
TECHNISCOPE**

Vecchioni & Guadagno - Via del Conte de Marolis, 8 - November 1966

IL BUONO, IL BRUTTO, IL CATTIVO.

ALDO GIUFFRE' ANTONIO CASAS · RADA RASSIMOV · ALDO SAMBREL   AL MULLOCH · SERGIO MENDIZABAL · MOLINO ROJO · LORENZO ROBLEDO · con MARIO BREGA
MUSICHE DI ENNIO MORRICONE   PRODOTTO DA ALBERTO GRIMALDI PER LA P.E.A. PRODUZIONI EUROPEE ASSOCIATE

EURO INTERNATIONAL FILMS PRESENTA

GIU' LA TESTA

ROD STEIGER · JAMES COBURN · ROMOLO VALLI in
GIU' LA TESTA
CON MARIA MONTI · RICK BATTAGLIA · FRANCO GRAZIOSI · DOMINGO ANTOIN

MUSICA COMPOSTA E DIRETTA DAL MAESTRO ENNIO MORRICONE REGIA DI SERGIO LEONE TECHNICOLOR · TECHN

Previous spread: **An Italian *fotobusta* for *Duck, You Sucker***

Above: **On the set with Peggy Ashcroft of the Fred Zinnemann film, *The Nun's Story*, for which Leone served as an assistant director in 1958**

Opposite: **Leone checking out a location in Morocco, on Robert Aldrich's *Sodom and Gomorrah*, for which he was second-unit director**

after World War II, Leone, too, remembered "the period of great indigestion – a time when dreams at last seemed to come true for Roman adolescents, the great return of the American cinema" (at the end of an official boycott, which had been imposed in 1941).

When he was nineteen years old, Sergio Leone wrote his first screenplay, for an autobiographical rite-of-passage movie called *Viale Glorioso* – after the street where his gang used to hang out – about his life in the late 1930s. It was not until the mid-1960s, just after completing *A Fistful of Dollars*, that Leone finally abandoned the idea of turning *Viale Glorioso* into a film: "Alas! Someone had already had the same idea and had already made an excellent film of it – Federico Fellini's *I Vitelloni*." Fellini's 1953 film concerned the listless lives of a group of five youths in the seaside town of Rimini: posing in the streets, lounging in the local café, visiting the music hall and the *palais de danse*, walking to the pier, picking up girls, and, of course, going to the cinema. Eventually, the Fellini figure, Moraldo, leaves Rimini to try his luck in Rome. The contrast between the deadening routines of everyday life in the provinces and the distractions of "the spectacle" is at the heart of Fellini's film. Leone's *Viale Glorioso* would have been about a similar contrast, but set in a darker time. The screenplay included a visit to see the *pupi siciliani* (Sicilian rod puppets) performing in a Roman park, childhood games in the street, under-the-counter American comics, and afternoon visits to the cinema.

Even after he had abandoned the project, fragments from *Viale Glorioso* kept turning up in his films. The opening of *Duck, You Sucker/A Fistful of*

Dynamite was based on a childhood memory about a urination contest down a flight of stone steps in Trastevere, while the scene where Rod Steiger thinks he is robbing a bank but is in fact releasing political prisoners was based on Charlie Chaplin picking up the red flag in *Modern Times*. *The Good, the Bad and the Ugly* reprises the old Buster Keaton gag from *Our Hospitality*, where a steam train cuts through the rope attaching Willie McKay (Keaton) to the bad guy. In addition, the film's Battle of Langstone Bridge is a reference to *The General*, where a reckless Union officer sends the locomotive to its doom across a burning bridge. In *Once Upon a Time in the West*, the Monument Valley scenes featuring Jill (Claudia Cardinale) with buggy driver Sam (Paolo Stoppa) and the heap-of-bones horse Lafayette were based on an incident that took place in famine-stricken Naples in 1941, when Leone was twelve and went for a harrowing carriage ride with his father.

Viale Glorioso was about a love affair – a love affair with cinema, hinging on the contrast between the richness and coherence of the onscreen world and the confusion and incoherence of the world outside the picture palace. As Sergio Leone said to me, "One of the first loves of Italians who grew up in the 1930s was America. Like all first loves, it may well be seen from a different point of view after the event, but it is never forgotten. And that was given to us by Hollywood, especially the epic of the West."

By the time Leone had decided to abandon *Viale Glorioso*, he had been working in the film business, off and on, for eighteen years. As an assistant director in the 1950s he had worked with some of the greatest directors of Westerns and Hollywood action movies, including Raoul Walsh, who headed the second unit on *Helen of Troy*. During lunch breaks, the eager young Leone would try unsuccessfully to generate multilingual conversations with Walsh about his past accomplishments, as he later recalled: "Walsh had been a master of the Western. I admired his work very much – *They Died With Their Boots On, Pursued, Colorado Territory* – and I wanted to take full advantage of my time with him on *Helen of Troy*. Alas! Whenever I brought up the subject, he always replied, 'The Western is finished.' . . . So I had to watch all these Hollywood cinéastes, like Raoul Walsh and William Wyler, sacrifice themselves to the taste of the moment by making sword and sandal films. And I was their assistant, the victim of some curse. I was more in love with the idea of the American West than anyone you could imagine. I had read everything I could on the conquest of the West, already building up a huge archive on the subject . . . While I organized chariot races, sea battles between triremes, and explosions on galleys, I was silently dreaming of Nevada and New Mexico."

The same thing happened with Fred Zinnemann, on the Belgian Congo location of *The Nun's Story*. Leone wanted to talk *High Noon* and "the way in

which space, time, and action were handled in those scenes at the railway station," but Zinnemann had other more pressing matters on his mind. And again with Robert Aldrich, on *Sodom and Gomorrah*: Here was a chance to work with the man who had made the action-packed "double-cross" Western *Vera Cruz*, a picaresque adventure set in Mexico involving two mercenaries – a particular Leone favorite – and the man who had made, more recently, *The Last Sunset*, featuring one of the great final duels between tortured, black-clad Kirk Douglas and angry nice guy Rock Hudson. But as had happened so often in the past, the experience of actually working with one of his cinematic idols turned out to be something of a letdown. Leone's eight-week stint in charge of the second unit ended with his being fired by Aldrich for taking overgenerous lunch breaks. His response to the man who shot *Vera Cruz* was to say that by far the most expressive actor in *Sodom and Gomorrah* had been the pillar of salt, so he was delighted to leave.

Somehow, Hollywood was no longer creating for him the magic he remembered from his youth. Westerns had become too formulaic and talky: A film such as *The Left-Handed Gun* seemed to be saying that if there had only been a social worker around, Billy the Kid would never have committed his crimes. The constant clichés in television Westerns were making it impossible to suspend disbelief anymore. Surely the whole point of fairy tales was that listeners would suspend their disbelief, would buy into the enchantment. If the stories started to feel silly or predictable, they could not expect to claim their audiences' attention for very long, and the enchantment would disappear. Leone sensed that the old fairy tales were slipping away and felt that "their loss would be irreplaceable." Focusing on convincing detail, making a concerted effort to keep the fairy tale as realistic as possible, putting an emphasis on the unpredictable, pumping up "the spectacle," and creating a hero in tune with the times could bring some of the enchantment back. He had enough experience to know that there was a world of difference between the mystifications of Hollywood and the facts of everyday life – a much more complex matter than just the contrast between "myth" and "reality." And he was fascinated by exactly how cinema functioned as a latter-day form of myth. In his films from *A Fistful of Dollars* onward, he wants us to believe in his fables – he goes to considerable lengths to ensure that we do – yet at the same time he doesn't want us to believe them. He distances himself through irony, humor, and the voice of a character saying, "It's like playing cowboys and Indians." He wants to have it both ways.

Instead of making *Viale Glorioso*, Sergio Leone made Westerns – set in another time and another country, in a scrupulously researched past that also resembled a dream. Instead of telling his stories in classic Hollywood fashion

Above: **The original Italian large-size poster for *A Fistful of Dollars***

Opposite: **Cinematic memories: Lee Van Cleef in an early role as a gunfighter**

(as his apprenticeship had trained him to do), he embellished them, turned the grammar of film into a kind of rhetoric, and generally behaved toward the Western like a mannerist artist confronted by a biblical subject. One of the defining features of the Western was the landscape, and Leone used landscapes in unsettling ways, making them either full of big faces or surprisingly empty and receding into the far distance. And rather than invoking the traditional morality of the Western, he turned the genre into a robust Mediterranean carnival peopled by tricksters and rogues.

When Leone cited Hollywood Westerns in his *Dollars* films – sometimes to reenchant them, sometimes to exorcise them – it was always in this fresh cultural context. When making *A Fistful of Dollars*, the Westerns he particularly had in mind, by his own account, were George Stevens's *Shane*, with its solitary rider from nowhere entering a valley range war, helping the "holy family," then returning whence he came; Edward Dmytryk's *Warlock*, with its reference to the townspeople waiting for a gunfight "like little boys waiting for the circus parade"; and Budd Boetticher's Ranown cycle of low-budget Westerns that contrasted the granite-faced stoicism of the hero (Randolph Scott) with a series of colorful, well-drawn villains. In Boetticher's Westerns, the hero brings a sense of worth and purpose to a surprisingly bleak wilderness. In *A Fistful of Dollars*, the hero much prefers to exploit the situation.

By the following year, in *For a Few Dollars More*, the mysterious stranger of *Fistful* had become a professional bounty hunter, a character who had also been explored in a group of 1950s Hollywood Westerns, including Anthony Mann's *The Tin Star* and André de Toth's *The Bounty Hunter*. These films concluded that there was much more to life than making money and that bounty hunting was almost a form of sickness. Leone referred to both of them in *For a Few Dollars More*: to the beginning of *The Bounty Hunter* in his opening sequence and to the end of *The Tin Star* in his climactic gun duel. He turned the morality of those films upside down, though, with the words that appear as an onscreen caption just after the credit titles: "Where life had no value, death, sometimes had its price. That is why the bounty killers appeared."

Then there was the "cinematic memory" of Lee Van Cleef, who brought with him to Rome the hard-won image he had created thirteen years before, in his *High Noon* debut as the expendable bad guy with the trademark "beady-eyed sneer" (as the actor liked to call it). Mark Twain once said that in America you are remembered for your latest work, in Europe for your greatest work – and Leone certainly had a photographic memory. In the script of *For a Few Dollars More*, the Van Cleef character, Colonel Mortimer, with his dandyish costume and box of tricks, was loosely based on the gambler Hatfield (John Carradine) in John Ford's *Stagecoach*. Mortimer is first discovered

Above: **An Italian fotobusta** for **The Good, the Bad and the Ugly**

Opposite: **A striking Italian monochrome poster for Once Upon a Time in the West**

reading Byron's *Poems*. But various elements from Van Cleef's film career were superimposed on this stock character: the pocket-watch from Henry King's *The Bravados*, which served a similar plot function in both films; the sneaky Derringer from John Sturges's *Gunfight at the OK Corral*; perhaps even the final settling of accounts in a circular clearing, resembling a bullfight in Boetticher's *Ride Lonesome* – which had involved the demise, as usual, of Van Cleef, playing Frank, a *really* bad guy. In *For a Few Dollars More*, Leone – bearing all these cinematic memories in mind – made Van Cleef the *nicer* of the two bounty hunters, the avuncular one who rides off into the sunset and forfeits the money to his younger, more reckless professional rival. This time, though, the key reference point was Aldrich's *Vera Cruz*, with its story of a mature Confederate major (Gary Cooper) and a younger itinerant gunslinger (Burt Lancaster) who are after the same quarry in post–Civil War Mexico.

One feature of *Vera Cruz* would be taken several stages further in Leone's third *Dollars* film, *The Good, the Bad and the Ugly*: the way in which Burt Lancaster's curses are interrupted by full-volume trumpet fanfares, so the audience can't quite hear what he is saying. This was to turn into the elaborate and convoluted insults yelled by Tuco (Eli Wallach), which segue into shrieking vocal lines on Ennio Morricone's soundtrack.

The most important Hollywood memory in this film – apart from the moment in *How the West Was Won* when Eli Wallach mimes gunplay for George Peppard's children (the scene that inspired Leone to cast Wallach as Tuco) – was the presentation of the Civil War. Since *Gone With the Wind*, Hollywood had traditionally depicted the North in terms of progress, industry, the city, and the triumph of national government from 1865 onward; the South was about feudalism, moonlight, and magnolias, "the good old cause," slavery, and plantations exclusively given over to cotton growing. Where the hero's loyalties lay was the moral touchstone of the movie. Whose side the hero was on really mattered in such films as Selznick's *Gone With the Wind*, Dmytryk's *Raintree County*, or John Ford's Shiloh segment of *How the West Was Won* (the classic credit read "The Civil War Directed by John Ford"). In *The Good, the Bad and the Ugly*, there is no moral touchstone – just a lot of dust. The Civil War is something very nasty going on in the background (the famous crane shot in *Wind* of hundreds of wounded troops at the railhead in Atlanta was influential here) against which the surreal adventures of the protagonists play out. It is someone else's war, like World War II must have seemed to the adolescent Leone growing up in Rome. "It does not involve a 'good cause,'" he said. "What interested me more was on the one hand to demystify the adjectives 'good, bad, ugly,' and on the other to show the absurdity of war." So there are numerous soldiers with missing limbs, as well as deliberate references to

C'ERA UNA VOLTA IL WEST

C'ERA UNA VOLTA IL WEST con HENRY FONDA CLAUDIA CARDINALE NEL RUOLO DI ARMONICA JASON ROBARDS

REGIA DI SERGIO LEONE GABRIELE FERZETTI CHARLES BRONSON PAOLO STOPPA

E IN ORDINE ALFABETICO

MUSICA DI E. MORRICONE JACK ELAM LIONEL STANDER WOODY STRODE FRANK WOLFF KEENAN WYNN

UNA PRODUZIONE RAFRAN-S.MARCO

LITOROMA

World War I's trenches and World War II's concentration-camp orchestras. Surface detail, added Leone, was not the same thing as historical accuracy. Because at the same time, *The Good, the Bad and the Ugly* was the most carnivalesque of all his films – a black comedy about the craziness of war, a *Catch-22* of the American Civil War.

And it was located in Texas. Historically, of course, most of the action in the Civil War happened east of the Mississippi. When Hollywood produced Westerns set at the time of the war, the stories tended to concern gunrunning, horse-trading, the shipping of gold, or the gathering of intelligence: supply lines, in other words, rather than battles; and certainly not concentration camps. In *The Good, the Bad and the Ugly*, there is a pitched battle in Texas.

After he had completed this film, Leone wanted to move into a different league. Just before Christmas 1966, he was in Rome at an early screening of *The Good, the Bad and the Ugly* with the young newspaper critic Dario Argento, when he was introduced to up-and-coming filmmaker Bernardo Bertolucci. Bertolucci said he had enjoyed the film a lot. Between January and March 1967, the three cinéastes – Leone, Bertolucci, and Argento – sat in the screening room of Leone's house on the Via Lisippo and together fantasized about making "the ultimate Western." Not a Mediterranean Western with noisy bandits, cynical *Americanos*, and a setting near the Rio Grande, but, in Leone's words:

"[A] dance of death, [in which] I wanted to take all the most stereotypical characters from the American Western – on loan! The finest whore from New Orleans; the romantic bandit; the killer who is half-businessman, half-killer, and who wants to get on in the new world of business; the businessman who fancies himself a gunfighter; the lone avenger. With these five most stereotypical characters from the American Western, I wanted to present a homage to the Western at the same time as showing the mutations which American society was undergoing at that time. So the story was about a birth and a death." Leone's ultimate goal was nothing less, he said, than a "cinematic fresco on the birth of America."

Leone, Bertolucci, and Argento viewed a great many Hollywood Westerns together: The resulting project was to contain a series of explicit references to favorite Westerns as elements in the "cinematic fresco." They pored over maps of Monument Valley on the Arizona-Utah border, where John Ford had filmed ten of his Westerns between *Stagecoach* in 1939 and *Cheyenne Autumn* in 1964. The film buffs at Leone's house played games of "spot the reference," and they invented characters' names such as Brett McBain, composed of two American crime writers' names, Ed McBain and Brett Halliday. In the process, the complex relationship between young Italian cinéastes and American cinema turned into a scenario where the socialism of Bertolucci met the melancholy and cinephilia of Leone.

Insofar as they were focused at all, the discussions seem to have centered on the many meanings of the phrase *C'era una volta, il West,* which means "Once upon a time, there was the West." The project's central theme was to be the arrival of progress on the desert frontier, in the form of the transcontinental railroad. There was nothing particularly original in that: John Ford's *The Iron Horse,* Cecil B. De Mille's *Union Pacific,* and more recently *How the West Was Won* had all given the theme epic treatment, and the writer Frank Gruber had categorized the Iron Horse formula as one of the seven basic plots in the Western genre. But Leone's particular interest in the story was to explore the relationship between popular fictions ("Once upon a time . . .") and their historical basis (". . . there was the West"), while lamenting the end of the Western's golden age and the demise of the Western as fable.

Leone told me that his starting point was a whole world away from *The Iron Horse* and Cinerama: "The basic idea, of course, was to use some of the conventions, devices, and settings of the American Western film and a series of references to individual Westerns – to use these things to tell *my* version of the story of the birth of a nation." So the story conferences included debates about the confrontation between Western heroes ("an ancient race" of rugged individualists) and the new era of the railroad boom, and the survival into the complex world of adults – through memorable images – of childhood fairy tales

Opposite: **Leone (standing) in an impromptu discussion near the Spanish Sweetwater set of *Once Upon a Time in the West***

Above: **Leone in Monument Valley with designer Carlo Simi (left), scouting the iconic Western location for *Once Upon a Time in the West***

EURO INTERNATIONAL FILMS PRESENTA

CLAUDIA CARDINALE
HENRY FONDA   in   JASON ROBARDS
"C'ERA UNA VOLTA IL WEST,,

C'ERA UNA VOLTA IL WEST

CON CHARLES BRONSON NEL RUOLO DI ARMONICA
GABRIELE FERZETTI · PAOLO STOPPA
E IN ORDINE ALFABETICO JACK ELAM · LIONEL STANDER
WOODY STRODE · FRANK WOLFF · KEENAN WYNN
REGIA DI   PRODOTTO DA   PRODUTTORE ESECUTIVO
SERGIO LEONE · BINO CICOGNA · FULVIO MORSELLA
UNA PRODUZIONE RAFRAN - S. MARCO
TECHNICOLOR TECHNISCOPE

of cowboys and gunplay. It was, as all the participants recalled, like playing an elaborate game.

At last, the treatment of *Once Upon a Time in the West* began to take shape. By now, Leone had visited the United States. He had made a reconnaissance in a hired jeep through the deserts of Colorado, Arizona, and New Mexico. He had even taken a guided tour through Monument Valley with cameraman Tonino Delli Colli and production designer Carlo Simi. This was to be the key cinematic reference point of the film – symbolized by a sequence actually shot in Monument Valley of a buggy passing through the Arizona side. Leone, however, took pains to point out that such references were not "calculated in a programmed kind of way; they are there to give the feeling of all that background of the American Western to help tell this particular fairy tale." He added that although the explicit references to Hollywood Westerns were intended to amount to "a kaleidoscopic view of all American Westerns put together," and although it was assumed throughout the film – via a process of intertextuality we would now call postmodernist – that the paying customers would recognize many of the citations in at least a vague way, the point of the exercise was to create the impression that the audience was watching a film they'd seen somewhere before, only to jolt them with the realization that they'd never seen the story told in *quite* this way before. There was the mix of recognition and surprise, visual clichés and trompe l'oeil, which Leone had determined since *Fistful* was the key to keeping ahead of his audience.

On one level, *Once Upon a Time in the West* is structured around a series of ironic reversals of famous and hallowed moments from the Hollywood Western. At the beginning, the three *pistoleri* are waiting at Cattle Corner Station for the hero (rather than the villain) to arrive on the noon train (which is, of course, running two hours late from Flagstone). The villain's name is "Frank" as it was in *High Noon.* Little Timmy McBain goes hunting with his daddy, like little Joey Starrett with his rifle in the opening sequence of *Shane.* But this time, instead of the white-hatted savior riding into view between the antlers of a deer, both father and son are ruthlessly gunned down. A series of sinister portents – cicadas suddenly going silent, partridges flying away from the sagebrush, sage hens squawking excitedly – herald not the arrival of Comanche warriors at the Edwards ranch (as in *The Searchers*) but the appearance of a gang of hired killers employed by the Morton Railroad Company. Maureen McBain sings "Danny Boy" – as Robert Mitchum does in *Pursued,* only this time it isn't supposed to connote family bonding and a shared history: It is the prelude to a massacre. No matter that the words of "Danny Boy" weren't actually written until 1913; Hollywood hadn't cared much about that either.

The most important reversal, permeating the entire film, is of the visual grammar and the ideology of the Western films of John Ford. To that extent,

WOODY STRODE:
"The first time I saw [*Once Upon a Time in the West*] was in Italy, in Italian. When the lights went down, I said to my wife, Luana, 'Here we go, Mama.' The scene with the water was a complete surprise. And the close-ups, I couldn't believe. I never got a close-up in Hollywood. Even in *The Professionals* I had only three close-ups in the entire picture. Sergio Leone framed me on the screen for five minutes. After it was over, I said, 'That's all I needed.'"

Opposite: **Two symbols of the American West, Henry Fonda and Monument Valley, are depicted together on this Italian poster for *Once Upon a Time in the West*.**

Once Upon a Time in the West can be interpreted as a key contributor to a European cinematic "moment" of the late 1960s, when ciné-literate filmmakers evolved a form of "critical cinema" (a phrase Leone wasn't too fond of, greatly preferring "cinema cinema") that made reference to the work of Hollywood directors about whom they had written. As Claude Chabrol was to Alfred Hitchcock, Jean-Pierre Melville to the gangster film, Bertolucci to film noir, so Leone, in Once Upon a Time in the West, was to Ford.

The sequence in Once Upon a Time where Leone most explicitly refers to Ford, and to the destruction by the railroad of his utopian dream, occurs when Harmonica (Charles Bronson) and Cheyenne (Jason Robards) are examining the kit of wooden parts that has been delivered to Brett McBain's farm, taking the measure of what will become the train station. Cheyenne catches on quickly: "Aha, he was no fool our dead friend, huh? He was going to sell this piece of desert for its weight in gold, wasn't he?" To which Harmonica replies, "You don't sell the dream of a lifetime." Not when you are "an Irishman" with a dream. But the agents of the railroad company have already massacred McBain and his entire family – Leone's most extreme take on what could really have happened to "the dream of a lifetime" and the utopian Irish community that supported it in the films of John Ford.

By the close of Once Upon a Time, the "worn-out stereotypes" of the Western have no further use. The railroad baron Mr. Morton (Gabriele Ferzetti), who has tried unsuccessfully to adopt the methods of a gunfighter, never gets to see the Pacific. Instead, he dies crawling like a snail toward a puddle in the desert. His funeral dirge is the music played earlier when he looked longingly at a painting of the ocean. Frank never succeeds in making the transformation from gunfighter to businessman. At death, he realizes that he is "just a man," while also discovering exactly who his nemesis is; the harmonica, stuffed into his mouth, plays his death rattle. Cheyenne, the romantic Mexican bandit, asks Harmonica to turn away as he dies, gut-shot, just out of sight of Sweetwater. John Ford's community square dance has, indeed, turned into a dance of death. By now an anachronism, Harmonica rides off into the hills, away from the new and "beautiful town." As parts of the rhetoric of the American Western, they have all played out their roles on the desert stage, only to be destroyed by real-life historical processes. Once upon a time there was the West.

After Argento and Bertolucci went their separate ways, Leone took the resulting treatment to his regular scriptwriter, Sergio Donati, who was upset at having been sidelined during the project's early stages. In three weeks flat, Donati turned the "slow and rhetorical" but suggestive treatment into a workable shooting script – after long story conferences with Leone –

Opposite: **Leone standing by Claudia Cardinale (Jill) while rehearsing the scene where she sees the body of her dead husband, Brett McBain, in** *Once Upon a Time in the West*

5169-33

enhancing in the meantime the "end of the West" theme and the character of Cheyenne, adding the character of Mr. Morton, and generally heightening the atmosphere of retrospective regret. I have seen Donati's script, and it is more or less identical to the finished movie. Some elements of the original treatment survived the transition to script, though – especially those that happen in the first twenty minutes before the story gets going. The unusual gestation of the treatment and screenplay help to explain why the finished film is so full of "quotes from all the Westerns I love" (as Bertolucci put it); "references, maybe quotations or references, some from me and some from Zinnemann, and . . . others" (Argento); or "references to individual Westerns" (Leone). This can be seen as the first truly postmodern movie, made by a cinéaste for other cinéastes, as well as the wider public, and deeply embedded in a culture of quotations. As Umberto Eco said of this film, "If you have one frozen archetype, everyone says the film is terrible: If you have a dozen of them, it becomes sublime, it becomes art."

The story has often been told about how the completed *Once Upon a Time in the West* had a lukewarm reception at its New York opening, had over twenty minutes cut from it, and *still* attracted the headline in *Time* magazine TEDIUM IN THE TUMBLEWEED. In the United States, the film made one-sixth of the gross of the faster-moving, more heavily plotted, less talkative *The Good, the Bad and the Ugly.* As Henry Fonda succinctly put it, "It didn't pull a dime." In France, it still holds the record for a continuous run at a single cinema – near the river Seine, at the end of the boulevard Saint-Michel. But, even in Italy, it didn't come near the success of the three Clint Eastwood movies. Then again, Sergio Leone had been pretty sure from the outset that you don't sell the dream of a lifetime . . .

Gradually, though, *Once Upon a Time in the West* started – as Leone recalled – to have the same kind of succès d'estime as Stanley Kubrick's *2001.* And today, *Once Upon a Time* is beginning to appear regularly on critics' and filmmakers' "best of" lists – not only as one of the best Westerns, but as one of the best movies. A filmmaker who rates the film very highly indeed is John Boorman. Boorman's *Point Blank* and *Deliverance* were two of Leone's

Opposite: **Henry Fonda as the veteran gunfighter Jack Beauregard, in *My Name Is Nobody***

Above: **West German poster highlighting the four stars of *Once Upon a Time in the West*, and introducing a garment that would become a fashion trend**

QUENTIN TARANTINO:
"I think Sergio Leone
will definitely be known
as the man who invented
the spaghetti Western.
Personally, for my money,
I think he is the greatest
of all Italy's filmmakers.
I would even go as far
as to say he is the greatest
combination of film stylist –
where he creates his own
world – with the storyteller
part of him as well.
These two are almost
never married."

personal favorites at the time, and Boorman returned the compliment in his diary, *Money Into Light*: "The Western," he concluded, "went into decline when writers and directors became self-conscious and introduced psychological elements. John Ford and others [on the other hand] worked from the blood. Sergio Leone's 'spaghetti' Westerns revitalized the form because he consciously reverted to mythic stories, making the texture and detail real, but ruthlessly shearing away the recent accretions of the 'real' West and its psychological motivations. Unfortunately, this was not understood in Hollywood . . . Sam Peckinpah was the only American director to take the hint from Leone . . . In *Once Upon a Time in the West,* the Western reaches its apotheosis. Leone's title is a declaration of intent and also his gift to America of its lost fairy stories. This is the kind of masterpiece that can only occur outside trends and fashion. It is both the greatest and the last Western."

Leone went on to make *Giù La Testa* – which is in dialogue with Hollywood movies about the Mexican Revolution of 1911–19 (especially Howard Hawks's and Jack Conway's *Viva Villa!*) as well as more recent Italian Westerns that, for Leone's taste, had taken their politics far too seriously. And in his first film as a producer, *My Name Is Nobody,* directed by Tonino Valerii, he blended references to his own earlier films, a critique of Sam Peckinpah's work up to 1970, an elegiac reflection on the relationship between his own work and – again – that of John Ford (represented in person by Henry Fonda), and the excesses of the Italian Western. *My Name Is Nobody* ends with elderly gunfighter Jack Beauregard (Henry Fonda) reading a long valedictory letter to the energetic Nobody (Terence Hill) who has at last proven that he is "Somebody" after all: "You can preserve a little of that illusion that made my generation tick. Maybe you'll do it in your own funny way, but we'll be grateful just the same. Because looking back, it seems to me we were all a bunch of romantic fools; we still believed that a good pistol and a quick showdown could solve everything. But then the West used to be wide-open spaces with lots of elbow room – where you never ran into the same person twice. By the time you came along, it was changed. It'd got small and crowded, and you kept bumping into the same people all the time. But if you're able to run around in the West peacefully catching flies, it is only because fellas like me were there first . . ."

This was Sergio Leone's *arrivederci* to the Western – the Hollywood version and the Italian version. He often said that his aim since *A Fistful of Dollars* had been to make "fairy tales for grown-ups," and that his Westerns – especially *Once Upon a Time in the West* – had been creative responses to, as well as exorcisms of, the Hollywood images that had colonized his head when he was growing up during the 1930s and 1940s in a Roman suburb. I grew up in a London suburb in the 1950s, the first television age, and I think I know precisely what he meant.

Opposite: **Leone directed the saloon sequence of *My Name Is Nobody*,** much to Terence Hill's delight.

THE WESTERN
FILMS OF
SERGIO LEONE

A FISTFUL OF DOLLARS [1964]

A stranger in a poncho rides on a mule into the small town of San Miguel, just south of the American-Mexican border. He learns from the bartender Silvanito that the town is being run by two rival gangs – the American Baxters (who are gunrunners) and the Mexican Rojos (who are liquor smugglers). First selling himself to the Rojos, he plays one side against the other and profits from both, to the great glee of the coffin-maker Piripero. The stranger witnesses Ramon Rojo steal a shipment of gold from the *federales*, at the Rio Bravo Canyon, and sees how ruthless he can be. Returning to San Miguel, the stranger secretly saves the lives of a Mexican family – Marisol, Julian, and little Jesús – but is discovered and savagely beaten by the Rojos. After the stranger escapes in a coffin, the Rojos assume he has joined the Baxter gang, and in reprisal they burn down the Baxter house and massacre the entire family. But the stranger is in hiding. He returns to town, signaling his arrival with a dynamite explosion, and has a shootout with the Rojos in the main square. Eventually, he defeats Ramon with help from a piece of iron that he wears beneath his poncho – proving that whatever the "old Mexican proverb" may say, when a man with a .45 meets a man with a Winchester, the man with a .45 can win. The stranger says farewell to the bartender and the coffin maker, and rides on his mule out of San Miguel, with more than a fistful of dollars.

This was not the first Italian Western, but earlier ones had, on the whole, been like pale imitations of minor Hollywood "cowboy and Indian" films. *A Fistful of Dollars* brought together director Sergio Leone, production designer Carlo Simi, and composer Ennio Morricone – each making a distinctive contribution in a relationship that would develop and deepen in the successive Westerns they worked on. *Fistful* also starred Clint Eastwood, who was at the time the second lead in the television series *Rawhide*.

Fistful was filmed between April and June 1964 on a tiny budget of two hundred thousand dollars. The main town's set had already been built for a low-budget Spanish *Zorro*, near Colmenar Viejo, north of Madrid; the riding sequences were filmed in the *ramblas* of Almería in southern Spain; the Rio Bravo Canyon sequence – filmed by second-unit director Franco Giraldi – was at Aldea Del Fresno on the river Alberche. Interiors were filmed in Rome.

The film was loosely based on Akira Kurosawa's samurai film *Yojimbo/The Bodyguard*, which Leone had seen in Rome in the autumn of 1963. Because someone forgot to clear the rights, the film became the subject

of a legal battle resulting in Kurosawa being awarded distribution rights in the Far East – where the film was a huge success – plus a slice of the worldwide profits. Apart from the Rio Bravo Canyon sequence and a cemetery gun battle with decoy corpses, the main differences between *Fistful* and *Yojimbo* include the absence in *Fistful* of reference to any "outside world"; the comic-book characterization of the stranger, with his stubble and cigar; and the story's complete indifference to law (or, indeed, to any form of legitimate authority).

Fistful also ignores any "civilizing" implications of settlement. In San Miguel, there is no sense of progress, resource, or development. This, too, was a radical departure from the traditional Western. Leone called this his "first personal film." It made Clint Eastwood a superstar in Europe, and it relaunched the entire Italian Western craze that would last until the early 1970s.

Before working on *Rawhide*, Clint Eastwood had appeared in ten features between 1955 and 1958, usually as a walk-on. His film career had actually been in decline when he accepted the role of ramrod Rowdy Yates in *Rawhide*. Although he had reservations about the *Fistful* script (it was badly translated into English), he took a

gamble on an Italian remake of a Japanese film to be shot on the plains of Spain. When he got there, he became one of the few actors in movie history to fight for *less* lines. He figured, as did Leone, that the more mysterious and silent, the more interesting the character would be.

Originally filmed under the title *The Magnificent Stranger*, *A Fistful of Dollars* was released in the United States – to big box office – in February 1967. The critics did not like it much, tending to dismiss the film as "an ersatz Western" and complaining about the dubbing and the brutality. The public, however, had discovered a new, up-to-date kind of fairy tale; a fresh, stylish, Western antihero; and a raucous musical score (Fender Stratocaster guitar, whip cracks, bells, yelling chorus, drum beats, and whistling) that was a world away from the traditional symphonic approach of the Hollywood Western. And the stranger, called Joe in the original Italian version, became the Man With No Name.

REGIA DI
BOB ROBERTSON

CON
MARIANNE KOCH

JOSEF EGGER

WOLFGANG LUKSCHY

JOHN WELLS

**DANIEL MARTIN
CAROL BROWN
BENNY REEVES**

TECHNISCOPE

TECHNICOLOR

DI DOLLARI

A. E. I. MCMLXIV

PRINTED IN ITALY BY POLIGRAM
Roma - Via Tiburtina Km. 24,500

FOR A FEW DOLLARS MORE [1965]

Two bounty hunters are working, with very different
methods, around New Mexico and Texas after the
American Civil War. One is the frock-coated Colonel
Mortimer, a Confederate veteran with a notebook and an
arsenal of weapons; the other is a younger man in a
poncho, with stubble and a cigar, who prefers more direct
methods. A psychopathic Mexican bandit called El Indio
is sprung from the Territorial Prison, with much killing,
and the price on his head rises to ten thousand dollars,
dead or alive – which attracts the attention of the two
American bounty hunters. Both of them independently
figure out that El Indio is likely to rob the El Paso bank,
mainly because such a feat is reputed to be impossible.
Mortimer and the young bounty hunter meet, ritually
try to humiliate one another, and then decide to work in
an uneasy partnership. The younger man infiltrates El
Indio's gang "from the inside," while Mortimer waits in
El Paso "from the outside." But the plan goes wrong, and
El Indio and his gang manage to ride across the border
to Mexico with the safe from the El Paso bank. The young
bounty hunter joins the gang again, while Mortimer
helps El Indio to open the safe – with the aid of chemicals
rather than explosives. In the flyblown Mexican town
of Agua Caliente, the two bounty hunters break into
El Indio's treasure chest and hide the El Paso loot. Caught
in the act, they are savagely beaten by the gang. El Indio,
by now self-destructive as well as destructive, frees the
two Americans, who then return and wipe out the bandit
gang. In a final settling of accounts, which takes place
in a circular threshing yard behind a farm, Mortimer
(under supervision from the younger man) kills El Indio
in a duel – in the process getting his revenge for the much
earlier rape and suicide of his sister. According to their
agreement, the bounty hunters should now split the
sixty-seven-thousand-dollar reward for the whole gang,
but Mortimer allows his partner to have all the money
(plus the El Paso loot) as he rides off into the sunset.

With a six-hundred-thousand-dollar budget, with
Clint Eastwood displaying a stronger sense of humor than
in *Fistful*, with witty scriptwriter Luciano Vincenzoni,
with veteran Hollywood bad guy Lee Van Cleef, and with a
story contrasting two generations of selfish bounty hunters,
Sergio Leone kept ahead of the other Italian Westerns
by at last getting into his stylistic stride. The interplay
of music, sound, and image; the design of "El Paso" and the
use of adobe Spanish villages; the expansive visual style

PM45 3342

LA RESA
DEI
CONTI

PER QUALCHE DOLLARO
IN PIÙ

RCA

MUSICHE DI ENNIO
MORRICONE

DALLA COLONNA SONORA ORIGINALE DEL FILM

PER QUALCHE
DOLLARO IN PIÙ

combining dirty realism in close-ups and exaggerated spectacle in an extended final shootout; the excessive behavior of the bad guy El Indio – all made *For a Few Dollars More* a much more confident film than *A Fistful of Dollars*. Ennio Morricone's score, with musical insignia for each character and "internal music" in the form of a chiming pocket watch, was more intricate than *Fistful*'s soundtrack.

For a Few Dollars More was filmed in twelve weeks between April and July 1965 at a variety of locations in Spain: "El Paso" was built, to Carlo Simi's design, near Tabernas in Almería; "Agua Caliente" was an existing Andalusian village called Los Albaricoques ["The Apricots"]; "Tucumcari" was a redesigned version of the *Fistful* set, and "Santa Cruz" was a standing set on the backlot of Rome's Cinecittà studios, where many of the interiors were also shot. With the increased budget, Sergio Leone could focus lovingly on the details of firearms, interior designs, and landscapes; he could also indulge his earthy sense of humor for the first time.

The older bounty hunter was played by Lee Van Cleef, who brought with him a history of performances as the bad guy in many Hollywood Westerns, from *High Noon*

(1952) onward. The younger bounty hunter, a variation on the Eastwood character in *A Fistful of Dollars*, was called Manco (Spanish for "one-handed") or Monco in European prints. Eastwood did not fancy smoking a cigar again, but Leone insisted, joking, "It's playing the lead!"

For a Few Dollars More became the most commercially successful Italian film ever made, beating Fellini's *La Dolce Vita* by a factor of 50 percent. It was released in the United States in July 1967, back-to-back with *A Fistful of Dollars*. The young bounty hunter was rebranded as the Man With No Name, and the film was a box-office smash.

PEA presenta   CLINT EASTWOOD   in un film di   SERGIO LEONE

PER QUALCHE DOLLARO IN PIU'

TECHNICOLOR - TECHNISCOPE

con **LEE VAN CLEEF - GIAN MARIA VOLONTE'**   MARA KRUP - LUIGI PISTILLI - KLAUS KINSKI - JOSEF EGGER - PANOS PAPADOPULOS - BENITO STEFANELLI - ROBERT CAMARDIEL
ALDO SAMBRELL - LUIS RODRIGUEZ e MARIO BREGA   musiche di ENNIO MORRICONE   sceneggiatura e dialoghi di LUCIANO VINCENZONI

"FOR A FEW DOLLARS MORE" 'X'

**It's the second motion picture of its kind!
It won't be the last!**

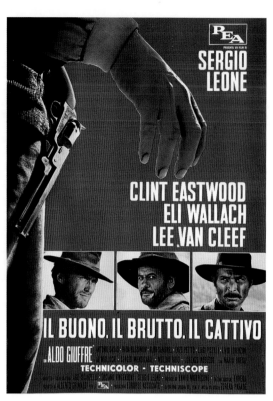

THE GOOD, THE BAD AND THE UGLY [1966]

It is 1861/62 during the American Civil War, and General Sibley is leading his Confederate troops from Texas into New Mexico, while General Canby with his Union troops is fighting back. But to the three main characters in this story, the Civil War is a bloody and dangerous distraction. Tuco is a Mexican outlaw who teams up with an American bounty hunter called Blondie to con the authorities out of reward money. Blondie turns Tuco in; then, after collecting the loot, he rescues him from hanging by shooting through the rope. Meanwhile, Angel Eyes – a hired gunman – hears about a consignment of Confederate army gold that has disappeared and goes looking for a Confederate soldier named Bill Carson, the one person who can locate its whereabouts. Blondie double-crosses Tuco, who in revenge forces the American to take a grueling trek across "miles of beautiful sun-baked sand" in the desert. Just as Tuco is about to kill Blondie, a Confederate coach full of corpses hurtles across the desert, and the dying Bill Carson tells each of the two con men one piece of information concerning the gold's whereabouts: Tuco hears that the location is Sad Hill, a military cemetery, Blondie hears the name on the grave next to Arch Stanton, marked UNKNOWN.

Dressed in Confederate uniforms stolen from the coach, the two visit a San Antonio mission headed by Tuco's priest brother Pablo Ramirez. Blondie and Tuco then meet a Union patrol, whom they mistake for Confederates because they are covered in dust. Captured, Blondie and Tuco are sent to the Union prison camp at Betterville, where Angel Eyes, still on the hunt for Carson, has become a sergeant. To find out the name of the cemetery, Angel Eyes tortures Tuco – while the camp orchestra plays a sad "ballad of a soldier" – then sends him off to jail. Blondie joins Angel Eyes and his gang in a plan to leave the war as fast as they can and find the gold. Tuco escapes by using a troop train to cut through his handcuffs; he rejoins Blondie, and together they kill Angel Eyes's gang in the town of Peralta – while it is being shelled. But Angel Eyes escapes, leaving a note that reads "See you soon, idiots." The two con men make their way toward the cemetery, but stumble into a major battle at Langstone Bridge. To get to the other side of the river, Tuco and Blondie blow up the bridge, much to the delight of a dying Union officer, who has recognized the battle's futility.

Finally Blondie, Tuco, and Angel Eyes meet for the final showdown in a huge military cemetery, where they face each other in a triangular duel. Having unloaded

Tuco's gun before the duel, Blondie kills Angel Eyes, then rides away with a hundred thousand dollars in gold, while Tuco is left alive with a rope around his neck and without a horse. Tuco yells an elaborate insult. But he is a hundred thousand dollars better off.

Inspired by an old Roman song about a cardinal who did bad things well and good things badly, Leone's cynical and comic epic interweaves historical events – between late 1861 and summer 1862 – with the picaresque adventures of "good" Clint Eastwood, "bad" Lee Van Cleef, and "ugly" Eli Wallach, whose noisy and carnivalesque performance dominates the film. The historical events were deliberately refracted through the two world wars of the twentieth century.

This time, the budget was $1.3 million – half of it from United Artists – and the settings, photographed by Tonino Delli Colli between May and July 1966, were correspondingly more elaborate. The Tabernas set was reused for Valverde, Santa Ana, and Santa Fe; Colmenar Viejo was chopped up to become war-torn Peralta; La Calahorra, outside Guadix, was the railroad station; and a derelict nineteenth-century big house called Cortijo de los Frailes ["The Brothers"], a few kilometers from Los Albaricoques, was the Franciscan Mission at San Antonio. The battle was staged north of Madrid, near the river Arlanza outside Burgos, and the cemetery was built nearby.

Eastwood played more of a con man this time (wearing his poncho only during the final duel), while Van Cleef, dark haired, played a more villainous character than he had as Colonel Mortimer. In the original Italian print, he is known as Sentenza (meaning "sentence"), but in the international print he became Angel Eyes. (In the shooting script he was called Banjo.) Wallach had a marvelous time playing Tuco, the foul-mouthed Mexican trickster, and his part grew as the filming progressed. The dance of death at the climax – Morricone's mariachi trumpet lament, Leone's cutting to the music, the rhetorical exaggeration, with a lot of staring, of the standard Western duel – was Leone at his very best. *The Good, the Bad and the Ugly* opened in the United States in January 1968, and the phrase soon entered the language.

ONCE UPON A TIME IN THE WEST [1968]

At a railroad station, three gunmen wait for a train that is two hours late. It brings Harmonica, who is looking for Frank and who shoots the gunmen when he discovers that Frank isn't with them. Meanwhile, Frank himself, a hired gun employed by a disabled railroad baron named Morton, massacres the Irish McBain family (Brett, his two sons, and one daughter) at their Sweetwater farm, in an attempt to get hold of their land. Sweetwater has a well, and the railroad will need water as it relentlessly pushes its way across the continent to the Pacific. Then Jill, recently married to Brett McBain, arrives from New Orleans via Flagstone and Monument Valley, to discover that her new family has been massacred – reportedly by a bandit called Cheyenne. Infuriated by the accusation, Cheyenne arrives at Sweetwater to clear his name. For mysterious reasons, Harmonica shows up to protect Jill from Frank's men, who are still after the McBain land. It transpires, through a series of flashbacks, that Harmonica is seeking revenge against Frank for some atrocity committed in the past. Harmonica is captured by Frank, but with help from Cheyenne shoots his way to freedom. Meanwhile, Frank forces Jill to sell Sweetwater for a knockdown price at a rigged auction. Again Harmonica protects her

by winning the auction with money he earns by turning in Cheyenne, who's got a price on his head. En route to Yuma Prison on Morton's train, Cheyenne is freed by his gang, who kill Morton in the process. Frank seeks out Harmonica "because now I know you'll tell me what you're after." Their final showdown takes place behind the Sweetwater farmhouse, as the railroad workers arrive. During the duel, Frank is forced to recall that many years earlier he had tortured and murdered Harmonica's brother. Harmonica kills Frank and rides off – ahead of the railroad – with Cheyenne's body strapped to a horse. Shot by Morton in the skirmish during his rescue, Cheyenne has died from his wounds just over the hill from Sweetwater. Sad to lose Cheyenne and Harmonica, Jill nevertheless busies herself taking water to the thirsty railroad workers who crowd around her. Now in charge of a booming railroad station, she has decided to stay on.

In preparation for *Once Upon a Time in the West*, Leone cut loose from his usual writers and spent time watching classic Hollywood Westerns with the young Bernardo Bertolucci and Dario Argento. He then asked Sergio Donati (who had contributed to the scripts of his last two Westerns) to help transform their treatment –

a mosaic of hallowed movie moments, held together by a simple story about water rights in the desert – into a brilliantly choreographed elegy on American myths ("Once Upon a Time") and grown-up historical reality ("In the West"). The Italian title translates as "Once Upon a Time There Was the West." From the opening sequences and their balletic remixes of moments from *High Noon*, *Johnny Guitar*, *Shane*, and *The Searchers*, to the climax inspired by John Ford's *The Iron Horse*, this dance of death – as Leone told me – collides the worn-out stereotypes of the Western with "the new, pitiless era that was advancing." It is an anthology of great sequences from the Hollywood Western, lovingly re-created before being turned inside out. The stereotypes include Henry Fonda – cast radically against type – as a blue-eyed sadistic killer, Charles Bronson as the avenger with no name who wears a musical instrument around his neck, Jason Robards as a romantic bandit, and Claudia Cardinale as a prostitute or, in contemporary Hollywood parlance, a "dance-hall girl."

Once Upon a Time in the West was filmed for Paramount between April and July 1968, with a budget of three million dollars. The opening sequence was filmed at La Calahorra, near Guadix, and, designed by Carlo Simi, the town of "Flagstone" was constructed next door; "Sweetwater" was built down the road from the El Paso set used in *For a Few Dollars More*, near Tabernas in Almería; and, for the first time, Leone filmed in America – in Monument Valley, no less, John Ford's great location, where Jill McBain arrives by buggy and where the climactic flashback occurs.

All of Morricone's main musical themes were written in advance of filming and played on the set "to create rhythms." Each main character had a theme, or leitmotif. *Once Upon a Time in the West* did not perform as well at the box office as Leone's *Dollars* Westerns, and in America, following lukewarm previews, it was abridged by more than twenty minutes. It has since been reappraised to the point that critics now rate the movie more highly than any other Leone film. In addition, it has had a lasting impact on the post-1960s generations of Hollywood filmmakers. The rock video starts here . . .

C'ERA UNA VOLTA IL WEST

PARAMOUNT FILM PRESENTERAR

AV REGISSÖREN
SERGIO LEONE
SOM GJORDE
"FÖR EN
HANDFULL
DOLLAR",

"FÖR NÅGRA FÅ
DOLLAR MER"
OCH
"DEN GODE,
DEN ONDE
OCH DEN FULE"

EN SERGIO LEONE FILM

CLAUDIA CARDINALE

HENRY FONDA   JASON ROBARDS

CHARLES BRONSON

HARMONICA
EN HÄMNARE

WOODY STRODE · JACK ELAM · LIONEL STANDER · PAOLO STOPPA · FRANK WOLFF · KEENAN WYNN   FÄRG TECHNICOLOR®
ONCE UPON A TIME IN THE WEST · REGI: SERGIO LEONE · PROD: FULVIO MORSELLA · EX.PROD: BINO CICOGNA EN RAFRAN-SAN MARCO PRODUKTION · TECHNISCOPE®

LEONE'S CITATIONS OF AMERICAN WESTERNS

Opposite: **Charles Bronson found stardom as Harmonica in *Once Upon a Time in the West*.**

I compiled the following chart of the explicit citations of American Westerns in *Once Upon a Time in the West* following conversations with Sergio Leone, Bernardo Bertolucci, Dario Argento, and Sergio Donati. Some citations they could remember clearly; some they were no longer certain about.

ONCE UPON A TIME IN THE WEST	FILM CITATIONS
Three of Frank's men pass the time as they wait at Cattle Corner Station.	*High Noon* (1952, Fred Zinnemann): Three men pass the time as they wait for Frank at Hadleyville Station.
One of them, Snaky, is played by Jack Elam.	Jack Elam was the heavy – with beetle brows over one good eye – of over thirty Westerns, including *High Noon* (as the town drunk), *Rancho Notorious*, *Vera Cruz*, *The Far Country*, *Man Without a Star*, *Wichita*, *The Man From Laramie*, *Jubal*, *Gunfight at the OK Corral*, *The Last Sunset*, and *Firecreek*.
Another, Stony, is played by Woody Strode.	The statuesque black actor Woody Strode starred in John Ford's *Two Rode Together* (as a Native American), *Sergeant Rutledge* (as a cavalryman), and *The Man Who Shot Liberty Valance* (as John Wayne's aged retainer). He was the most athletic of *The Professionals* (1966, Richard Brooks) hired to rescue Claudia Cardinale from Mexico. Of his part in *Rutledge* he memorably said, "You never seen a Negro come off a mountain like John Wayne before."
Another, Knuckles, is played by Al Muloch.	The pockmarked face that filled the screen at the beginning of *The Good, the Bad and the Ugly* belonged to Muloch. In *The Fastest Gun Alive* (1956, Russell Rouse), the gunslinger (Broderick Crawford) noisily clicks his knuckles while preparing for showdowns. The sound resembles the scrunch of Martin Landau's shoe as it descends on Cary Grant's hand – while Grant clutches the concrete edge of Mount Rushmore in *North by Northwest*.
The locomotive arrives.	It travels over the camera, as happens in *The Iron Horse* (1924, John Ford) – after which such a shot became an essential element of visual grammar in Westerns.
It brings the mixed-race stranger (Charles Bronson) to his appointment.	The granite-faced actor originally known as Charles Buchinsky played villains or Native Americans in *Apache*, *Vera Cruz*, *Jubal*, *Run of the Arrow*, and *A Thunder of Drums* – as well as the courageous and sympathetic Mexican-Irish Bernardo O'Reilly in *The Magnificent Seven* (1960, John Sturges).
He announces his presence by playing the harmonica.	This is a reference to Sterling Hayden's guitar in *Johnny Guitar* (1954, Nicholas Ray); the bell on James Stewart's saddle in *The Far Country* (1954, Anthony Mann); the mute Sioux boy Silent Tongue's harmonica playing – "the only sound to ever come from his mouth" – in *Run of the Arrow* (1957, Sam Fuller); and James Stewart's accordion playing to celebrate the laying of the railroad track in *Night Passage* (1957, James Neilson). (That sequence was prepared and directed by Anthony Mann.)
Little Timmy McBain (Enzo Santaniello) mimes the shooting of a bird, near Sweetwater.	*Shane* (1952, George Stevens): Little Joey Starrett mimes the stalking of a deer, with his rifle.
In Sweetwater, there is a prominent tree stump on the farmyard.	*Shane* again: The hero and Joe Starrett wrestle with a tree stump, clearing the wilderness to make a garden.
Maureen McBain (Simonetta Santaniello) sings, "Danny Boy, the pipes, the pipes are calling," as she prepares the wedding feast.	*Pursued* (1947, Raoul Walsh): Mrs. Callum and family, with adopted Jeb Rand, sing the "Londonderry Air" – "an old-fashioned tune" – with musical accompaniment, to reassure themselves that "the best and finest thing there is – is family." *Pursued* has a very similar flashback structure to *Once Upon a Time*.
The tables are draped with red gingham tablecloths.	The tablecloths were featured in so many Western ranch interiors that art theorist Erwin Panofsky called them "the icon of domesticity."

Brett McBain (Frank Wolff) is an Irish Roman Catholic.	Like John Ford, who was a second-generation immigrant. In *The Iron Horse* and *Union Pacific* (1939, Cecil B. De Mille), the Irish play a big part – as laborers – in building the railroad. Ford's softhearted and hardfisted Irish sergeant (played by Victor McLaglen) is a stock character in the cavalry trilogy.
McBain's older son does not approve of his father's remarriage following a holiday romance in New Orleans.	*Last Train From Gun Hill* (1958, John Sturges): Anthony Quinn's son does not approve of his father's remarriage to an ex-"dance-hall girl" who dresses in scarlet.
McBain notices suspicious signs in the desert scrub: The cicadas become silent; the partridges fly away; the sage hens squawk excitedly.	*The Searchers* (1956, John Ford): Aaron Edwards notices suspicious signs of Comanche activity in the desert scrub: A coyote howls; the partridges fly away; a mirror flashes a signal; the sage hens squawk excitedly.
The gang of hired gunmen emerges in formation from the dust and the sagebrush – wearing long duster coats.	Dusters are worn by old man Clanton and his clan in *My Darling Clementine* (1946), Uncle Shiloh Clegg and his nephews in *Wagon Master* (1950), and Liberty Valance and his subnormal henchmen Floyd and Reese – all directed by John Ford.
Their leader is the blue-eyed, unshaven Frank (Henry Fonda).	Fonda was the noble, gentle, baby-faced Western hero – also capable of violent action when pressed – who played the backwoods lawyer in *Young Mr. Lincoln* (1939); the man who shames the lynch mob, and himself, at the end of *The Ox-Bow Incident* (1942); Wyatt Earp in *My Darling Clementine* (1946); the inflexible lieutenant colonel from the East, called Thursday, in *Fort Apache* (1948); the embittered bounty hunter who is socialized into domestic values in *The Tin Star* (1957, Anthony Mann); the Earp-style gunfighter called in to tame the town of *Warlock* (1959, Edward Dmytryk); and the grizzled buffalo hunter who retreats to the hills in *How the West Was Won* (1962). Fonda's "image" of quiet-spoken integrity came as much from his non-Westerns *The Grapes of Wrath*, *Twelve Angry Men*, and *The Wrong Man*. According to Leone, "The glacial Henry Fonda in *Once Upon a Time* is the legitimate son . . . of the intuition that John Ford brought to *Fort Apache*."
Frank chews on a wad of tobacco.	As did another Frank – Frank James (Henry Fonda), the victim of injustice in *The Return of Frank James* (1940, Fritz Lang).
Jill McBain (Claudia Cardinale) arrives at Flagstone Station and waits for Brett to meet her.	*My Darling Clementine*: Clementine Carter (Cathy Davis) arrives at the Mansion House Hotel in Tombstone (while a slow version of the theme song plays); later, she will return to the hotel lobby, deciding whether to "leave town on the eastbound stage."
Jill and Sam (Paolo Stoppa) travel in a buggy through the sandstone rocks of Monument Valley.	Although Monument Valley had first been used as a Western location in *The Vanishing American* (1925, George B. Seitz), the setting was so indelibly associated with John Ford – who made ten Westerns there, in which it "stood for" various desert regions of America – that many Hollywood filmmakers felt it would be a form of plagiarism to shoot there. *How the West Was Won* (1962) concludes with Lilith (Debbie Reynolds) traveling in a four-wheel buggy through Monument Valley with the Prescott family, and a horse called Sam.
The buggy ride is interrupted by a rail gang laying tracks; Sam drives the buggy through the building site.	Johnny Guitar's journey, on horseback, is interrupted by the blasting of the railroad; Johnny rides through the railroad workers.
Sam talks to his beloved "heap of bones" and "stinker of coal" – his horse Lafayette.	Influences include William S. Hart and Fritz; Tom Mix and Old Blue/Tony; Ken Maynard and Tarzan; Buck Jones and Silver; Gene Autry and Champion; Roy Rogers and Trigger; and all the hard-riding heroes from the days before the cowboy stopped kissing his horse. Hart, incidentally, first coined the phrase *horse opera*.
Jill asks, "Why are we stopping?" Sam replies sharply, "Don't the trains stop?"	*Dodge City* (1939, Michael Curtiz): In the opening sequences, a buggy races against a locomotive, and Colonel Dodge contentedly observes, "Iron men and iron horses – that's progress."
They enter an elaborate wooden trading post in the middle of the desert, where the stout cigar- smoking bartender (Lionel Stander) tells Jill, "Just happen to have a full tub in the back . . . Only three people have used it this morning!"	*Winchester '73* (1950, Anthony Mann): Vin (James Stewart) and his young companion Johnny enter Riker's wooden Hotel and Bar, an emporium that sells "pelts, whiskey, steak dinners, water cans, repeating rifles, and pistols." Jack Riker is the stout, cigar-smoking host. "You know, I ain't felt so naked since the last time I took a bath," says Vin. "You've got a long memory," replies Johnny.
The bandit Cheyenne (Jason Robards) drinks from a jug, revealing in the process that he is in handcuffs.	*The Comancheros* (1961, Michael Curtiz): Paul Regret (Stuart Whitman) drinks from a bowl at a watering trough, revealing in the process that he is in handcuffs. In the same film, the John Wayne character goes by the pseudonym of McBain and the main plot begins in the town of Sweetwater.

Harmonica plays some "false notes" on his instrument.	*Night Passage*, the Anthony Mann sequence: A fight breaks out at the end of the railroad track, and James Stewart says, "I guess I must have squeezed out a couple of wrong notes."
Jill and Sam arrive in Sweetwater, where they are greeted by the sight of the McBain family corpses laid out on trestle tables.	*Tribute to a Bad Man* (1955, Robert Wise): The tough rancher (James Cagney) discovers the corpse of L.A. Peterson laid out on a farm wagon, with a well in the background, at the Peterson ranch – in a dust storm.
The McBains are buried in rough coffins, following a frontier funeral ceremony.	*Shane*: One of the sodbusters is buried in a similarly rough-hewn coffin – Shane and the Starrett family looking on – following a frontier funeral ceremony.
The disabled Mr. Morton (Gabriele Ferzetti), proprietor of the Morton Railroad Company, sits in his executive carriage.	Influences include a succession of wheelchair-confined – and tyrannical – patriarchs, who try to run their landholdings with a rod of iron. Among the most memorable are Lionel Barrymore in *Duel in the Sun* (1946, King Vidor), Walter Huston in *The Furies* (1950, Anthony Mann), and Melvyn Douglas in *Hud* (1962, Martin Ritt). The closest to Morton is Edward G. Robinson in *The Violent Men* (1955, Rudolph Maté), who has lost the use of his legs in a range war, walks on crutches, and wants to control the whole valley, from end to end, before he dies. His brother Cole (Brain Keith) kills one of the small holders who is in the way, and Robinson says, "My orders were to do it without spilling blood."
Morton and Frank discuss business: "It's almost like holding a gun, only much more powerful."	*The Man Who Shot Liberty Valance* (1962, John Ford): Ranse Stoddard makes his reputation in the Shinbone business community and eventually becomes a senator on the strength of his claim of having shot the outlaw Valance. He also teaches the local inhabitants about Washington, Lincoln, law and order – and progress.
Meanwhile, the bandit Cheyenne searches the Sweetwater ranch house in hopes of discovering the reason why the McBains were slaughtered.	*Johnny Guitar*: In her saloon, Vienna displays the wooden model of a railroad, with surrounding town. "When the railroad track reaches here, how much do you think this property will be worth?"/"Its weight in gold."
Cheyenne tells Jill that she reminds him of his mother; later he compliments her, saying, "My mother used to make coffee this way – hot, strong, and good."	*Warlock*: Reformed bandit Gannon (Richard Widmark) talks with Miss Dollar (Dorothy Malone), as she passes him a cup of coffee. "You didn't finish your beans."/"My mother used to say that."/"It's a thing women say. Where is she?"/"She's dead, Miss Dollar . . . She died, oh I don't know, nineteen years ago, back in Nebraska." In the same film, gunfighter Clay (Henry Fonda) says to Miss Marlowe, "My mother played the melodeon . . . Yes, even killers and gunmen have mothers."/ "And I'm sure you loved and respected her."/"Yes, ma'am."
Cheyenne tells Jill, "You make good coffee, at least . . ."	Gags about making coffee around the campfire abound in the 1950s Western – including in *The Tall T* (1956, Budd Boetticher) when reluctant badman Usher (Richard Boone) says to Pat Brennan (Randolph Scott), "You make good coffee," and in *Three Rode Together* (1961, John Ford), when cynical sheriff James Stewart says to cavalry officer Richard Widmark, "You make lousy coffee, I'll tell you that for sure." But the actual line seems to come from the film noir *Farewell, My Lovely*.
Jill McBain spends an uneasy night at Sweetwater, armed with a farmer's rifle.	*Sergeant Rutledge* (1960, John Ford): The heroine spends an uneasy night at the remote Spindle Railroad Station in Arizona, with a rifle in her lap, "trying to stay alive."
Harmonica strips Jill of her fashionable New Orleans clothes to prepare her for her role as water-bearer.	*Man of the West* (1958, Anthony Mann): Billie Ellis (Julie London), singer at the Longhorn Palace, is stripped of her scarlet saloon-girl outfit – at gunpoint – by Dock Tobin's (Lee J. Cobb) henchmen at their wilderness hideout. And in *River of No Return* (1954, Otto Preminger), as Kay (Marilyn Monroe) floats downriver on a raft, she changes from her saloon-girl outfit to jeans, boots, and patterned shirt: "My things!" she cries, as the suitcase containing her fine dresses floats downstream.
Harmonica shoots Frank's men as they ride toward Jill at the Sweetwater well. Cheyenne wryly observes, "He not only plays, he can shoot, too."	*Rio Bravo* (1958, Howard Hawks): Stumpy (Walter Brennan) says to Sheriff Chance (John Wayne) during the climactic shootout, "Can you shoot as good as you say you can?"/"Can you throw?"/"Near as good as you can shoot." In *Johnny Guitar*, Johnny asks the Dancing Kid (Scott Brady), "Can you dance?" The laconic reply is, "Can you shoot?"
Harmonica boards Morton's train to settle his account with Frank – who repeatedly asks, "Who are you?" Harmonica replies with a list of dead men's names, "All alive till they met you, Frank."	*The Bravados* (1958, Henry King): As lawman Jim Douglas (Gregory Peck) tracks down and kills the men he thinks raped and killed his wife – Lee Van Cleef, Stephen Boyd, Henry Silva – they all ask at the point of dying, "Who are you?" or "Who is he?"

Frank asks Wobbles (Marco Zuanelli), "How can you trust a man who wears both a belt and suspenders? Man can't even trust his own pants."	Kirk Douglas says exactly the same thing in *Ace in the Hole* (1951, Billy Wilder).
Unbeknown to Frank and Morton, Cheyenne is traveling on the metal chassis beneath the executive carriage; he announces his arrival by flushing Morton's newfangled water closet.	*Man Without a Star* (1955, King Vidor): Jeff (William Campbell), known as the Kid, travels in the same way – beneath a railway carriage, on the Kansas City–Wyoming train – while drifter-from-Texas Kirk Douglas travels with his saddle in the cattle truck, and Jack Elam stows away on the roof. The film, which features the arrival of interior plumbing in the West, contains one of the best "bathtub gags" in the genre: "D'you know what we're putting in? A bathroom in the house."/"In the house . . . Well, that ain't decent!"/"Only someone from the East could think of that!"
The wooden component parts of the town of Sweetwater are delivered to the site.	*Cimarron* (1960, Anthony Mann): On the eve of the first Oklahoma Land Rush in April 1889, the future town of Osage is laid out (as Yancey Cravat/Glenn Ford puts it), "with certain sections plotted off like town lots, and all the rest divided up into farms." The film shows Osage's development from shacks to brick-built mansions, from frontier main street to skyscrapers.
Cheyenne asks, "What are we going to do? Build a station, idiots . . . !"	In *How the West Was Won*, Mike King (Richard Widmark) says after the Arapaho attack, "The rest of you get back to work, we've got a railroad to build."
The Sweetwater site is auctioned by the sheriff (Keenan Wynn), while Frank's men terrorize the bidders.	*The Man Who Shot Liberty Valance*: Liberty (Lee Marvin) and his henchman (Lee Van Cleef and Strother Martin) terrorize the inhabitants of Shinbone during a local election meeting. In *How the West Was Won*, Gregory Peck's San Francisco mansion – complete with solid gold model of a locomotive – is sold for a song. The auctioneer asks, "Is that your last bid?" and the widow Lily (Debbie Reynolds) is told, "It's a bad day . . . if there had been some other way" to meet her debts.
Meanwhile, Frank calmly pays a visit to the town barber [scene excised from the final cut] "Shave and haircut?"/"Shave and silence . . . Perfume!"	*My Darling Clementine*: Wyatt Earp (Henry Fonda) gets a shave and is sprayed with "sweet-smellin' stuff" in Tombstone's Bon Ton Tonsorial Parlor and Dentist.
The sheriff puts a handcuffed Cheyenne onto the train from Flagstaff to Yuma: "I'm sending you to Yuma . . . It's got a modern jail there." Cheyenne's men get on the same train to rescue him.	*3:10 to Yuma* (1957, Delmer Davis): Rancher Dan Evans (Glenn Ford) escorts outlaw Ben Wade (Van Heflin) through the town of Bisbee to the Yuma train, which will transport him to jail – having protected him, in the hotel's bridal suite, from all intruders. Wade's exit line is, "I've broken out of Yuma before."
In Flagstone's Gold Coin Palace Hotel bar, Frank pays for his whiskey by tossing a dollar coin into his empty glass. He says to Harmonica, "You're entitled to your profit, same as the next man."	*Two Rode Together*: James Stewart tosses a dollar coin into his empty whiskey glass. "What was that, sir?" asks trader John McIntyre. "That's for the drink. You don't even store honest whiskey."
Frank walks cautiously from the hotel, across the street and toward his horse – while Harmonica watches from a balcony.	*Rio Bravo*: Chance (John Wayne) and Dude (Dean Martin) walk through the urban landscape of a Texas town, in a dust storm. *Forty Guns* (1957, Sam Fuller): Griff Bonnell (Barry Sullivan) walks down the main street of town, Wyatt Earp–style, toward a nervous gunman.
Outside Scott's Retail Store, Frank passes a painted clockface without hands. The shadow of a rifle across the clock elicits Harmonica's words: "Time sure flies; it's already past twelve."	*High Noon*: The hands of the clock in Sheriff Will Kane's office tick away to noon, in real time.
Harmonica protects Frank from his own armed employees, in order to save him for the final settling of accounts: "You saved his life."/"I didn't let them kill him – and that's not the same thing."	*Rancho Notorious* (1950, Fritz Lang): Vern Haskell (Arthur Kennedy), whose own revenge is constantly being thwarted, says, "I'm going to kill you, Cinch, but I'm not going to murder you."
Mr. Morton dies in the desert, crawling like a snail toward a puddle from his own locomotive. In his mind, he's made it from sea to shining sea.	*Western Union* (1941, Fritz Lang): Edward Crayton, surveyor for the Western Union Telegraph Company, falls off his crutches and lands facedown in a puddle of water.

Cheyenne, having escaped from the Yuma train, tells Jill to "make believe it's nothing" when the railroad workmen pat her on the behind: "You can't imagine how happy it makes a man feel."	*Jubal* (1956, Delmer Davis): Foreman Jubal Troop (Glenn Ford) and simpleminded rancher Shep (Ernest Borgnine) sit in the wilderness discussing how to look after a woman. "Well – there's a lot of things a man does that bother a woman, like whackin' her on the behind when she isn't looking."/"Well, I always do that."/"You mean in front of company?"/"Well, sure – well, if I just swat her in private . . .?"/"You think she likes being swatted?"/"Well, don't all women? Shows 'em you love 'em, don't it?"/"Well, there's other ways, you know, Shep. She's just fed up with bein' whacked on the rump."/"Thanks for the tip, Jube. I guess you know women after all, better'n I do." Shep's wife (Valerie French), meanwhile, says of her relationship with Shep, "I'm livestock."
Sitting outside the Sweetwater ranch house, Harmonica whittles on a piece of wood. "I've got a feeling, when he stops whittling," says Cheyenne, "something's gonna happen."	*The Magnificent Seven*: Bernardo O'Reilly (Charles Bronson) whittles on a piece of wood to entertain the Mexican children. As he dies in the final gun battle, he says to the children, "What's my name?"/"Bernardo."/"You're damn right."
Harmonica discusses "an ancient race" with Frank: "Nothing matters now – not the land, not the money, not the woman. I came here to see you."	Influences include Budd Boetticher's "Ranown" cycle of Westerns – especially *The Tall T* (1956), *Ride Lonesome*, and *Comanche Station* (1959) – in which stoical Randolph Scott is usually on a mission of honor to avenge a personal tragedy, and in which he acknowledges at the climax that "there are some things a man can't ride around." *Man of the West*, too: In the ghost town of Lassoo on the Mexican border, reformed badman Gary Cooper settles accounts with his cousin Claude, who used to ride with him in the bad old days. "We're all alone now, Claude. Just you and me . . . This is the moment. You've been planning for it all your life. Now it's finally here. Just like you knew it always would be."
Harmonica and Frank fight a gun duel in the backyard of the McBain ranch, while Jill waits inside the house to learn the result.	*The Last Sunset* (1961, Robert Aldrich): Black-clad O'Malley (Kirk Douglas) and wholesome Mr. Stribling (Rock Hudson) meet for a gun duel in the stockyard beside the town of Agua Caliente, while Dorothy Malone waits inside to learn the result. The formalized presentation of the duel (rhythmic cutting, matching shots, extension of real time, electric guitar accompaniment) resembles the Harmonica/Frank confrontation.
At his moment of death, Frank "shares" in Harmonica's flashback memory of the day he was first given his harmonica – the day his brother was tortured and hanged from a brick arch in Monument Valley.	*Pursued*: Flashback to the massacre of Jeb Rand's family, when Jeb was a child – in the New Mexico desert – starting with flashes of light and a close-up of a pair of spurred boots, which we see in greater detail as the story progresses. All is revealed when murderous lawyer Grant Callum (Dean Jagger) puts a noose around Jeb's neck at the climax. Jeb has had the feeling "something's after me," throughout the story. *Run of the Arrow*: the mute Indian child plays a death rattle on his harmonica as Jeb falls into the quicksand.
Cheyenne warns Jill that people like Harmonica "have something inside – something to do with death."	*Warlock*: It is said of gunfighter Clay (Henry Fonda) that "trouble and death follow you." But the line most likely came from *High Sierra* (Raoul Walsh, 1941): Doc Banton says, "Remember what Johnny Dillinger said about guys like you and him – he said you were just rushing towards death – yeah, just rushing towards death."
Jill says to Harmonica, "I hope you'll come back someday." He replies without conviction, "someday," and leaves behind all possibility of "family" as he goes through the door.	*Sergeant Rutledge*: A friend says to Braxton Rutledge of the Ninth Cavalry, "Maybe someday, but not yet." He replies, "Someday . . . You always talk about someday, Brax." *The Searchers*: Ethan Edwards (John Wayne) goes through the door of the Edwards' ranch house – which is shut behind him – his mission accomplished. Ford called the film "the tragedy of a loner who could never really be part of the family." In Europe the film was titled *The Prisoner of the Desert*.
Cheyenne dies of gunshot wounds in the desert – killed by Mr. Morton's derringer.	As if Liberty Valance, the wild man, *had* been shot by Senator Ransom Stoddard after all.
Sweetwater: Thirsty railroad workers finally arrive at the McBain ranch by locomotive; Jill takes water to them.	*The Iron Horse*: The railroad is blasted through the mountains; a locomotive reaches the "end of [the] track" with just wooden sleepers ahead at North Platte; a locomotive enters the makeshift town of Cheyenne, with the workers crowding onto the rolling stock; two locomotives meet at Promontory Point just as the metal rails finally link the Union Pacific (which has gone west from Nebraska) and the Central Pacific (which has gone east from California). Uniting North and South, as the prologue says, by binding together East and West. Most of these sequences were visually re-created, in one form or another, for the equivalent moments in *Union Pacific* and the track-laying episodes of *How the West Was Won*. In Leone's film, the Morton Railroad Company has started at the Atlantic and reached Arizona on its way to the Pacific.

DUCK, YOU SUCKER/A FISTFUL OF DYNAMITE [1971]

The Mexican Revolution, 1913. After the early successes of Villa and Zapata, and President Madero's land reforms, Victoriano Huerta, whose downfall is imminent, is trying to put the revolutionary impulse into reverse. Against this bloody and confusing background, Juan Miranda – a naive Mexican bandit with a large extended family – hitches a ride on a luxurious stagecoach and robs its rich passengers, who have been humiliating him by talking offensively about the Mexican peasantry. He crosses the path of Sean Mallory, an ex-IRA terrorist who rides a motorcycle and is an expert on explosives. Miranda tells Mallory of his plans to rob the fabled bank at Mesa Verde. After blowing up the stagecoach, Sean goes with Juan and his family to Mesa Verde where they eavesdrop on a backroom meeting of a revolutionary cell led by Dr. Villega. Juan and his family break into the bank, only to discover that it has been converted into a political prison; after releasing the inmates, Juan is hailed as a "great, grand hero of the revolution." Sean Mallory, it transpires, is working with Villega's revolutionaries and has been using Juan Miranda, seeing in him the potential to become a new Pancho Villa. Government troops, under the unpleasant Colonel Gunther Ruiz (or Reza), lead the

inevitable reprisals. Sean and Juan temporarily hold up an armored advance of Ruiz's troops by ambushing them at a bridge with a big explosion, but this only leads to Juan's family being massacred in a cave and Dr. Villega being tortured into betraying his comrades. Sean has periodic flashbacks of the time in a Dublin pub when he was betrayed by an IRA comrade, whom he then shot. Finally, the remaining revolutionaries agree to derail Ruiz's troop train with a head-on collision. Dr. Villega, unlike Sean, does not save himself by jumping from the revolutionaries' train at the last minute, and he dies as the train spectacularly collides with Ruiz's locomotive. In the ensuing carnage, Juan kills Ruiz and Sean is badly wounded. While Juan goes to get help, Sean kills himself in a nitroglycerin explosion. Before he dies, he dreams of an idyllic Ireland when the issues seemed so much simpler, before he realized that "revolution means confusion."

A delayed reaction against the idealistic, late-1960s Italian "political" Westerns – set during the Mexican Revolution – the film was also Leone's statement about his own disillusionment with politics. Leone, who had "fallen out of love with the things associated with the West" was originally going to produce the picture, with

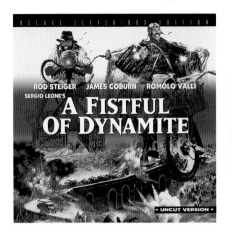

Opposite: **Juan Miranda (Rod Steiger, center, standing) and his extended family of bandits in** *Duck, You Sucker*

Left: **When** *Duck, You Sucker* **bombed in U.S. theaters, it was rereleased as** *A Fistful of Dynamite*, **in an attempt to capture audiences who remembered the Leone** *Dollars* **films.**

Right: **Sean Mallory (Coburn) shortly before his explosive death in** *Duck, You Sucker*

Following left: **A German lobby card for** *Duck, You Sucker*

Following right: **James Coburn as explosives expert Sean Mallory, a former IRA terrorist, in a German lobby card for** *Duck, You Sucker*

Peter Bogdanovich as director. But late in the day, United Artists persuaded Leone to direct. Although the part was originally written for Eli Wallach, Juan Miranda was played by Rod Steiger, whose method-acting approach caused some friction on the set. Sean Mallory was played by James Coburn, with whom Leone had wanted to work since casting *A Fistful of Dollars*; his part was originally slotted for Jason Robards or, failing him, Malcolm McDowell (as a much younger IRA man). As a matter of historical fact, the Irish Republican Army did not exist until 1919, but Leone's vision of Ireland is more about John Ford's films *The Informer* (for the betrayal) and *The Quiet Man* (for the greenery) than about history. Dr. Villega was played by Leone's close friend Romolo Valli, who had been a medical student before becoming a stage actor in the 1950s and a character actor in Visconti's *The Leopard* and *Death in Venice*. Before preparing *Duck, You Sucker*, Leone had toyed with the idea of remaking the 1934 film *Viva Villa!* (possibly using Toshiro Mifune in the Wallace Beery role as Pancho Villa), and one of his ambitions was to challenge "the Hollywood romance of the sombrero."

His film was shot – this time by Pasolini's cinematographer Giuseppe Ruzzolini – between April and July 1970 in Guadix (the old quarter), Almería (the railway station), near Gérgal (the stopping of the coach), at a disused sugar factory on the outskirts of Guadix (the firing squads), and in a small village called Medinaceli, near Guadalajara – where production designer Andrea Crisanti (substituting for Carlo Simi, who was unavailable) built the bank and main square of Mesa Verde. With fewer variations, Morricone's music was slower and more lyrical than usual, and had a strong emphasis on the soaring soprano voice of Edda dell'Orso, used as if it were a musical instrument.

In Italy, the film was called *Giù La Testa*, meaning "keep your head down" or "get out of the way." In France, it had the best title: *Il était une fois la révolution* ("Once upon a time, the revolution"). In America, it was originally called *Duck, You Sucker*, then retitled *A Fistful of Dynamite*. It was not a commercial success under either title. Among critics in Italy and France, however, the film was better received than Leone's earlier films. In particular, it was noted that the two central characters develop a relationship, and both of them "grow" during the story – a Leone first. The film has been reappraised following the release of the full 152-minute version.

SERGIO LEONE
PRÉSENTE

TERENCE HILL · HENRY FONDA

**MON NOM
EST "PERSONNE"**

UN FILM DE
TONINO VALERII

Left: **At the climax of
My Name Is Nobody,
Jack Beauregard
(Henry Fonda) faces
the new fast gun
in town, Nobody
(Terence Hill),
in a gun duel, as
shown on this
French lobby card.**

Opposite left: **A
French poster for
My Name Is Nobody
featuring the duster
from *Once Upon a
Time in the West***

Opposite right: **A
French lobby card
showing "the Wild
Bunch" in *My Name
Is Nobody***

Following: **Illustrations
by Renato Casaro
grace the amusing
front and back
covers of the Italian
45 rpm soundtrack
single for *My Name
Is Nobody*.**

MY NAME IS NOBODY [1973]

It is 1899, and aging veteran gunfighter Jack Beauregard is planning to retire to Europe. His eyes are not what they once were, and there are too many youngsters wanting to challenge him. At the beginning of the film, he demonstrates his prowess against three bad guys in a barbershop. When he discovers that his brother has been killed by Sullivan, a corrupt businessman who runs a phony gold-mine scam, Beauregard postpones his departure to claim his share of the loot. "Is there anyone faster than him?"/"Faster than him? Nobody!" Enter an energetic and self-assured drifter with a gun, called Nobody, who has hero-worshiped Beauregard since he was a child, and who wants the veteran to bow out in style rather than quietly to retire. He keeps egging the older man on, but Beauregard thinks Nobody is far too reckless. Amazingly quick on the draw, Nobody shows off his skill at a carnival and in a saloon. Eventually, Nobody stage-manages a mighty confrontation in the desert between Beauregard, on one side of the railroad tracks, and "the Wild Bunch," on the other – 150 riders in long dusters who are employed by Sullivan to do his dirty work but who are, in fact, manipulating him. Beauregard scores well (the Wild Bunch are carrying dynamite in their saddlebags),

earning his place on the sepia pages of a history book. Now he must retire to make way for Nobody. A duel is fought – and photographed – on a period street in New Orleans, in front of a large crowd, and Nobody wins. But the duel has been set up to allow Beauregard to bow out in a fitting way, and he is next seen on a stern-wheel boat, writing a valedictory letter to Nobody: "You can preserve a little of that illusion that made my generation tick." It is Nobody's turn to become famous, to become Somebody after all, and to step into the shoes of the legend. He enters a barbershop similar to the one where the story began.

Full of references to Leone's earlier films (the opening scene and duel scene of *Once Upon a Time in the West*; the old prophet from *For a Few Dollars More*), to children's games, carnivals, and nursery rhymes, and to the work of Sam Peckinpah (*The Wild Bunch*; the elderly gunfighter with eye trouble from *Ride the High Country*), *My Name Is Nobody* started life as an attempt to turn Homer's *Odyssey* into a Western – hence the title, an echo of what the Cyclops says to Ulysses. But as the project developed, it also became a commentary on the incredibly popular *Trinity* comedy Westerns starring Terence Hill, and an *arrivederci* to the Italian Western.

Terence Hill plays the hyperactive Italian hero, and Henry Fonda – in his farewell to the Western – gives a dignified performance as a fading "national monument." In fact, by coincidence, the great Western director John Ford died, clutching his rosary, just after *My Name Is Nobody* finished principal photography. Morricone's music picked up on the elegiac, twilit atmosphere with a slow variation on the opening bars of "My Way," before parodying his own "Like a Judgment" theme from *Once Upon a Time in the West* for the final duel, and accompanying the rides of the Wild Bunch with a jokey version of Wagner's *Ride of the Valkyries* played on car horns. The music exactly matched the tones of the movie: part lyrical "end of the West" lament, part zany comic strip, Italian-style. *My Name Is Nobody* was directed by Tonino Valerii, Leone's assistant from *Dollars* days who had since directed four Westerns of his own, as well as a couple of thrillers. He was conscious that, for Leone's first film as a producer, he might favor "a young man trained in the Leone school of direction" and that Leone might also think that "he could influence me in a certain direction." In the event, Valerii was proved right on both counts: *My Name Is Nobody* is often mistaken for a Leone-only film, and Steven Spielberg is reported to have called it his favorite Leone film – much to Valerii's annoyance.

My Name Is Nobody was filmed on location in America – in Taco, New Mexico, Arizona, and New Orleans – and then around Guadix, partly on the Flagstone set at La Calahorra from *Once Upon a Time in the West*. Armando Nannuzzi photographed the American scenes, then, after quarreling with Valerii ("He wanted to intervene in the film's direction"), was replaced in Spain by Giuseppe Ruzzolini. Meanwhile, there were delays in Spain, so Sergio Leone took over the second unit, filming, among other scenes, the saloon sequence and the carnival with Terence Hill, who was thrilled to be directed by the maestro. When the film was released, Sergio Leone's name appeared three times on the credits – "Sergio Leone presents," "From an idea by Sergio Leone," "Produced by Sergio Leone" – while the director's name appeared only once. The public was eager for a new Leone film.

My Name Is Nobody overtook *They Call Me Trinity* at the Italian box office and was a huge hit in France and Germany, but it did not do well in America, where it had a lackluster marketing campaign ("Nobody but 'Nobody' knows the trouble he's in!"). It is fascinating to compare *My Name Is Nobody* with John Wayne's farewell Western *The Shootist* (1976), which was also produced by an Italian: Dino De Laurentiis. The "national monuments" were saying goodbye.

GENERAL MUSIC

stereomono zge 50469

Distribúzione RCA s.p.a.

MUCCHIO SELVAGGIO

dalla colonna sonora originale del film

IL MIO NOME E' NESSUNO

ENNIO MORRICONE

PRINTED IN ITALY CAMPI FOLIGNO 1 74 grafica

GENERAL MUSIC

stereomono zge 50469
Distribuzione RCA s.p.a.

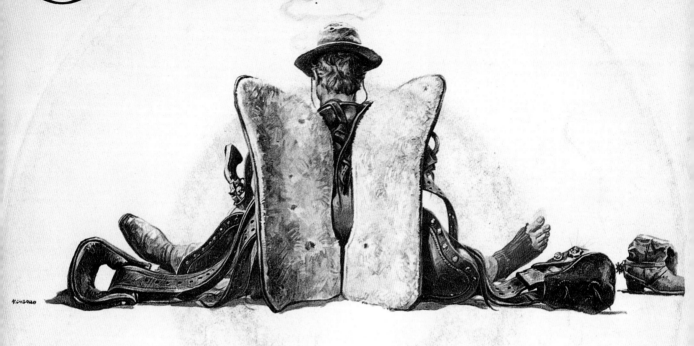

IL MIO NOME E' NESSUNO

dalla colonna sonora originale del film omonimo

ENNIO MORRICONE

INTERVIEWS

THE DIRECTOR
SERGIO LEONE

This conversation took place at the Dorchester Hotel, London, on an evening in February 1982. Sergio Leone had phoned me earlier that day to thank me for the research into his father, Vincenzo, which I'd put into my book Spaghetti Westerns. *That afternoon, he visited George Lucas, who was working on* The Return of the Jedi *at Elstree.*

CHRISTOPHER FRAYLING: **Many critics now take your films seriously – and particularly *Once Upon a Time in the West*. But for a long time, they gave your work a very rough time.**

SERGIO LEONE: The day after *A Fistful of Dollars* opened in Rome, one of the reviews really got to me – because it was written by an enemy of mine. It was a thoughtful review which even suggested connections between *Fistful* and the films of John Ford . . . So I picked up the telephone and said to him, "I'm touched, truly touched by your support. Thank you so much. I'm so glad you were able to bury our disagreements." And this was his reply: "But what on earth have *you* got to do with *A Fistful of Dollars*?" It was then that I realized he was the only critic in town not to have found out that behind the name of "Bob Robertson" on the credits was Sergio Leone. Since then, with monotonous regularity, he has always panned my films. You know that the name "Bob Robertson" was chosen with reference to my father's chosen name "Roberto Roberti" – and by the way, I was very touched by the material you found about my father in your book *Spaghetti Westerns*.

But, of course, you are right about the critics in general. The newspaper reviewers always accused me of trying to copy the American Western, from the very start. Later, the critics wrote that I was trying to create a form of "critical cinema." Both were missing the point, in their different ways. Because, in fact, I brought to the Western some strict conventions of my own, which did not include imitations of the American ones. And obviously, there's a culture behind me that I can't just wish away. I can't

Opposite: **Steiger and Leone locked horns during the making of *Duck, You Sucker.***
Above right: **Leone gets his own close-up, circa 1971.**

just negate it. For example, we live and breathe Roman Catholicism, even if we don't believe all of it. So perhaps this comes through in aspects of my films, as you say in your book *Spaghetti Westerns*. It is in the air.

I also have my own things to say when I make a Western. At the time I was preparing my first Western, *A Fistful of Dollars*, in some ways I really felt like William Shakespeare. It occurred to me that William Shakespeare could have written some great Westerns!

Shakespeare. Why?
Because Shakespeare wrote some great Italian romances without ever having been to Italy – far better than the Italians did. Apart from the fact that a few people claim that Shakespeare really *was* an Italian [*laughter*]. But that's another story.

And in any case, how long do you want to go back in history? I am convinced that by far the greatest

writer of Westerns was Homer, for he wrote fabulous stories about the feats of individual heroes – Achilles, Ajax, and Agamemnon – who are all prototypes for the characters played by Gary Cooper, Burt Lancaster, Jimmy Stewart, and John Wayne. Homer's stories are the great mythological treatments of the individual hero, as well as being prototypes for all the other Western themes – the battles, the personal conflicts, the warriors and their families, the journeys across vast distances – and, incidentally, providing the first cowboys. The Greek heroes entrusted the short span of their lives to their dexterity with lance and sword, while the cowboys entrusted their survival to the quick drawing of a pistol. Basically, it all comes down to the same thing. These are the great myths about individualism. The warrior. The pistolero.

In my films, the women tend not to play a very important role because my characters had no time to fall in love or to court someone. They were far too busy trying to survive – to pursue what it was they were after. So the roles for women in Western films usually tend to be kind of ridiculous. The Rhonda Flemings in *Gunfight at the OK Corral*. What's she there for? To make Burt Lancaster seem even more of a hero. If you had taken her out altogether, the film would have worked better and moved faster. Now, if the female character is at the center of the story – like Claudia Cardinale in *Once Upon a Time in the West* – then that is very different. What I suppose I'm saying is that I was able to approach the Western with detachment, from a European point of view, while still being a lover of the genre.

You've mentioned in interviews that another Italian source for your Westerns – let's accept that Shakespeare *wasn't* Italian! – was the puppet tradition in Sicily.

As I say, when I started my first Western, I had to find a psychological reason inside myself – not being a person who ever lived in that environment! And a thought came to me spontaneously: It was like being a puppeteer for the *pupi siciliani*. The pupi siciliani are an old Sicilian

tradition. The players tour around in a painted carriage performing shows which are both historical and legendary – based on the *Song of Roland*. They stop with their puppets and their carriage in every village square and put on a performance. However, the skill of the puppeteers consists of one thing: to give each of the characters an extra dimension which will interest the particular village the pupi are visiting; to adapt the legend to the particular locality. That is, Rolando takes on the faults – and the virtues – of the village mayor. He's the good guy in the legend. His enemy, the bad guy, becomes – say – the local chemist . . . The puppeteers take a legend or fable and mix it with the local reality. The relationship with everyday life is a two-way one. You get the parallels? As a filmmaker, my job was to make a fable for adults, a fairy tale for grown-ups, and in relation to the cinema I felt like a puppeteer with his puppets. *The Song of Roland* was absorbed into Italian art by the poet Ludovico Ariosto as *Orlando Furioso*. Ariosto adapted it to become Italian, as he rewrote the Middle Ages. The puppeteers by the same token made this story more interesting for local

Above: **Leone and his daughter Raffaella on the White Rocks set of *For a Few Dollars More*, May 1965**

people because they added to a character the public did not know much about, all the characteristics of a real local person. That is what I tried to do with the Western. You see? There was a strange fraternity between the puppets of the traditional Sicilian theater and my friends of the Wild West . . .

You call your films "Fairy tales for grown-ups." Can you explain what you mean?

The films are for grown-ups, but they remain fairy tales and have the impact of fairy tales. For me, cinema is about imagination, and the imagination is best communicated in the form of parables – meaning fairy tales. Not in the Walt Disney sense, though. They draw attention to themselves as fairy tales – everything is made up and cleaned up and sugary sweet, and this makes the tale less suggestive. To me, anyway. I think that fairy tales capture the audience's imagination when the setting is realistic rather than fantastical. The fusion of realistic setting and fantasy story can give film a sense of myth, of legend. Once upon a time . . .

You've also related your films, especially *The Good, the Bad and the Ugly*, to the picaresque tradition in literature – books such as *Don Quixote*.

In films of adventure, and especially serious Westerns, directors are scared of letting the audience laugh – of allowing a picaresque spirit to intrude on tragic adventures. The picaresque genre in literature isn't *exclusively* a Spanish literary tradition, you know: There are also equivalents in Italy. The picaresque and the *commedia dell' arte* – an Italian theatrical tradition – have this much in common: They do not have true heroes represented by a single character. Take Harlequin in the Goldoni comedy: He serves two masters and is a trickster. He sells himself to one master and then to the other without either knowing about it. So he is not a "true hero." The same with Clint Eastwood in *The Good, the Bad and the Ugly*. Again, my background, my formation, contains things which have inevitably influenced me and which have nothing to do with Westerns.

But there was this extraordinary interest in Westerns among Italian audiences in the mid-1960s. Your *Fistful of Dollars* started an avalanche.

When they tell me that I am the father of the Italian Western, I have to say, "How many sons of bitches do you think I've spawned?" There was a terrifying gold rush after the commercial success of *A Fistful of Dollars*, and I felt – and continue to feel – a great responsibility for this phenomenon. It wasn't as if the Italian Western had been taken up by many serious producers or serious directors; it was simply a terrifying gold rush, and most of them built castles in the sand instead of on rock – the foundations just weren't there. A stampede! Imagine the affection with which people must have viewed my first film, when they were prepared to put up with four hundred more as they searched for the same thing. There was pressure from all sides to reveal the exact location of a second gold mine. By 1968, they were turning out about a hundred Westerns a year in Italy – six of them being shot on the same day! Incredible. And it ended up with the *Trinity* films with Terence Hill and Bud Spencer, which came as a reaction after all these ugly Italian Westerns. There was a title of one of these films in Italy: *If You Meet Sartana, Tell Him He's a Dead Man*. Well, a joke was going around in Rome, based on this, which said: "If you meet Sartana, tell him he's an asshole." This was what Enzo Barboni, the director of the *Trinity* films, had an instinct about. He would take these stock characters from the Italian Westerns and present them to the same audiences who had sat through four hundred ugly films – only this time around, he spat in the characters' faces, made fun of them, and treated them badly. Then he would have success with them again. Psychologically, the trick worked . . . for a time. But it was an easy game to play. Along came a film where pistol duels were replaced by slaps in the face! The audience felt liberated. It was a form of retaliation . . . [The second *Trinity* film, *Trinity Is Still My Name*] was released at a very precise moment of exasperation with a genre which had run out of breath. When the film was later reissued, it had no success at all.

When you made *Once Upon a Time in the West*, you seemed to be deliberately distancing yourself from this assembly-line approach to filmmaking.

Well, when I made *Once Upon a Time in the West*, I was originally supposed to be making *Once Upon a Time in America*, my film about gangsters in New York. And *West* was a side issue to begin with. I was finishing *The Good, the Bad and the Ugly* and really did not want to do any more Westerns. The horses, the guns, the costumes, the settings – they didn't excite me as they once did. Remember that I'd made three films in three years, one after the other. But unfortunately, success has more of a stigma than lack of it. People may pardon you over and over again for the fact of *not* being successful, but they never pardon you for a success. So I went to America with the intention of – with the proposal for – making *Once Upon a Time in America*, and they said, "This one is rather expensive. I'll tell you what – first we'll do another Western and *then* we'll talk about *America* . . ." I said, "Fine, but I will do a Western the way *I'd* like to do it." And I began to think about this story, which honestly I never estimated would have a commercial success. The basic idea, of course, was to use some of the conventions, devices, and settings of the American Western film, and a series of references to individual Westerns – to use these things to tell *my* version of the story of the birth of a nation.

You've called *Once Upon a Time in the West* "a dance of death."

Yes, I wanted to do a film which was a dance of death, or a ballet of the dead. I wanted to take all the most stereotypical characters from the American Western – on loan! The finest whore from New Orleans; the romantic bandit; the killer who is half-businessman, half-killer, and who wants to get on in the new world of business; the businessman who fancies himself as a gunfighter; the lone avenger. With these five most stereotypical characters from the American Western, I wanted to

Opposite: **Japanese poster for *Once Upon a Time in the West***

present a homage to the Western at the same time as showing the mutations which American society was undergoing at that time. So the story was about a birth and a death. Before they even come onto the scene, these stereotypical characters know themselves to be dying – in every sense, physically and morally – victims of the new era which was advancing . . . I wanted in this way to tell the story of the birth of a nation which is America . . . In fact, Claudia Cardinale represents the water, the promise of the West; the plot revolves around her, and she's the only one who survives. Charlie Bronson represents the last frontier, the end of the frontier. Henry Fonda is torn between being a cowboy, a killer, and a businessman. Jason Robards represents the last romantic, the last romantic who is possible. Gabriele Ferzetti is the relentless force of capitalism, at whatever the personal cost.

***West* is full of "citations" of American Westerns. Opening with *High Noon*, going on to *Shane* and *The Searchers*, the whole story being a variation on *The Iron Horse* and *Union Pacific* and even *How the West Was Won*.**

Certainly those references are all in there. We wanted that feeling throughout of a kaleidoscopic view of all American Westerns put together. But you must be careful of making it sound like citations for citations' sake. It wasn't done in that spirit at all. The "references" aren't calculated in a programmed kind of way; they are there to give the feeling of all that background of the American Western to help tell this particular fairy tale. They are part of my attempt to take historical reality – the new, unpitying era of the economic boom – and blend it together with the fable. Once upon a time, there was the West . . . For example, the harmonica is a direct descendant of the guitar in *Johnny Guitar*.

Bernardo Bertolucci reckons that amidst all the cinematic game playing and the use of references to moments in Westerns, he may have slipped in one or two even you didn't notice!

テクニスコープ／テクニカラー

パラマウント映画

CIC配給

First of all, I'd like to say that Bertolucci remembers less vividly than he might. He worked on the treatment and not the script of the film. I made all the decisions as director, but he really did bring something personal to his work on the treatment. The script was prepared, after Bernardo had worked on the treatment with me and Dario Argento for about two months, from their outline suggestions. I, in fact, prepared the script with Sergio Donati, very quickly indeed. The actual script writing took less than a month.

Why did you decide to adopt a different cinematic style for this film?

The rhythm of the film . . . was intended to create the sensation of the last gasps that a person takes just before dying. *Once Upon a Time in the West* was from start to finish a dance of death. All the characters in the film, except Claudia, are conscious of the fact that they will not arrive at the end alive . . . And I wanted to make the audience *feel*, in three hours, how these people lived and died – as if they had spent ten days with them: for example, with the three *pistoleri* at the beginning of the film, who are waiting for the train and who are tired of the whole business. I tried to observe the character of these three men, by showing the ways in which they live out their boredom . . . So we had the fly and the knuckles and the dripping water. They are bored because they are inactive. You get the feeling that all the characters in the film *know* that they will not arrive at the end. They all take pleasure in each passing second, as though it is their last. The rhythm – short time, long time – is like the last gasp that a person takes. This style was in some ways a *reaction*. As I've said, I wanted to make a film for myself rather than for the public. I can still remember, after the opening in Rome, one person in particular – a greengrocer who worked near the Piazza Venezia – coming up and saying, "Leone's gone crazy – he can't say a fucking thing

Top: **Cardinale as Jill McBain on a Spanish lobby card**
Bottom: **Leone reversed Henry Fonda's usual Western character by making him the sadistic killer Frank.**

straight anymore. America must have had a bad effect on him!" Eventually, though, *Once Upon a Time in the West* had the same kind of succès d'estime as Stanley Kubrick's *2001*. When they were first released, both films had a rough ride in the first instance – and it was only after a few months that the word of mouth began to spread, among students and cinéastes, in colleges and schools, particularly in France and West Germany. Even in Australia. Critics all over the place began to reappraise my earlier films, which I thought was hilarious. In Paris, *Once Upon a Time in the West* really took off. It ran in a cinema on the Boulevard St. Michel, uninterrupted, for two years. When I visited the cinema, I was surrounded by young cinéastes who wanted my autograph. All except one, the projectionist, who approached me and said, "I kill you! The same movie over and over again for two years! And it's so slow." There was a phrase going around the Paris menswear houses just after *Once Upon a Time in the West* opened. The phrase was "This year, the style is Sergio Leone." Somehow the French film-going public was better prepared for a kind of cinema which was slow and reflective.

Where did the idea for those "duster coats" – the *spolverini* – come from?
When the Americans spoke about the costumes in *Once Upon a Time in the West*, as they did, and asked where I had copied them from, I said, "I haven't invented anything – I've just gone back to the original." The canvas "dusters" were a practical kind of garment, because they were the only protection a cowboy had when he stayed away from town out in the desert for several days at a stretch – the only protection against the terrible dust of the desert in the daytime and the downpours of rain at night. And the dusters were good with whiskey stains, too. Sometimes they were covered in buffalo grease, as a protective surface. So when the cowboys took them off they almost stood up by themselves! American directors depend too much on other screenwriters and don't go back enough into their own history. Actually, some of the Westerns that were made at the very beginning of the century were

closer to actuality. But with the expansion of Hollywood, the films came to diverge more and more from historical reality. For one thing, the Western was sidetracked by the influence of rodeos and radios, which had little to do with the real West.

One or two critics writing about the late 1960s have said that a distinctive feature of the period was the way in which some European filmmakers "commented" in a conscious way on Hollywood films – Claude Chabrol and Alfred Hitchcock, Bertolucci and film noir, yourself on the films of John Ford.
There's something in that. Ford is a filmmaker whose work I admired enormously, more than any other director of Westerns. I could almost say that it was thanks to him that I even considered making Westerns myself. I was very influenced by Ford's *honesty* and his *directness*. Because he was an Irish immigrant who was full of gratitude to the United States of America, Ford was also full of optimism. His main characters usually look forward to a rosy future. If he sometimes demythologizes the West, as I had tried to do in the *Dollars* films, it is always with a certain romanticism, which is his greatness, but which also takes him a long way away from historical truth (although less so than most of his contemporary directors of Westerns). Ford was full of optimism, whereas I, on the contrary, am full of pessimism. So there is a great difference in our conceptions of the world – but outside of that, if anyone influenced me, it was Ford. There is a visual influence there as well, because he was the one who tried most carefully to find a true visual image to stand for "the West." The dust, the wooden towns, the clothes, the desert. The Ford film I like most of all – because we are getting nearer to shared values – is also the least sentimental, *The Man Who Shot Liberty Valance*. We certainly watched that when we were preparing *Once Upon a Time in the West*. Why? Because Ford, finally, at the age of almost sixty-five, finally understood what pessimism is all about. In fact, with that film Ford succeeded in eating up all his previous words about the West – the entire discourse he had been

promoting from the very beginning of his career. Because *Liberty Valance* shows the conflict between political forces and the single, solitary hero of the West. A conflict and a more attentive eye looking at the implications of the conflict. And in the end a pessimistic look at the conflict. That's what I take from *Liberty Valance*. Ford loved the West, and with that film at last he understood it. Someone pointed out to me that *Liberty Valance* also has a *triello*, like the ones in my stories – a three-way duel between Stewart, Wayne, and Marvin.

The conflict between the solitary hero and political forces beyond his control was once turned by Karl Marx into the classic question: "Is Achilles still possible side by side with powder and shot? Or is *The Iliad* at all compatible with the printing press or even printing machines . . . ?"
Yes, I know that quotation. My father was a socialist, and so that makes me a disillusioned socialist, and I tend to pour all my disillusionment – my disillusionment with dreams – into my films. But my inspiration comes also from films that chime with this feeling. For example, Charlie Chaplin's film *Monsieur Verdoux* had a strong influence on *The Good, the Bad and the Ugly*. In my film, we find two killers who are confronted by the horror of an entire war – the war between the North and the South – and one of them says, "I've never seen so many men wasted so badly." In *Monsieur Verdoux*, the protagonist, who is a murderer, says when he defends himself, "I am just an amateur at homicide compared with Mr. Roosevelt and Mr. Stalin and Mr. Churchill, who do such things on a grand scale. I am just a little dilettante."

What do you think your influence has been on the American Western?

Partly secondary, partly primary. *A Fistful of Dollars* certainly had an influence, as did later films. For example, Sam Peckinpah told me that *The Wild Bunch* could not have been made if it hadn't been for my films. He said that *A Fistful of Dollars* launched "a new kind of cinema." Up to a certain time, Westerns were more like children's games, with people dying by falling forward – instead of being propelled backward. The lead bullet would enter like this and stay there without leaving a mark. I feel that *A Fistful of Dollars* made a certain breakthrough in terms of the presentation of violence and ushered in the kind of realism that now can be used in these films. The producers did not think before this that it could be done. In this sense, my films have not only influenced the Westerns that came after, but also other films. Stanley Kubrick could not have made *Clockwork Orange* without this breakthrough in the treatment of violence in cinema. Not just violence, but cultivating the look of *verismo* to tell a fable. While he was preparing *Barry Lyndon*, Kubrick phoned me and said, "I've got all Ennio Morricone's albums. Can you explain to me why I only seem to like the music he composed for your films?" To which I replied, "Don't worry. I didn't think much of Richard Strauss until I saw *2001*." Kubrick was at that time preparing to make a kind of *Once Upon a Time in Eighteenth-Century England* . . .

It seems difficult these days to find a theme for the Western that "fits" the American experience of life. The function of Western as myth seems to be in trouble now.
Even when it was a successful form of cinema, the Western was always underrated by the film establishment. When you think that John Ford never won an Academy Award for his Westerns – and some of them were very good

indeed. Now audiences are not so interested. They are no longer so fascinated by the Western. Maybe this has got something to do with the use Hollywood and American television have made of this genre in the past. Or the fact that rural themes no longer appeal to an urban audience . . . Also Westerns cost just as much as any other films – and sometimes much more these days – when everything has to be done almost from scratch. Howard Hawks or someone once said that you can't make a good Western without dust, rocks, and actors who know how to have gunfights and get on a horse. That costs money. But in the history of American Western films, there's never been one that has made a great deal of money. Unless you count *Gone With the Wind* (which I don't) or a Broadway satire like *Blazing Saddles*. These days, with rising costs, the Western is not seen as that good an investment.

The genre became self-conscious long before *A Fistful of Dollars*, didn't it? Think of *Shane*, a story that is presented as a myth seen through the eyes of a child.
Yes. *Shane* shows up – by contrast – the repetitiveness and the lack of attention to detail in most Westerns made after that. And it wasn't a big film by today's standards. It was important to me when I was preparing *A Fistful of Dollars*, much more so than with *Once Upon a Time in the West*. Remember the scene where Jack Palance challenges the little man outside the saloon? When the little man is shot, he staggers six yards back into the mud. It is a very realistic presentation of death. And it is the result of careful thought . . . When you think of all the Westerns you've seen, I'm sure you'll agree that as a rule the producers shied away from a realistic approach and turned the whole thing into a prepackaged formula kind of entertainment that paved the way for the empty clichés of television – with a few exceptions, of course.

After a while, if you had seen one Western you had seen them all. One of the reasons why the Western began to induce sleep – why the public lost interest – was because of repetition and because of that prepackaged approach to filming action and violence. And the characters talked so much! The producers laid so much vocalizing on top of the gunshots and the hoof beats that they lost sight of what the Western stories were all about. All those voices! They superimposed the most positive and reassuring values of the day onto a brief period of American history, which was in reality amazingly violent – what I've called the rule of violence by violence. But you wouldn't know that from the films. Talk, talk, talk. For example, they ought to make a film set in Andersonville Camp in the American Civil War. No one has dared to do that. Another film they ought to make instead of *Patton* is *Sherman*. I'd like to see someone try *that* in a film!

The serious Western has become almost synonymous with the American films of Clint Eastwood. He's carrying the genre single-handed. What do you think about the Westerns he's made since leaving Italy?
I'd like to hear what you think.

I think *Josey Wales* is a terrific film. *High Plains Drifter* was like an Old Testament parable.
Yes, to mix the morality of the story with my protagonist . . . But what fascinated me about Clint above all [when we first met] was his external appearance and his own character. The first thing I ever saw him in was a fifty-minute episode of the television series *Rawhide*, and that particular episode was called "Incident of the Black Sheep." I took Clint Eastwood on above all because Jimmy Coburn cost too much at that time. He cost about twenty-five thousand dollars and we only had fifteen

thousand dollars to spend. When I saw "Incident of the Black Sheep," I noticed that Clint didn't speak much . . . but I noticed the lazy, laid-back way he just came on and effortlessly stole every scene from Victor, I mean Eric Fleming. His *laziness*, his laid-back quality is what came over so clearly. When we were working together, he was like a snake, forever taking a nap five hundred feet away, wrapped up in his coils, asleep in the back of the car or on the set. Then he'd open his coils out, unfold, and stretch . . . When you mix that with the blast and velocity of the gunshots, you have the essential contrast that he gave us. So we built his character on this, as we went along, physically as well, giving him the beard and the small cigar that he never really smoked. When he was offered the second film, *For a Few Dollars More*, he said to me, "I'll read the script, come over

Above: **Lee Van Cleef, looking like "a hairdresser from the south of Italy," according to Leone**

and do the film, but please, I beg of you, one thing only – don't put that cigar back into my mouth!" And I said, "Clint, we can't possibly leave the cigar behind. It's playing the lead!"

Have you wanted to work with Clint Eastwood since *The Good, the Bad and the Ugly*?
I made him a proposal once, which he in good humor refused. I wanted to say farewell to the three characters from *The Good, the Bad and the Ugly* and to do so in style. I wanted to say farewell to them and to the rules of the game, which I had imposed. So I hoped that the three *pistoleri* who are killed by Charlie Bronson at the beginning of *Once Upon a Time in the West* would be Clint Eastwood, Lee Van Cleef, and Eli Wallach. The other two agreed, but Clint was the only one who didn't want to do it – so there wasn't any point in using Lee Van Cleef and Eli Wallach. It wasn't a question of expense – he just couldn't see the funny side of it . . .

You've talked about your first sight on film of Clint Eastwood. What about Lee Van Cleef?

This is a marvelous story. Lee Marvin was supposed to play the part of Colonel Mortimer in *For a Few Dollars More*. I thought he was terrific as the badman with a whip in *The Man Who Shot Liberty Valance*. But this agreement fell through a few days before filming was scheduled to begin. Lee Marvin had accepted the leading role – actually two roles – in the film that was to make his fortune, *Cat Ballou*, for which he also won an Oscar. So I found myself without a leading actor, with only a few days to go, and I flew to Los Angeles to find another Colonel. I had with me a very old photo of Lee Van Cleef from the *Academy Players* directory, in which he looked like a hairdresser from the south of Italy. But he also had a hawklike nose and the almond-shaped eyes of Van Gogh. I had absolutely no idea what he looked like in 1965. How could I have? I remembered having seen him in *High Noon* – where he had a walk-on part – and *The Bravados* and *Gunfight at the OK Corral*, but that was several years earlier. He might have changed his appearance since then. I made a calculation that he must have been about forty then, so now he would be about forty-eight, forty-nine, or fifty – just the right age for the Colonel.

When I got to Hollywood, he seemed to have completely vanished. Finally, after a lot of running around, we managed to find an agent called Sid. This agent told me Lee Van Cleef was no longer a film actor, that he was a painter, and that he had been in hospital for a long time, because he had been in a head-on car accident in a canyon at Beverly Hills. He had been in hospital for a long time, and after coming out he had decided to take up a new profession . . . But I said, "Well, I must see him at all costs, because physically when I think of this character I picture him." And a few hours before my plane left, Lee Van Cleef came to this small hotel on the outskirts of Los Angeles where I was staying. It was a drive-in, motel kind of place – Canyon Dry or something like that. I was staying there because it was close to Clint Eastwood, who lived outside Hollywood. Anyway, I saw Lee Van Cleef walking

in the distance. I was with my production manager, Ottavio Oppo. From a distance, he looked just exactly right. He was wearing a long trench coat, very dirty, with long black boots and short hair. He looked like a grizzled old eagle. I turned to my production manager and said, "Just sign him up here and now. I don't even want to speak to him, because if I do it might decide me not to take him, and I might not take him because I don't take to him, and if I did that I would be making a big mistake. A big mistake. He is so *perfect* for the film that I don't want to hear a word of what he has to say." And that is what happened. Then I did start to speak with him and found him to be a pleasant and intelligent man. I gave him the script of *For a Few Dollars More* so he could read it on the flight to Rome. When we got there, a car came to collect us and take us to Cinecittà, where we had to start shooting the first setup right away. Straight down to business, without even a couple of hours' rest. Anyway, he read the script, and when he'd finished I came up to him on the plane and asked, "Well, what do you think of it?' And he said, with a smile, "It's Shakespearian." He was so shaken by events that he hadn't really understood the script very well. I don't know what was going on in his head at that moment – coming over to play a leading role when he was least expecting it. Up until then, he'd decided to give up films for good. And the script was a bit unusual, something different from the usual Western script. But still . . .

You mention the cinematic memory of Lee Van Cleef, and we've talked about the Western references in *Once Upon a Time in the West*. Can you remember any of the other American Westerns you had in mind for the first two *Dollars* films?

One of the first loves of Italians who grew up in the 1930s was America. Like all first loves, it may well be seen from a different point of view after the event, but it is never forgotten. And that was given to us by Hollywood, especially the epic of the West. The exploits of these larger-than-life characters became events in our own personal lives. When I was making my own Westerns,

I wanted to try and recapture some of the excitement of that first love – which had since become a distant memory, it is sad to say. I wanted to make the myths come to life again. And in this project, I called to mind certain films. *Shane* was important. Remember the way Jack Palance gets off his horse very, very slowly and stylishly? And, of course, the scene with the little man outside the saloon. What else? I'd seen so many Westerns. There was John Ford's *My Darling Clementine* with the gunfight in the dust, whipped up by the stagecoach. There was *Rio Bravo* by Howard Hawks, where John Wayne and Dean Martin take one side of the street each on their so-careful night patrol. The Budd Boetticher films. And *Warlock* I liked very much. Many films, many Westerns. People have said that I chose Eli Wallach for *The Good, the Bad and the Ugly* because of his performance as the bad guy in *The Magnificent Seven*. It wasn't because of that. It was because in *How the West Was Won*, when he acted for the children, he showed that he could be a great clown as well.

If you were going to make a Western today, what theme do you think would be right for the times?
That is very difficult. *Once Upon a Time in the West* was the summa of everything for me. It would need a story and a type of discourse that fascinated me in a very particular way, for me to enter into all that again. Maybe an epic film about the American Civil War would be interesting, dealing with Andersonville and problems of that nature.

So many Hollywood films since 1967 have tipped their hat in the direction of your films.
They don't even do it mysteriously. They even say openly: "That's where we got it." It's not that anyone is trying to hide it.

***Once Upon a Time in the West* seems like a very expensive film. I gather that the set for the town of Flagstone cost more than the entire budget of *A Fistful of Dollars*.**

It was a miracle, the way it happened. A Hollywood producer told me that "if it had been made by us at that time, the film would have cost us ten million dollars. Minimum." Remember, we're talking about 1968. The above-the-line cost was in the region of one and a half million dollars – but the total cost came to only about three million dollars. The cost of the film, less the above-the-line, was only just over one million dollars. Which really is miraculous, given the cost of the main set. And for that Paramount allowed me to make a Western the way I wanted to make it.

***Once Upon a Time* is the film that seems to have had the most impact on the 1970s generation of Hollywood filmmakers. John Carpenter, George Lucas . . .**
Maybe. They set their films in the future, but a lot of them are really Westerns. For example, when I saw the opening sequence of Steven Spielberg's *Close Encounters*, I thought, "That was made by Sergio Leone." You know, the dust, the wind, the desert, the planes, the sudden chord on the soundtrack. And it was the same with John Carpenter's *Escape From New York*: They even say my early Westerns had an influence on him. George Lucas has told me how he kept referring to the music and the images of *Once Upon a Time in the West* when he cut *Star Wars*, which was really a Western – series B – set in space. All these younger Hollywood directors – George Lucas, Steven Spielberg, Martin Scorsese, John Carpenter – they've all said how much they owe to *Once Upon a Time in the West*. Perhaps they like it because it's a real *director's* film . . . But none of them has ever been tempted to make a Western that is actually a Western. Some of these younger directors – who are no longer very young! – make films that are evidently American, but seen in a European way. And this "contamination" has produced some excellent results. I particularly admire the films of Spielberg, which are about much more than meets the eye. But as to my influence . . . well, I don't know. I did receive a very warm reception from the students at the two most important film schools in Los Angeles. They told me that they study

extracts from my films, such as *The Good, the Bad and the Ugly*. They actually use these extracts for lessons on editing technique, which is, I must say, gratifying.

And yet at the time, *Once Upon a Time in the West* – and indeed *The Good, the Bad and the Ugly* – were cut in America before they were released.
With *West*, the decision to cut the film was particularly disastrous. The film was constructed comma by comma, carefully constructed like a geometric exercise – or rather, like a riddle taking the form of a rebus – with all the fine little components playing their part in the whole, and with all the component parts revolving around a center. Like a labyrinth. Or maybe more like a chess game. It's a concept that appeals to me very much, and I will be using it in *Once Upon a Time in America*.

I've been speaking to a number of American film directors about the Western today – and most of them confirm that the real challenge is to find a theme that chimes with audiences while retaining the best traditions of the Western movie.
As I've said, American directors depend too much on previous scripts and don't go back enough into their own history. When I was preparing *The Good, the Bad and the Ugly*, I discovered that there had only been one big battle in Texas during the Civil War, which was really about the ownership of gold mines in Texas. The point of the battle was to stop one group of guys from getting their hands on the gold first, before the other group of guys. So when I was visiting Washington, I tried to get some more documentation on this incident. The librarian there, at the Library of Congress, the biggest library in the world, said to me, "You can't be right about this. Texas, you say, signore? You must be mistaken. There's never been a battle fought over gold mines in America, and certainly not in Texas. Come back in two or three days, and I'll do some checking for you. But I'm quite certain you are wrong." Well, I returned after two or three days, and this guy looked at me as if he'd seen a ghost. "I've got eight

books here," he said, "and they all refer to this particular thing. How the hell did *you* know about it? You read in the Italian language, so how did you manage to find out? *Now* I understand why you Italians make such extraordinary films. Twenty years I've been here, and not a single American director has ever bothered to inform himself

Above: **Sergio Leone was a serious collector of antiques and paintings, and it shows in his Westerns.**

JASON ROBARDS:
JASON ROBARDS:

"The atmosphere – I didn't find it tense; I found it a joy, a lot of fun. I felt that was Sergio. Now, some people, I'm sure, find it tense if he gets very demanding. But he said to me, 'You and Hank do the acting, and I'll just shoot, make photographs of the others.' Making us feel good, you see."

about the history of the West." Well, I've got a huge library myself now – they'll photocopy a whole book for you for eight dollars in Washington! That's the great thing about going there for research. You can have any book you want photocopied. I have stacks of them.

You obviously take a lot of trouble over the details in your films – props, weapons, decor.
On *Once Upon a Time in the West*, I was even more meticulous and detailed than a Visconti. Do you know that when we were shooting interiors, I even had brought that particular dust of that particular color all the way from Monument Valley. I think a meticulous approach to the particular is a great help and support to an actor . . . Visconti has sometimes been criticized for being too fussy. You can't be.

Have you ever been tempted to make a film about Italy and Italian society – set in the present?
I like to make films that are spectacular . . . Unfortunately, although Italy is a great nation and has a high profile in some things – Italian fashion and design are successful throughout the world – it still does not offer much in international terms. One of the reasons that prompted me to make Westerns was because they are part of a tradition that is becoming lost to the Americans themselves. Now it belongs to all of us. The Western is a consumer item in Japan, Nigeria, Colombia, England, Italy, Germany, and France – all over the place. It belongs to the world now. But Italy, on the other hand, has a big problem in this respect. Take a fine film like Visconti's *The Leopard*, for instance. It is incomprehensible in America. Visconti did a marvelous job on it, but it was a huge flop in America. They said, "We're not interested in this story about Southern Italy in the last century, which we know nothing about." When you write a story about Italy, unfortunately, you can write only about Italy. In America, though, even in the smallest town, you can write about the world. Why? Because it is a conglomeration of all these communities. You can find the world in America. I mean the world, with

all its customs, defects, and strengths. As a European, the more I get to know of America, the more it fascinates me *and* the more distant I feel – light years away.

You sound pessimistic! Finally, would you like to say whether you think the ending of *Once Upon a Time in the West* is pessimistic or optimistic?
From one point of view, it is optimistic – in that a great nation has at last been born. "Great" because after all the killing, so many cadavers, some building, something constructive is at last going on . . . It's been a difficult birth, but all the violence has made the greatness possible. From another point of view, it is pessimistic, undoubtedly – because the West has given way to the great American matriarchy, the worship of "Mom." America has come to be based on this, and the arrival of the railroad ushers in the beginning of a world without balls, if I can put it that way. The great force in American life – part of its formidable success story – is based on women with iron balls, so to speak. I'm pretty sure that Rockefeller's grandmother came from a whorehouse in New Orleans – or if not her, someone similar – and behind the American success story, there is this awesome force of women who are extraordinarily strong.

Like Jesse James's mother, you mean . . .
Si, si.

Opposite: **Leone, on horseback, surveys the set of Sweetwater (*Once Upon a Time in the West*) in Almería.**

THE COMPOSER
ENNIO MORRICONE

A Fistful of Dollars
For a Few Dollars More
The Good, the Bad and the Ugly
Once Upon a Time in the West
Duck, You Sucker
My Name Is Nobody

This conversation was recorded in November 1989 in Rome for the BBC2 television documentary Viva Leone! *for which I was consultant. (Thanks to codirector Nick Freand Jones for supplying the full transcript.) I subsequently met Ennio Morricone in March 2001, when he was in London for a sold-out pair of concerts at the Barbican. On both occasions, when the orchestra started playing the opening bars of* The Good, the Bad and the Ugly, *the audience erupted.*

VIVA LEONE!: As a musician and composer, how did you start in films?

ENNIO MORRICONE: You want to start your questions in the distant past! At the Santa Cecilia Conservatoire where I studied, I wasn't thinking of becoming a composer of film music . . . I continued with my classical music studies, because I wanted to increase my musical culture. After leaving the Conservatoire, I started writing chamber music, and little by little I realized that I couldn't live on the very meager income from composing contemporary music, and so I competed for a job in the Conservatoire in Sardinia, at Sassa, but didn't get there because others were ahead of me. At that point I started working as an arranger for records, songs, radio, television, theater – and gradually I got to know [director] Luciano Salce, who asked me to write music for two comedies on the stage in Rome, then for my first film. It was *Il Federale/The Fascist*, and it was a great success – not so much for the music, but the success meant that people could get to know me. Then I did other Salce films, and other directors began to offer me work.

How did you come to be working with Sergio Leone on *A Fistful of Dollars*?

We met because he had heard two of my film scores – one for a Spanish director and one for an Italian. They were both Westerns. And Sergio Leone asked me to write the music for his film *A Fistful of Dollars*, only then it was still called *The Magnificent Stranger*. Clint Eastwood became the magnificent stranger who comes into this small town, with its two rival families. Finally they changed the title.

Sergio Leone came to my house to talk to me about the film, and I recognized him because of this funny way he had of moving his lips. We had been at school together in the third grade. The last time we'd seen each other we'd been playing cops and robbers in the courtyard during break time. I even remembered his name, and that's how we recognized each other; but I recognized him first. Twenty-five years had passed . . .

Did you read the script of *The Magnificent Stranger*?

He asked me *after* the film had been shot and edited. After that, our method changed a lot. Sergio became more and more meticulous. We went together to see *A Fistful of Dollars* again at the Quirinale Cinema here in Rome. It was already a success. It was one year later, and the film was still on its first run. We came out of the side door of

Opposite: **Two great collaborators: Ennio Morricone (left) and Sergio Leone (center), circa 1972**
Above: **Early Italian Morricone 45 rpm single soundtrack recording of *Fistful***

the cinema and stood in the street, and both of us realized that it was a good film but perhaps it could have been made much better. Sergio felt he could do better and I, too, thought I could do much better. We weren't happy with it. As it turned out, this feeling was justified because the second film, then the third, the fourth, the fifth . . . Sergio and I, too, continued improving. The success of *A Fistful of Dollars* spurred us on. We knew the film had value, and that both he and I had to maximize that value. We wanted to make our work a thing of perfectionism. When I think of Sergio, I often ask myself what he could have done for cinema if he had continued living. He could have done so much.

How did you work with Sergio Leone on that first film?
He told me about this film, all his thoughts about *A Fistful of Dollars*. We went to see *Yojimbo* together, and he told me that the spirit of his leading man was like Toshiro Mifune's – that the character was exaggerated and that the film was picaresque. I understood that Clint's expression was a little like that of a Roman bully, and I liked him right away. Sergio told me the story of the film, always making gestures with his hands. I understood the film very well by what he told me. He seemed to know exactly what he wanted, and some of my music, which he'd listened to, already contained a grotesque, slightly comic irony, which suited the Clint character. Sergio

Above left: **Japanese soundtrack recording of** *Fistful*
Above right: **Spanish soundtrack recording of** *The Good, the Bad and the Ugly*
Opposite: **French soundtrack recording of** *Once Upon a Time in the West*, **where this single was especially popular**

heard an arrangement I'd made for an American piece, an arrangement where I'd deliberately left out some of my ideas. Those ideas I'd left out were to let people hear, behind the musical theme, the nostalgia of a character, Mister X, for the city. As the city was heard in the distance, I could use the city sounds coming from far away – the sound of a church bell, a whistle, percussion, and a guitar. He listened to this and liked it very much and wanted it at once as one of my themes – without the vocal. He told me to practically leave it as it was. That was the main title.

Then, when we arrived at the final scene where there's that trumpet, he had gone back to the Mexican *deguello* from the film *Rio Bravo*. Sergio and Roberto Cinquini had actually set up in their minds the images to go with this deguello by Dimitri Tiomkin. I said, "Sergio, if you put that deguello in the film, I won't do it – because I have no interest at all in doing that kind of work." I've always rejected those sorts of compromise. So he said, "Okay, you compose it, but do it in such a way that it sounds like a deguello." I didn't take very kindly to that either, so I took an old theme of mine that I'd written for a friend, a lullaby for some sea dramas by Eugene O'Neill, a television series of these three sea dramas. This lullaby was sung by one of the Peters sisters. The choice of this piece of music, written long before *A Fistful of Dollars*, relieved me of the distressing burden of having to write an imitation of that deguello – in the sense that the theme was far removed from the lament. What made the theme resemble the lament was its performance, played in a quasi-gypsy style on the trumpet, with all the melismas that go with that kind of

trumpet playing. In the second film, we had the trumpet again; in the third; and in the fourth we were finally just about liberated from this thing . . . In *Fistful*, I told Sergio later that I'd used an old theme of mine. This led him, on all his subsequent films, to select musical themes that other directors had rejected. He would reevaluate them in his own context. It became almost a point of honor. "Okay, let's take that one – it's really very good even if they rejected it." And in other cases, I had written themes that hadn't been rejected, but just left in a drawer.

When did the idea arise of writing the music first?
It developed from *The Good, the Bad and the Ugly* onward. Because *For a Few Dollars More* was made by Sergio almost at once after the success of *A Fistful of Dollars*, so there was no time for us to work out themes in advance. But for *The Good, the Bad and the Ugly*, there was.

How did your relationship with Sergio evolve from film to film?
It didn't really evolve. It was our *resolve* that became stronger. His stories became more complex, funnier, and more dramatic. In his third film, the story of the American Civil War was introduced. In the fourth, the story of the building of the railroad from East to West. In *Giù La Testa*, the story of a revolutionary who fits into the environment of a Western film. His stories evolved, and as a result my musical ideas got better, too. Already in *The Good, the Bad and the Ugly*, the idea of having the main musical theme based on the sound of the coyote was a step forward – the theme that took on three different

ALESSANDRO ALESSANDRONI:
"*A Fistful of Dollars*? Nobody believed in this kind of movie. I remember that all the people in the studio were laughing because we saw on the screen lots of *deads*, lots of corpses. And also the RCA, who were the music publisher, they didn't believe in this film. They wouldn't spend much money on the soundtrack. Anyway, Ennio Morricone had chosen the whistle and the trumpet – the mariachi-style trumpet. So he asked me to whistle for him. 'Alessandro, come here to RCA – there is a little whistling to do.' And I was used, because before I had whistled for Nino Rota – just a small piece – and then I discovered that my whistle was very good for the microphone, because the microphone doesn't like the breath and I have just a small amount of breath and the most part of my whistle is whistle. Everyone can whistle, but most people have 50 percent of air, 50 percent of sound. My whistle is 90 percent sound, 10 percent of air. The microphone is very sensitive. So my sound is pure. Sergio Leone used to joke with me, I remember. He was so big, you know. 'So you have to whistle the best you can this morning – because it is very important.' And we used instruments that were unusual in a Western. A wooden flute, for the scale. A whip. Bells. The Sicilian *maranzano* – '*dang*.' The use of instruments was quite different from the traditional approach; it made a kind of Italian folk sound. Also the harmonization. Very simple, but dramatic. And for *A Fistful of Dollars*, I played my 1961 electric Fender Stratocaster guitar, as well."

ENNIO MORRICONE

RCA VICTOR
47-9615

Für eine Handvoll Dollar
(aus dem gleichnamigen Constantin-Farbfilm)

Vorspann-Musik
(aus dem Constantin-Farbfilm „Für eine Handvoll Dollar")

aspects, reflecting the three main characters. There was an articulation in the thought and form of these pieces that didn't even exist in *A Fistful of Dollars* – *A Fistful of Dollars* was the starting point.

After *Fistful*, did you work from scripts?
No. Generally, Sergio did not give me the script. He told me the story, his take on the characters, and even what the design of the sets would look like. Then I would compose the music. Since I knew him very well, I knew just how to proceed. I would play him the themes [on the piano], he would discuss them – like them or not like them. Usually he was happy with what I did.

The phrase "internal music" – justified from within the scene – has been used about your musical scores for Leone.
Sergio understood very well – and it is important in his films – how music that is internal to a scene, which grows out of the scene, retains and carries all the expressiveness it acquired during the scene. For instance, the organ that plays the *Toccata* by Bach for the duel scene in the church in *For a Few Dollars More*; or the harmonica in *Once Upon a Time in the West*. The first time we hear the harmonica, it is internal to the scene; when we hear it subsequently, it is no longer internal but it has retained all the dramatic strength, the irony, and the tragedy it originally attracted from its internal setting. The sound of the harmonica was born "by chance" from the harmonica in the mouth of the brother who supported his elder brother on his shoulders, an elder brother who would die when the younger man collapsed from fatigue. The sound

was a symbol in the viewer's memory and also a dramatic representation of the story of the entire film – therefore, it remains present throughout the film. This is something that Sergio really understood . . .

The sound of the chiming watch in *For a Few Dollars More* – the Colonel's watch – was fundamental, too, with the rape and the explanation at the end. The chime starts as an internal sound, passes through being a mediated sound, and becomes an external one. Technically, Sergio did not know much about music, but his intuition was extraordinary. I would never have spoken to him using terms like the ones I've just used. But he had great intuition.

By the time of *Once Upon a Time in the West*, you were writing all the music in advance.
The main themes for *Once Upon a Time in the West* were ready before filming. So I recorded them in advance and he shot the film with the theme music on the set. I believe Sergio regulated the speed of the crane that follows Claudia Cardinale when she comes out of the station, in time with the musical crescendo. But for the first twenty silent minutes as well, there was something very important that I'd told Sergio. I'd been, some time before, to a concert in Florence where a man came onto the stage and began in complete silence to take a stepladder and make it creak and squeak. This went on for several minutes and the audience had no idea what it was supposed to mean. But in the silence the squeaking of this stepladder became something else, and the philosophical argument of this experiment was that a sound, any sound at all from normal everyday life –

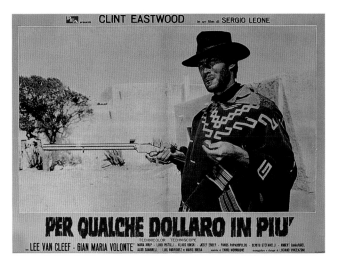

PER QUALCHE DOLLARO IN PIU'

...LEE VAN CLEEF · GIAN MARIA VOLONTE'...

isolated from its context and its natural place and isolated by silence – becomes something different that is not part of its real nature. I talked about this with Sergio, who already had these things in his blood – in his ideas about silence. He made those extraordinary first twenty minutes of *Once Upon a Time in the West* from that idea. I really believe that. Everything in that silence: the drop of water, the fly, the wind, the mill, the crunch of footsteps – all isolated and yet all mixed together. All isolated, and then there are the moments of the reality of the sound.

In a way, it becomes a kind of fantasy. In my opinion, this was one of the best things that Sergio did in his film.

You've said that Sergio "always respected the work of musicians and of the orchestra . . . other directors don't mix the music well, they keep it too low or they cover it with sounds."

The orchestration is, for me at least, a fundamental thing – and the theme is very important in the orchestration. But the place where a theme itself is put is the decisive thing for the success of the film and for the theme itself. I'd say that the theme itself is almost not so important as where it is inserted and in what instrumental setting it is put. So even if I've worked very hard to find a good theme, and Sergio has been very careful in his selections, this remains an irrefutable fact – from the work I've done with Sergio and with other directors . . . Out of his intuition,

Opposite left: **German 45 rpm soundtrack single of *Once Upon a Time in the West***
Opposite right: **French single of *My Name Is Nobody***
Above: **Eastwood holds the chiming watch in an Italian *fotobusta* for *For a Few Dollars More*.**

Sergio understood a very important thing – that film and music share a temporal dimension; they rely on time for their existence. We need to see a film in the time it takes to screen it. We need to listen to music in the time its composer imposes on us. It is not like a painting, which you can enjoy in a few seconds, during which time you can be struck by the greatness of a picture or a sculpture or even a grand palace designed by a great architect. You can come back and admire it later. Film and music need attention, transmission, that makes use of time. If you respect the temporal nature of both film and music, you get the best results. Sergio had this intuition, and so for some scenes he left the music alone and gave it time to express itself . . .

Sergio, famously, spent a lot of time on the sound design for his films.

It was very important to him that he rid his films of inessential sounds. He not only wanted to strip away all inessential sounds, he wanted to isolate sounds and improve their quality. He pushed the soundmen like I'd never seen anyone do – with big fights sometimes. That's how he was. On the one hand, very conscientious about what he was doing – a great creative crisis – and on the other, he was open to anyone who had any kind of criticism to make. He was presumptuous and modest both at the same time. This sensitivity to external criticism was what helped him to get better and better. Sometimes, external critics caused him to make some mistakes – for example, some cuts that shouldn't have been made that instead of improving a scene may have made it worse. For example, the cut at the end of *Giù La Testa*. He cut all the flashback about Ireland, at least in the Italian version, and it was a cut that saddened those who had viewed this scene. It happened by accident. My brother-in-law stood up in a screening just before that flashback, and Sergio – who was watching the audience, not the screen – noticed. He didn't say a word to anyone, but he cut the scene. Maybe my brother-in-law's fault! Often he had been accused of overelaborate endings, so he

plucked up his courage and made the cut. And I think it was an error. He was sensitive to criticism, both explicit and implicit.

Is there a scene in Sergio's films that you are particularly fond of?

There are some moments in Sergio's films that have already become historic moments in the story of cinema. The pre-finale in *The Good, the Bad and the Ugly* – which is called "the ecstasy of gold" – when Tuco arrives at the cemetery to find the grave where the gold is hidden. Those three minutes and twenty seconds are a cinematographic moment of enormous expressivity – but also great editing techniques, great camera techniques, and a great way to think out a scene. Also, I must say, the music did its part . . .

Was it different, when scoring Tonino Valerii's film *My Name Is Nobody*?

With Valerii's film, my discussions were not only with Valerii but also with Sergio, who was the producer and who took an interest in everything – conscientious as he was – in everything that happened in a film he was involved in. Besides, it was the first production he'd made, so he was very particular about everything. He had to be, because by now he had become an important director of Westerns – and not only of Westerns. Sergio insisted on being present at the discussions between me and Valerii and naturally supervised all the things we discussed.

In English, we sometimes refer to Westerns as "horse operas" . . .

I don't think Sergio's films are horse operas . . . The real importance of Sergio's films, I think, especially the later ones, is that the films might well not be Westerns . . . They are about humanity.

Were you both surprised by the success of the first film, *A Fistful of Dollars*?

We were both surprised. Sergio, as well. As I told you, we returned to the Quirinale Cinema where the film was still on its first run, a year later. And we both came out thinking we could have done it much better. That was a lesson in modesty, to see it again after one year. This desire for perfection, born of the re-viewing of that film, those words we spoke to each other outside the cinema, remained with us to the end. Sergio and I always wanted to improve the quality of our work – with application, with love, even with our quarrels, sometimes stormy, but always friendly – in our search for the best. That's what I remember about Sergio. Always the wish to become better. If he had made the film he was planning to make, after the beauty of *Once Upon a Time in America*, I do wonder what he could have achieved – this extraordinary friend and film director.

Above left: **French 45 rpm soundtrack recording of *Once Upon a Time in the West***
Above right: **Morricone soundtrack recording of *Duck, You Sucker***
Opposite: **Japanese Morricone soundtrack recording of *Duck, You Sucker*, coupled with *Shaft***

●ユナイト映画「夕陽のギャングたち」主題曲

¥500

夕陽のギャングたち

Duck You Sucker From "Duck You Sucker"

●MGM映画「黒いジャガー」主題曲

黒いジャガーのテーマ
Theme From "Shaft"

THE ACTORS
CLINT EASTWOOD

A Fistful of Dollars
For a Few Dollars More
The Good, the Bad and the Ugly

This conversation took place at Claridge's Hotel, London, in May 1985. Clint Eastwood was in London to promote Pale Rider *and to appear on the stage of the National Film Theatre for a question-and-answer session. Having spent a long day talking to journalists about* Pale Rider, *he seemed at the end of it to enjoy reminiscing about his Italian experiences.*

CHRISTOPHER FRAYLING: **Could we talk about the origins of the "Eastwood style," in the Italian Westerns of the mid-1960s? In retrospect, they changed both the look and the feel of the traditional Western.**

CLINT EASTWOOD: Yeah, I think they changed the style, the approach to Westerns. They "opera-cized" them, if there's such a word. They made the violence and the shooting aspect a little more larger than life, and they had great music and new types of scores. I wasn't involved in the music, but we used the same composer, Ennio Morricone, in *Sister Sara* and I worked with him a bit there . . . They were scores that hadn't been used in other Westerns. They just had a look and a style that was a little different at the time: I don't think the stories were any better, maybe they were less good. I don't think any of them was a classic story – like *The Searchers*, or something like that – they were more fragmented, episodic, following this central character through various little episodes.

Someone once wrote that Leone's films are "operas in which the arias aren't sung, they are stared" [*laughter*]. But when you say "a look and a style," do you mean that their main contribution was a technical one?

Uh-huh. I think the technical effect is the biggest – the look and the sound. A film has to have a sound of its own, and the Italians – who don't record sound while they're shooting – are very conscious of this. Sergio Leone felt that sound was very important, that a film has to have its own sound as well as its own look. And I agree . . . Leone'll get a very operatic score, a lot of

Opposite: **Leone and Eastwood on the set of** *The Good, the Bad and the Ugly*

trumpets, and then all of a sudden *ka-pow*! He'll shut it off and let the horses snort and all that sort of thing. It's very effective. So, yes, I think you've hit on it when you say "technical" – that was the star: technical changes. The lighting was different, too. It wasn't flat-lit. A little more . . . style.

I've read somewhere that, when you were preparing for the role of the Man With No Name, just before you left the Universal Studios set on *Rawhide* for Rome and Almería, you bought the costume at a Santa Monica wardrobe store and borrowed the leather gunbelt, pistol, and suede boots from *Rawhide*. Yet Sergio Leone has told me that the transformation of Rowdy Yates into the Man With No Name – the basic change of "look and style" from which everything else followed – was mostly *his* idea.

[*Eyes narrowing momentarily*] He didn't accept that . . . ? Well – I guess I heard that, too, and I heard stories where people would say that he would lay a rope down the line on the ground where I should walk – and all that stuff – and I thought, "Funny, he's the only one who ever had to do that." But I guess it's normal for him – all of a sudden I go off back to America, and he does several films in the same vein and then drops out for a while, and he sees me going on to do other things and maybe that affected him. Who knows why a person says different things?

[*Not feeling lucky, not pushing it*] Whoever it was, the character's sense of visual style – the poncho in *A Fistful of Dollars*, the long-waisted coat in *The Good, the Bad and the Ugly* – was a world away from the fringed buckskins of Alan Ladd in *Shane*, or all those well-scrubbed army scouts in 1950s Westerns.

[*Visibly relaxing again*] Yeah, that was accepted at the time – sixties – and yeah, that buckskin does look a little drugstorish now. But we did similar things in *High Plains Drifter* and *Pale Rider*, where he's kind of a stylized character, with a little bit of a different look – the hats, the long coats, and various other things. But it was

mostly the people who were *in* the clothes. Gian Maria Volonté had a good face, and all those Spanish, gypsy faces – that was just general . . . everything kind of tied together and made an interesting-looking film. You ask most people what the films were about, and they can't tell you. But they tell you, "the look" [*he mimes throwing the poncho over his shoulder*] and the "da-da-da-da-*dum*" [*he hums the opening notes of* The Good, the Bad and the Ugly *theme*], and the cigar and the gun and those little flash images that hit you, and we get back to "technical" again, technical changes. Maybe I had some contribution in there, and, er, maybe not . . . I remember we cut out quite a bit of dialogue together, on *Fistful*, before and during.

I don't know if you recall, but I'm told that in the Italian press of 1964 you were billed as "Western consultant" on *A Fistful of Dollars*.
[*Laughter, and a quizzical look*] Uh-huh?

A lot of the technical lessons of the Italian films seem to me to have been carried over into your first Western as a director, *High Plains Drifter*: the sound effects, the heavy framing, the way in which the hero is presented . . .
Yeah. I don't really associate *High Plains Drifter* as closely with those films as maybe some do – other than

Above: **Silvanito, the bartender (José Calvo), and Joe, in *A Fistful of Dollars***

the same actor and this mysterious drifting character who comes in, which is like the character in *Fistful of Dollars*. But then that's sort of the classic Western – that's been done so many times before – with *Shane*, with William S. Hart, with . . . [*pause*] there's nothing really new under the sun there; it's just a question of styling. And it was the same actor playing it. Some elements that come with that character are going to come into other characters that I play, too, along the line. You adapt it to yourself, you know . . . *The Fistful of Dollars* character, also – it was fun for me to do everything that was against the rules. For years in Hollywood there was a thing called the Hays Office: There were certain taboos that were put on the Western, even more so than other things. One was that you never could tie up a person shooting with a person being hit. You had to shoot separately and then show the person fall – and that was always thought sort of stupid, but on television we always did it that way . . . We did it that way on *Rawhide* – and everybody talked about it, and it was sort of a thing that hung over there. And then, you see, Sergio never knew that, and so he was tying it up and that was great – that's terrific, tie up the shots. You see the bullet go off, you see the gun fire, you see the guy fall, and it had never been done this way before. Those things seemed to me very bad for television. Where everybody was shooting sort of standard things. The typical television filming would be where the person is in the door: CUT. CUT around to other person who says some lines. CUT: walks up to him. Two head close-ups. You never do see the two people together. So that was part of it.

Turning to *The Outlaw Josey Wales* [1976, or twelve years after *Fistful*], which I think is one of your finest films as a director so far, there's much less emphasis on "style," on the detached, comic-strip aspects of the Italian Westerns, and much more on the kinds of things that might be on Americans' minds after the Vietnam War. It's about the rebuilding of a small community

after the bloody dislocation of the American Civil War – but it could just as well be about post-Vietnam America. How conscious was that?
Right. It was inherent in the story, but I guess it made it attractive to me; but I didn't sit there and say, "Well, I'm doing this now because this parallels some situation in history, then and now, like Vietnam." But I think the dislocation could be the same after every war . . . *is* the same.

In a way, *Josey Wales* puts the morality – the American morality – back into the character of the Man With No Name. Josey is determined to get his revenge on the Kansas Redlegs – "I don't want nobody belonging to me," he says – yet he's constantly being deflected from his quest by various drifters who refuse to take his macho image seriously. Even the hound dog he picks up along the way isn't taken in by the image. The punch line is that we should choose – whatever the odds against – "the word of life" rather than "the word of death." It's the gentle option, rather than the violent one . . .
Well, the thing that I liked about it was that it was a Western with a very good story and a central character, and the effects on this character and what life had done to this guy, and his search for something it would be easier to run away from – and by accident things always happen to him that make him a better person. He starts out as a farmer, becomes a killer, and in the end, I think, becomes a farmer again – although the audience decides that. Because, like I said, the films that I did with Sergio, if they'd been done with less style, they would have been very poor shows because they weren't really very good, strong stories, and I like stories. It's not that we drifted apart, but I think we just became philosophically different. I was drifting – naturally, being an actor – toward more personal, more real stories. And he wanted more production values as a director, so he was always going toward vaster and vaster scenes, with trains blowing up, and more Indians over the hill, or whatever – I'm just using examples,

nothing specific . . . and I wanted more personal stories. He got into larger, epic pictures, and I got into smaller pictures. In *Josey Wales*, there was a personal story that also had a large landscape to it, and that was ideal for me.

It must be unique for an entire cinematic genre to depend on the fortunes of one individual, but, through the 1970s and 1980s, the future of the Western has to a large extent hinged on the box-office performance of your work . . . What do you think *your* particular contribution has been to the American Western of the 1970s and 1980s?
Well, the answer maybe is just what you said. Maybe that I was lucky enough to make a few of the most successful ones of that period. I don't have any great bolt of lightning from the sky about that one. I just feel the Western is part of the American heritage; the earliest American film, as you'll know, was *The Great Train Robbery*. Americans don't have many art forms that are truly American. Most of them come from Europe or wherever. Westerns and jazz are the only two I can think of that are American art forms. But *High Plains Drifter* was great fun because I liked the irony of it. I liked the irony of doing a stylized version of what happens if the sheriff in *High Noon* is killed and symbolically comes back as some avenging angel or something – and I think that's far more hip than doing just a straight Western, the straight old conflicts we've all seen. *Josey Wales* just had a much stronger story as far as the personal – the individual – was concerned, and a good character. *Bronco Billy* wasn't really a Western at all . . . More Frank Capra than Western.

Today, country-and-western music, "new" and "old," has never been more popular – and Willie Nelson and Kenny Rogers have made Westerns (*Barbarosa, The Gambler*) on the strength of their success as singers. So maybe the way forward might be in modern Westerns. Urban cowboys. Electric horsemen . . .
Well, I think the Western *has* to be, period. I don't think it can be modern. I don't think anybody's interested in

a Western set today necessarily – or maybe they might be, depending on the film. I hate to say that definitely. Perhaps a picture about rodeo riding or something like that might help to excite somebody. Maybe. But I think a period Western is always that kind of escape – another time, time when things were more simplified . . .

What of Sergio Leone's development *since* you worked with him in 1967?
I wish Sergio would make a film from a really tight script – a tight story. Ford, Hawks, Anthony Mann, they didn't start with the details and then find the story later – "Let's start with that great shot of an Indian on the horizon." They chose good, tight stories. Sergio sometimes seems to start with "Look at that bottle, how it spins, what its symbolism is" and *then* thinks about the story.

But at the time, he definitely filled a gap . . .
Yeah, at that time a lot of the older directors were not making good movies anymore, and Westerns weren't as *special* as they had made them, maybe. Sergio filled the gap. But when I was a kid, I didn't think about who the director was – Howard Hawks, for instance. I liked Howard Hawks films, but to me they were John Wayne films.

Above: **Leone directs Eastwood in the "Socorro" scene that was cut from** *The Good, the Bad and the Ugly*.
Opposite: **Eastwood returns with his poncho and cigar in** *For a Few Dollars More*.

LEE VAN CLEEF

For a Few Dollars More
The Good, the Bad and the Ugly

This conversation – between my good friend Alex Cox and Lee Van Cleef – was recorded on May 10, 1978. Alex went on to UCLA film school shortly afterward, and his subsequent cult movies – including Repo Man, Straight to Hell, *and* Walker *– have reflected his continuing admiration for Italian Westerns. Alex even lived for a time in Tabernas, just down the road from the El Paso set that Carlo Simi designed for Leone's* For a Few Dollars More. *I'm grateful to Alex for letting us publish, for the first time, this conversation.*

LEE VAN CLEEF: I came into this town in a stage play called *Mr. Roberts*. Stanley Kramer saw it and put me in a picture called *High Noon*. The first time I went into his office he told me to go fix my nose and I told him to go fuck himself. So he told me that instead of playing the second lead I would have to play one of the silent heavies. I said, "Fine – silent is the way I play." In fact, in the middle of the picture, Fred Zinnemann, the director, said, "I want you to say 'Howdy' or something to Ian Macdonald when he's getting down off the train," and I said I didn't think I should – "I've been playing this silent, and if I open my mouth one iota it's going to destroy the strength of the character." And he agreed with me. Most actors like to talk a lot – I don't. I read scripts, and I cut the dialogue down to the barest essentials. I've always done that.

ALEX COX: Is that what you'd call an approach to acting?
There is no approach to acting other than sharpening your tools. You learn how to use a sword, stunt fighting, how to use your voice, how to dance – all this is sharpening your tools. It's a basic necessity for all actors. But I don't think too many actors are doing that today.

Of the American parts you played, which were you happiest with?
I got happiness out of every damn one I did. I'm not just saying that to sound off – I really did. Even the old *Range*

Rider series, even *Space Patrol* on TV. We had some fun with them. I got knocked out in one – some old character actor hit me on the head with a plastic gun, and down I went. And we were doing that live.

How did you meet Sergio Leone?
Leone came over in 1965, looking for one or two actors he had in mind for his second Western. The moment we met, he made up his mind and said, "That's it – that's the guy to play Colonel Mortimer in *For a Few Dollars More*." Well, I wasn't going to argue with him – hell, I couldn't pay my phone bill at the time. I went over and did the thing, I paid my phone bill, and exactly one year later to the day – April 12, 1966 – I was called back to do *The Good, the Bad and the Ugly*. And back-to-back with that, I made *The Big Gundown* [Sergio Sollima, 1966]. But now, instead of making seventeen thousand dollars, I was making a hundred and something – which was Leone's doing, not mine. And I was doing leads and heavies in Italy from then on.

What was the set of an Italian Western like?
It's a lot of fun. I tried to learn the languages – Spanish and Italian and German – not too successfully. Working on a European set isn't a hell of a lot different from working on an American set. I think the Europeans are a lot more spontaneous, more artistic to some degree. But I don't think that they have the technical talent we have here in the states. Here people have been trained much more specifically – they know exactly what they're doing. The Europeans are perhaps slower, but, in the end, damn near as good.

How much did the characters you played differ from the ones in the original scripts?
The one area that I disagreed with in the Italian scripts was the dialogue. There was too much of it. I'd be given a goddamn half-page paragraph and say, "Look, I can get

Opposite: **The bounty hunter protagonists of *For a Few Dollars More***

this across in two words." Maybe it's a difference in the languages, but I had to rewrite every damn scene I was in. I reduced the whole thing – cut it down to a "Hello" or a "Pardon me, ma'am." A lot of actors think that the more words they have, the more attention they get. That's bullshit. I make people *look* at me. I don't have to say a lot of words.

Did Leone speak much English in the early days?
On *For a Few Dollars More*, no. He did the next year . . .
But it caused no problems – I understood exactly what he wanted. It was an instinctive thing. He would demonstrate a little bit, and there was always an interpreter on the set. But I knew from the script what was expected of me. The next year, he'd learned more English and we got along even better. He would walk through what he wanted done, then I'd do it my way . . . and he always accepted the difference.

Above left: **Italian poster for For a *Few Dollars More***
Above right: **Lee Van Cleef's career took off after *For a Few Dollars More*, and he briefly became an action superstar.**
Opposite: **Leone (wearing gunbelt) on the set of *The Good, the Bad and the Ugly* with Van Cleef (center) in Almería**

Did the Italian directors play music on the set?
I never experienced that. But Leone did play the Morricone score for me beforehand. It didn't help me any. I don't act to music, not unless I'm doing a musical.

Did making two films back-to-back create any problems?
No. Different parts doesn't mean a thing – not for somebody who thinks he's an actor. *The Good, the Bad and the Ugly* was strictly a heavy, just a mean son of a bitch – nasty, because he could smile doing it. *The Big Gundown* was a surly character, but not a heavy. The guys behind me in that picture wanted me to become a politician, but I had no such aspirations and I erased that from my mind as an actor.

Do you have any regrets about the Italian Westerns you made?

No. I don't care where I work – films are an international business, not just an American institution. You go where the work is. It can be in my own backyard, Israel, Spain, or Yugoslavia. We may have the greatest technical efficiency in the world, but our artistic values are not necessarily the best.

You rate the art direction in European pictures?

Yes. And the timing. Editing is where Leone's really at the top. His timing is great – our own directors are involved in the editing, but they don't do it. Leone does it himself – he's inspired by it. He even had me come into the cutting room while he was putting *The Good, the Bad and the Ugly* together, to show me something he'd done. It was a beautiful experience.

Did he ask you to be in *Once Upon a Time in the West*?

I turned it down. I don't remember now exactly why. I didn't like the way it was written.

THE ACTORS
ELI WALLACH

The Good, the Bad and the Ugly

This conversation occurred in two places – at the Madonna di Campiglio "Western All'italiana" festival in Northern Italy, on July 15, 2001, and in Sicily on July 13, 2002, at the Taormina Film Festival, which featured a Sergio Leone tribute and symposium. At Madonna di Campiglio, I had the special experience of watching the latest Italian print of The Good, the Bad and the Ugly *with Tuco himself.*

CHRISTOPHER FRAYLING: One of the reasons Sergio Leone cast you as Tuco in *The Good, the Bad and the Ugly* was that he remembered a moment of mime in your performance as the outlaw Charlie Gant in *How the West Was Won* – when you mimed the firing of a gun, to scare George Peppard's children. That, and your Mexican bad guy Calvera in *The Magnificent Seven*.

ELI WALLACH: You remember that Calvera had two gold teeth? Well, when I thought it out, I realized that in Westerns you never see what they do with the money. They hold up a bank, they stop the train, they kill the sheriff – they do all that, but they never spend the money. So when I started to work with John Sturges, I said, "Do you mind if I show where I used the wealth?" So I had a silk shirt, I put two gold teeth in, I had a beautiful horse and a lovely silver saddle so that they'd say, "Oh, this man lives high!" All the rest of his gang were dirty. The Mexican audience, incidentally, had had a riot five or six years before, with a movie with Gary Cooper and Burt Lancaster called *Vera Cruz*: They'd ripped the seats out of the theater and thrown them at the screen because the Mexicans were portrayed as usual – as dirty, vengeful, yelling, and shooting. So if you watch *The Magnificent Seven* carefully, you'll see the villagers are always in white clothes – all neat, all well dressed. There was a censor on the set when we shot it in a little Indian village in Mexico.

How did you come to specialize in "Latin" characters on the screen, from Silva in your first film, *Baby Doll* (1956), to Calvera, to Guido in *The Misfits* (1961), to Tuco in *The Good, the Bad and the Ugly*?

Well, I was brought up with Italians in Little Italy, Brooklyn, where all the Mafia people lived! They are still there. And so, for example, the sign of the cross I do in *The Good, the Bad and the Ugly* – it's a shorthand way of doing it. You know, they do it so many times – they do it this way. Those are the kinds of things I observed when I was growing up and I used. But I don't know how the hell it happened that I played so many Mexican bandits, to tell you the truth.

Where and how did you first meet Sergio Leone?
I was in Los Angeles, filming, and my agent called me and said, "There's an Italian director who saw your films about the West and bandits, and he would like to interview you for a movie," and I said, "What sort of a movie?" and he said, "An Italian Western," and I said, "I've never heard of an Italian Western – it sounds like a Hawaiian pizza!" Well, I then met Sergio, who spoke no English. He said – in French – "I would like you to be in my movie." He weighed about 290 pounds, and he said, "I will show you. Can you see a little piece of my film?" And when I saw the

Opposite: **Italian poster for *The Good, the Bad and the Ugly***
Above: **Eastwood (left) slaps Leone in rehearsal for the first arrest scene in *The Good, the Bad and the Ugly*, with Eli Wallach (at right) at Elios Studio in Rome.**

way they shoot his name down as a director, in the credits of *For a Few Dollars More*, I thought, "This guy has his tongue in his cheek, and he has a sense of what's right." So I said, "Where do you want me to go?" and he replied, "I want you in Rome on such and such a date . . ."

Various details were added to the character of Tuco, after the initial script stage.

As soon as I knew I was going to do it, I went to see a great Western director named Henry Hathaway. I'd done two films with him [*Seven Thieves*, 1960; *How the West Was Won*, 1963]. Once Leone called me and said, "I want you to be in this movie," I said, "Can I see the script?" He sent me two pages! I said, "I can't – with two pages." He said, "Listen, it's going to take me almost two and a half weeks to shoot those two pages, and you are going to do it!" So I went to Western Costume, in California, with Mr. Hathaway, and he helped me pick out the first hat I wear – kind of a straw hat – and the chaps, which go over the knee – because in Mexico they wear those, it protects you against the brush; that's why they wear those leather chaps. And it's a vestige, a rollover from what it used to be used for – into a mannerly kind of thing. So I brought them to Italy, and Sergio was enchanted with that. One thing I loved about Sergio was that he was willing to gamble on what I wanted to do with this character Tuco. When I first met him in Rome, he was wearing suspenders *and* a belt, and I thought he must be afraid his pants are going to fall down. So I said, "Oh, do you mind if *I* wear suspenders and a belt?" and he said, "No, *certo*, do it." He adapted well to my requests, and if I did something – for example, putting the gun together from different parts, in this little shop – I seem to know what the hell I'm doing, but actually I knew nothing about any of it! Then after I've put the pieces together, I walk out into the yard and shoot at these cutouts of Indians, which is also a racial comment, you know. When it came to a holster, he said, "No holster for your gun – you'll have a concealed gun tied to a rope or lanyard round your neck and let it dangle between your legs." So I asked him to show me how I could

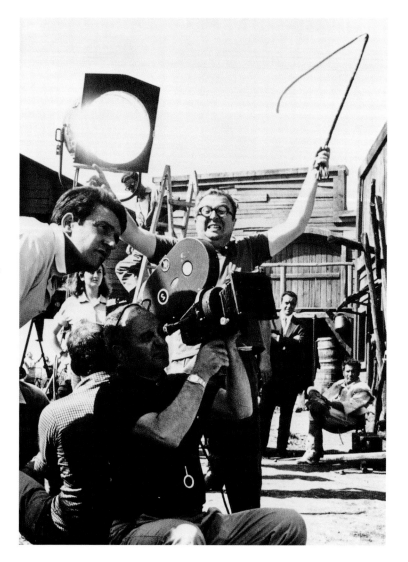

shoot it that way. He said, "Like this," and shot himself in the groin! From then on, he said, "Forget it, just put the gun in your pocket."

The way Tuco crosses himself, was that your idea?

Yes, it was. I thought, "Wouldn't it be wonderful if I did that a couple of times," and he said, "Keep it, keep it."

The part seems to have grown as the shooting of the movie progressed.

Yes, the eye patch and crossing myself and praying at the monastery. And getting up in the morning after the big explosion and walking down and peeing. You know, the act of peeing and how a person might do that in the morning? Well, Sergio loved that. I don't know if Clint resented the part growing, but he seemed not to.

Above: **The whip-cracking maestro on the set for *The Good, the Bad and the Ugly*, with Tonino Delli Colli behind the camera and Wallach (far right) observing the shot**

You got on so well with Sergio Leone that he subsequently offered you the part of Juan in *Duck, You Sucker/A Fistful of Dynamite*.

Yes, he begged me to do the part, and I said, "I have another commitment." "No," he said, "you've got to do it." Finally, I said I would do it. Then he goes to California to raise the money, and the studio tells him they have Rod Steiger committed for a number of weeks. So he used Rod. That's where our disagreement came in. I said, "Well, what happened with the promise to me?" And he said, "*C'est la guerre.*" I said, "Well, I'm gonna sue you – give me something, when I've turned down other movies." "No," he said. "I'm gonna sue you," I said. And he said, "Get in line." And then I realized he's concerned about his movie and not me, and I stopped speaking to him. But yesterday I saw Carla Leone again – for the first time since *The Good, the Bad and the Ugly* – and I thought, "It is ridiculous to punish her for this." I used to spend Sundays with them on the beach and we had tapas together – little appetizers – and I'd be with Carla and the kids and Sergio. And then we would have a big dinner – with pasta the Italians used to buy from Italy so it would not be contaminated in Spain! I hadn't seen Carla since then.

What was the atmosphere like, on the sets of *The Good, the Bad and the Ugly* in Almería?

Well, I was a stranger to Sergio Leone's films. The other two [Clint Eastwood and Lee Van Cleef] had made movies already with Sergio. Clint took me by the hand and led me through it all. He said, "Don't go anywhere near explosives, you never know what's going to happen." There was no real union guidance. You'd get up at dawn, go out, and shoot till seven o'clock at night. All day long, on that horse in the desert. One morning we were in the desert at about 6:30 a.m., and the sun came up and there was the man with the reflector, and the director, and me. And I said, "Sergio, I have to go to the bathroom." And he pointed to the desert and said, "There." I thought, "Well, there are no luxuries in Italian moviemaking!" The Italians would work the Spanish workers hard on the set – "Get this, do that" – but on the

weekend they would play soccer, and the Spaniards would get their revenge. They would take a sweet revenge.

Clint Eastwood gave you good advice, about the explosives . . .

Yes, he said to Leone, "Where are you going to stand when the explosion comes?" If you look when we jump into that pit, you'll see flying past the camera a lot of debris, real stuff coming. Well, they used doubles for our scene in the pit. Sergio wanted Clint and me to be in that pit. So Clint asked Sergio where *he* was going to be when the bridge blew up, and Sergio said, "Right here, with the cameraman." "Okay, if *you'll* stand right here I'll do the scene." We did a run-through, and Sergio wasn't there. He was up at the top of the hill. So they used doubles! And there's that marvelous story about them blowing up the bridge by mistake. I love that story. What happened? Well, Sergio had this superb effect planned for when the bridge was to be blown up. Three cameras: one close to the bridge, one quite a distance away, and one in slow motion so the pieces would explode slowly. Most of the soldiers in the scene were Spaniards who were loaned by the Franco government to the film to play Civil War soldiers. They built a big bridge over a tiny little stream and had to pour water into it to make it look like a river. The captain – a Spanish army captain – put the dynamite around so it would blow up. The Italian special-effects man had told the captain what an honor it was to have him help on the set, and therefore the honor of putting the two wires together to blow up the bridge should be his. The captain said, "No, I don't want to do it," but the special-effects man insisted, "It would be an honor for me and the Italian producers. And when I say '*Vaya!*' [which means 'go'] just put the two wires together." As all this was going on, one of the assistants came up and said, "You want me to put one of the cameras over there?" and he answered, "Yes, *via*, go." The captain misheard the word *vaya*, put the wires together, and the bridge was blown up. Leone was looking up at the sky, looking for clouds to go by, and the bridge blew! He was furious. It's the old "Ready when you are, Cecil B. De Mille"

story. And the Spanish captain said to Leone, "I will rebuild the bridge, just do not fire that effects man." So the bridge was rebuilt, and the man was not fired.

Were you often in danger?
Well, in the cemetery, when I had to cut the bag open with the gold in it, I nearly died. Because they had a certain acid to weaken the bag where the gold was. And I used to like drinking this Spanish lemon soda – very refreshing. And the propman had put the acid in the bottle I liked drinking from, and I took a sip. As soon as it hit my mouth, I knew it was acid and I spat it out.

That was a near one! And there was a story about a frisky Spanish horse, I believe.
Yes, in one of the scenes where I was about to be hanged and Clint shoots through the rope. The propman put a little charge of dynamite in the rope so it would break.

Above: **Wallach looks on as Leone works with the actor playing Bill Carson (Antonio Casale), in the desert sequence of** *The Good, the Bad and the Ugly*.

The horse I was sitting on was jittery when he first heard the shot, so I suggested to Sergio that he put some cotton in the horse's ears. He said he had never heard of such a thing. I told him that in Hollywood they sometimes put cotton in the horses' ears to calm them down. Sergio wouldn't do it. So when the horse heard the sound, he got scared and took off with me on his back. But you know these stories . . .

Well, it certainly sounds like a grueling project. And with Sergio Leone's well-known obsession for detail, you must have been sitting around a lot as well – on the thirteen-week shoot in Rome, in the Spanish desert, and near Burgos.
They didn't have the equipment you have today. I mean, with a zoom lens you sit there and press a button and zoom in and out. When we were shooting the gunfight at the end – waist here, hands here, face here, eyes here – they had to change lenses all the time for different shots. Three lenses: One went right into your eyeballs! And after that he wanted very much to have a helicopter shot – leaving me

as a small antlike figure in the middle of the cemetery. But Sergio couldn't get the helicopter camera to really work because it shook. Today, they can do it better.

Was the Ennio Morricone music played on the set, for the cemetery scenes? Sergio clearly had the music in his mind when he shot your marathon run around the cemetery and the final duel . . .

The first time I heard Morricone's music was when the movie was released. I told Sergio: "In silent movies they played music that the audience never heard, but it moved the actors in certain ways." I wasn't joking when I said to him, "I wish I'd heard the music; I would have ridden the horse differently; I would have moved differently." It would have been beautiful. You know, in *The Magnificent Seven* Elmer Bernstein wrote the music – that became the music for the Marlboro Man – and the movie begins with us riding across from the distance with this wonderful music. And I thought, "I'd have ridden better if I'd heard that music." John Sturges once said to me, "Why do you type when you're riding a horse?" I said, "What do you mean, *type*?" He said, "Holding the reins, and this hand is going like this – like typing." I said, "All right, I'll hold on. I won't do that." Music on the set of *The Good, the Bad and the Ugly*? No. But Sergio shot a lot of footage so he could use it in the way he wanted.

The music was certainly written and recorded in advance for Leone's next film, *Once Upon a Time in the West*.

That was good. You know, I spent two years on the stage with Henry Fonda in *Mr. Roberts*. He called me once and asked what I knew of an Italian director named Sergio Leone. I said, "Hank, by all means do it." "But he wants me to play a heavy." "You've done enough Westerns. It'll be a great ride for you, great experience." And he did it. I visited them on the set of *Once Upon a Time in the West*, and he said he really enjoyed working with Leone because Leone was not afraid to allow his actors to develop and grow. Now the movie is a classic.

HENRY FONDA:

"I went to the studio, and I sat by myself at Goldwyn for three-and-a-half hours, and I watched all of *A Fistful of Dollars*, all of *For a Few Dollars More*, and about half of the third one. I had a lot of fun, all by myself. I thought they were very funny and entertaining in every possible way. I called Eli Wallach, who was in the last one and who is a friend of mine, and he said, 'Don't miss it. You will love every minute of it. You'll love Sergio . . . ' So I accepted. Now I read the script again, and I know that the guy he wants me to play is a heavy. I've got several months before I have to go over there to report, and I'm thinking about playing this guy. So I went over to a guy in the Valley, an optometrist, and I had myself fitted for contact lenses that would make my eyes dark, because I didn't think my baby blues would be the proper look for this heavy character. I grew a moustache that was a little bit like John Booth's, who shot Lincoln. I was trying every way I knew to look like a period heavy. I arrived in Rome and went on the set, and Sergio took one look at me and said, 'Off!' He wanted the baby blues; he wanted the Fonda face. If you remember my first scene . . . the camera comes around very slowly until you can recognize the killer – and Sergio Leone was waiting for the audience to gasp, 'Jesus Christ, it's Henry Fonda!' It was all fun. I loved every bit of it."

In a way, Tuco is Sancho Panza to Clint Eastwood's knight of the rock-hard countenance. You know that shortly after *The Good, the Bad and the Ugly*, Sergio Leone announced that he was hoping to make a version of *Don Quixote* – with Sancho as the Mediterranean carnival figure and the Don as a traditional kind of hero . . .

I did Sancho Panza to Lee J. Cobb's Don Quixote on television. So I could have played that for Sergio. When I was asked to speak at Jason Robards's memorial, I couldn't think of what to say. I couldn't sleep, and I dreamed the speech verbatim. I got up the next day, went to the theater – more than a thousand people – without notes or anything. I said: "I was Sancho sitting on a little white ass. Jason was this lanky fellow sitting on his white mare, not wearing a helmet but an Austrian hat. He doesn't have a lance, he has a ukulele, and he's singing, 'Swanee, how I love you . . .' And we start to ride across the desert, and I say, 'Oh sire, it's very hot in the desert,' and he says, 'Don't worry, kid, *The Iceman Cometh*.' " And I put in the titles of all the great plays he did, until the end: "I said, 'I'm depressed and unhappy, sire,' and he says, 'I know, kid, it's been *A Long Day's Journey Into Night*.' " And I put it all in there. It worked well.

Sergio Leone had a very strong visual culture and a strong sense of exactly how his shots should look.

I'll never forget him saying to me, "I want it all shot like Vermeer, with the light coming through the windows," or "I want some dark colors in there like Rembrandt." He knew what he wanted the picture to give, and he leaned on the painters to get it. *The Good, the Bad and the Ugly* is very well lit. He used the cameraman Tonino Delli Colli from then on. What I always say about Sergio is that he dreamed a dream. He took Kurosawa's *Yojimbo* and shot the exact same picture, only with Italians. The Japanese sued him and won the suit. But what he did learn was: "I will approach the Western in another way; I will not dress

them as they do in all the American Westerns. I will go back to Mathew Brady's prints of the Civil War, and I'll dig out these long dusters that men wore in the picture, and the clothes." A detail: He always showed people with fingers cut off. Lee Van Cleef had a finger part missing, he had a man with no legs outside the saloon, a man spread-eagled on the train as it came into the station – *I Was a Spy*. That came directly from Mathew Brady prints. So did all the military men posing for pictures just as I'm being led to the train. He was meticulous about these things. The cannons and the machine guns were from the military museum in Spain. The train was a small, old, old train and, if you remember, I was handcuffed to the guard who was taking me to the prison. The only way I could get away was to put the body of the guard on the tracks and have the train run over the handcuffs. Well, those handcuffs were made of very soft lead – the strap was made of soft lead so when the train ran over it, it would be cut. Leone wanted me to do the whole scene, where I'm watching the train come, then turn my head so the audience can see my face and see it was really me, not a stuntman; it was not a trick. So the train comes – about eight miles an hour, but it comes –

and at the last second I turned my head like he wanted. But I saw each of these cars had a step made of iron, so if I raised my head just a little higher I would have been decapitated! And Sergio said, "Good shot. Wonderful, Eli. But we do it one more time with your head raised a little more." And I said, "No." People think it's easy to do stunts!

What about the dubbing? It can't have been easy to sustain your performance as Tuco – after it was all over.
We spent seven straight days in New York City dubbing the dialogue. Sergio had shot the film silent, which is how they do an Italian production. So every single line had to be dubbed. You spoke the language you knew. The man who plays my brother spoke not a word of English, not a word. It was a very difficult thing to recapture the outdoors, the shootings, the battle, the desert – in the dubbing room. Sergio stood beside me for seven straight days. He checked each line, even though he spoke no English. I'd say to him, "But I'm on a horse, I'm in the desert!" "Don't worry, just do it. Just say the line the way you think you would say it." So I'm standing in the studio in New York pretending to be on a horse in the desert. While we were shooting a scene with one old man, not an actor – who had one arm – he just counted

from one to ten angrily. I went to see the movie and the man was wonderful. I thought, "I've spent my whole life studying acting, and this man's counting and he's wonderful!"

Looking back, do you have a favorite scene in *The Good, the Bad and the Ugly*?
One of my favorites is when I'm being hanged for the third time, and there were a lot of English extras who lived down around Almería, listening to the man reading: "And Tuco is being held for arson, rape, incest . . ." – he names sixteen crimes. As I'm sitting on this horse, my hands tied behind me, thinking, "What am I doing in southern Spain sitting on a horse? I could be doing Chekhov somewhere," and this little lady looked up at me, and she's in the sun and fair-skinned, and I looked down at her and went, "*Grrr*" as part of my attitude about being stuck on a horse. And Leone couldn't contain himself with delight because I did something human. And he kept it in, and it's in the movie. That's one of my favorite moments.

How would you sum up Sergio Leone?
He was an all-movie man. I'm sure at night he would lie there thinking about how he was going to set the next scene. He slept it, ate it. He was tense, but he had some kind of magical touch. The director is a kind of conductor with his orchestra. He has hired the musicians and he's the one who has the flavor and control of what you're doing. As an instrumentalist, I enjoyed having him wave the baton. I think it is one of the best performances I've done in the movies. You know, a sequel was written by Vincenzoni that I liked very much. It occurs fifteen years afterwards. But Tuco is still searching for that son of a bitch. And he discovers that the Clint character has been shot, killed. But his nephew is still alive, and he knows where the treasure is. Now Tuco starts to pursue him. Well, for some reason Sergio wouldn't give the title up. I don't know why. To sum up? Little did I know when I jumped out of that window with a bottle of wine and a chicken at the beginning of *The Good, the Bad and the Ugly*, I'd be opening the door on working in Italy for the next ten years!

EURO INTERNATIONAL FILMS presenta

CLAUDIA CARDINALE e "JILL"

C'ERA UNA VOLTA IL WEST

un film di SERGIO LEONE

LITOROMA via A.Fontanesi 11

CLAUDIA CARDINALE

Once Upon a Time in the West

This conversation was recorded by British filmmaker Howard Hill for the television documentary Once Upon a Time – Sergio Leone *(Point Sound and Vision, 2000) for which I served as consultant and which used material from my collection. I'm grateful to Howard for letting us publish it here for the first time.*

HOWARD HILL: Do you remember when Sergio Leone asked you to make *Once Upon a Time in the West*?
CLAUDIA CARDINALE: I remember how he told me about the movie. He had no script, and I spent an entire day in his house, and he explained the movie with all the tiniest details and the shots and the traveling and the music. He even played me the music of the movie. He had such a passion for cinema, and it was so marvelous to talk to him because of that. And also the part that he wanted me to do – a marvelous part. I understood everything already. I knew the film, image by image, before the starting of the movie.

He loved cinema, and he loved his work, but he could be tense.
I remember during the scenes when he wasn't very happy, he was holding a packet of cigarettes and was doing all the time *tack tack tack*. He was very nervous, that was the only thing. You could see he was very nervous, if he wasn't very happy with a scene. But on the set, one thing was marvelous: He loved the actors, and for him the actors were queens and kings.

Did he give you much direction?
The most important thing was the music. He used to put it on just before he started shooting. Just before the camera was rolling, he put the music, the music of Jill in the film, and then he stopped it, and we went. And then we were in the mood, and it gave you the energy and the poising and everything, and it was so easy to act, to become the character.

Opposite: **Italian large-scale poster for *Once Upon a Time in the West*, featuring Claudia Cardinale**

It was the first time a woman had played a central role in one of his Westerns.
It was the first time in one of his Westerns, though they had done it another time [in *Johnny Guitar*, 1954]. This was fantastic because usually the woman was like an object – she had a limited space – but in this film the woman was the center. Everything revolved around her. The way Sergio looked at women – the way he looked at me, the cuts, and every detail, the makeup, the hairdo – no improvisation – everything was perfect.

Can you tell me about the shooting schedule?
Yes. The first scene, I remember it well, was the love scene with Henry Fonda in Cinecittà. We were surrounded by hundreds of journalists from everywhere in the world, and the wife of Henry was sitting just next to camera. "The first time he'd done a love scene," they said. I was a bit nervous, and he was very tense, too. It was a marvelous love scene, and, in fact, a lot of people remember this scene as a really special scene. This was the first day. I mean, to start with a love scene with an actor you don't know, with all the people around you. They were sitting all around us on chairs, like the movies, looking at us during the scene. I remember very well Sergio, who was on top of us filming the close-up of me. Then after Cinecittà we went in Spain, and I'm sure you remember the scene when I'm arriving with the train. Fantastic, the dolly and the crane. You discover all the town with the music of Morricone. Then we went to America, to Monument Valley to do exteriors.

Was Sergio Leone pleased with the result?
I think he loved the movie. I think he was very happy with it. What I think is that in Italy they didn't respect him. He was a marvelous director, and for some Italians, very snobbish, it is not a film on a big level. And now they say he is a genius. He was a marvelous technician, a marvelous director of actors, and he knew everything of the camera, the lights, the shots, the angles, and the music.

JAMES COBURN:

"Sergio was like a kid with a big toy, and the motion-picture camera was the toy, and he had all these wonderful things to play with."

Can you say something about Sergio Leone's attention to detail?

Every detail was discussed. There was no improvisation, and he was doing some long scenes. I remember the scene after the beginning, when Jill thinks that there is a mystery, and she is looking all around the room, in the mirror; and at the end she is lying on the bed, filmed from above. I think Sergio was thinking of Visconti when he did this. And after, when he did *Once Upon a Time in America* with Robert De Niro, he did more or less the same scene at the end, and I told him, and he said, "Yes, Claudia."

Do you have a favorite scene in *Once Upon a Time in the West*?

Maybe the scene where I am arriving at the town on the train, because I think this scene is absolutely marvelous; also the scene when I am lying on the bed in the ranch; but many others.

What sort of a character was Sergio Leone?

He was living for cinema, for movies. He loved this work – life on the set and the finished films – and we were talking a lot about movies together, and he was a real friend. He was very close, and we were talking all the time, and even when we finished the movie, we continued seeing each other. For me, cinema is really him: Sergio Leone. When he was shooting with Robert De Niro on *Once Upon a Time in America*, I was shooting a movie in Canada with friends, and we were spending every night with Robert and Sergio and the crew; my crew of the other film were furious and jealous because I was every evening with Sergio Leone. At the end of a day's filming on *West*, in the evening, I was always going out with him to a restaurant. He couldn't eat very much, and he would say, "Claudia, you should eat this and this and this" – all the things that he couldn't eat. The pleasure of Sergio was watching me eat all these things he was always saying he couldn't eat, but then he would say, "You have to eat" – and so he was eating, too! Even though he was supposed to be on a diet. Then he wanted me to eat just so that he could in his imagination enjoy it, as if he could eat these things himself. I miss him a lot. He had so many dreams of things he wanted to do and realize. Many times, when I am shooting a movie with a director, and the director is placing the camera, I think of Sergio: I think, "Sergio, unfortunately it is not you here today." Often I say that.

Opposite: **Pages from the Japanese press book for *Once Upon a Time in the West***

■ チャールズ・ブロンソン
CHARLES BRONSON

この映画の実質的な主役、何か謎めいた「その男」を演ずるには、うってつけの個性的な演技者である。

1923年11月3日、ペンシルバニア州アーレンフェルドに、リトアニアからの移民の炭坑夫の息子（14人中、9人目）として生まれた。映画界に入るまではレンガ職人・料理人・ボクサーなど…転々と職を変えて生き抜き、第2次大戦のときは航空兵として従軍、戦後、小さな劇団に入ったのが、俳優としてのスタートだった。

それから映画界で活躍するまでには、長い苦闘が必要だったが、53年の「肉の蝋人形」以来、着々と地歩を固め、「荒野の七人」（60年）「大脱走」（63年）「いそしぎ」（65年）「特攻大作戦」（66年）「アドベンチャー」（70年）「レッド・サン」（71年）「バラキ」「メカニック」（72年）「さらばバルデス」（73年）など数多くの大作で活躍、人気を高めている。

女優ハリエット・テンドラーと結婚（49年）、2児をもうけたが離婚。68年、同じ女優のジル・アイアランド（デヴィッド・マッカラム前夫人）と再婚、1児がある。

■ クラウディア・カルディナーレ
CLAUDIA CARDINALE

「CC」のイニシャルで親しまれている、世界的な大スターの1人。ソフィア・ローレンと並ぶイタリア映画の代表的な女優である。

1938年4月1日、北アフリカのチェニスで生まれた。両親は、イタリアからの移民。教師志望だったが、チェニスの美人コンテストで当選、そのときのベニス旅行で、カメラマン等の目にとまり、映画に入った。のちに彼女の夫となったフランコ・クリスタルディの暖かい注視を浴びて女優としての技量を身につけた。

家庭では、夫と息子によくサービスする良妻賢母の評価が高い。

デビュー作は「いつもの見知らぬ男たち」（59年、マリオ・モニチェリ監督）。その後、またたく間に素晴しい成長を遂げ、「鞄を持った女」（60年）「山猫」「8½」「ブーベの恋人」（以上63年）と話題をさらった。それだけでなく、フランス語・イタリア語・英語・スペイン語と4ヵ国語ペラペラの語学力にものを言わせて、外国映画にも数多く出演している。

その他の主要作品…「プロフェッショナル」（66年）、「赤いテント」（68年）、「太陽の200万ドル」（70年）、「華麗なる対決」（71年）、「ラ・スクムーン」（72年）。

■ ヘンリー・フォンダ
HENRY FONDA

いまさら、こまごまと紹介する必要のないほどの、アメリカ映画の代表的な名優である。デビュー作品「運河のそよ風」（35年）以来、60余本の映画に出演、30年を越えるキャリアを誇る人である。その知性的な名演技は、「怒りの葡萄」「荒野の決闘」「ミスター・ロバーツ」「十二人の怒れる男」など、数々の記念碑的名作の主演者として、そのいぶし銀の如き魅力を、いかんなく発揮している。西部劇は、この作品で、10本目であった。

1905年5月16日、ネブラスカ州グランド・アイランド生まれ。ミネソタ大学中退後、地方劇団に加わり、長い舞台経験を経て、映画界に迎えられた。それからは、急速に映画出演が多くなった。

第2次大戦のとき、海軍士官学校に入り、優秀な成績を収めて実戦に参加、海軍大尉まで進んだ。

私生活では、3度離婚、1度死別、65年にシャーリー・アダムスと5度目の結婚をした。新進スターであるジェーン・フォンダ、ピーター・フォンダの2人は、死別した2度目の妻フランセス・ブロッカウとの子である。

その他の主要作品…「戦争と平和」（56年）「スペンサーの山」（63年）「バルジ大作戦」（65年）「わが緑の大地」（71年）など。

■ ジェイスン・ロバーズ
JASON ROBARDS

大げさに言えば、アメリカ最高の俳優と呼ばれるほどの、芸達者である。もともと、アメリカ演劇アカデミーで演技を学び、ユージン・オニールからアーサー・ミラーまで、さまざまの役柄をこなした舞台俳優で、力量は確かなものだ。「氷運搬人」の舞台で注目され、「夜への長い旅路」（ともに、オニールの作）で声価が定まった。

1922年7月26日、シカゴ生まれ、父は同名の舞台俳優で、以前は「Jr.」をつけて呼ばれた。ハイスクール時代は長距離ランナーのスターであり、野球の選手でもあって、プロになろうとさえ考えたというが、太平洋戦争（海軍に入って参戦）の後、俳優で立つ決意を固めた。演劇学校に入れと教えたのは、父である。

映画のデビュー作は「夜」（58年）。その後は「夜は帰って来ない」（61年）「テキサスの五人の仲間」（65年）「マシンガン・シティ」（67年）「裸足のイサドラ」（68年）「トラ・トラ・トラ！」（70年）「ジョニーは戦場へ行った」（71年）と好調。

エリナー・ビットマン、ローレン・バコールと2度離婚し、現在はロイス・オコーナー夫人との間に2児がある。

PER UN PUGNO DI DOLLARI

regia s. leone

THE VISUALIZERS
CARLO SIMI

PRODUCTION DESIGNER:

A Fistful of Dollars
For a Few Dollars More
The Good, the Bad and the Ugly
Once Upon a Time in the West

This conversation with the great production designer was recorded at the Montpellier Festival of Mediterranean Cinema, in France, on October 23, 1998. That same evening, Carlo was about to participate in the opening of an exhibition of drawings of his sets and costumes for Sergio Leone. His voice was weak – from a serious illness – and I was grateful that he was prepared to spend so much time with me. When my Leone biography was first published, Carlo wrote to say that at last Sergio's contribution to cinema was being recognized and "on behalf of the Italian film industry I salute you!"

CHRISTOPHER FRAYLING: How did you first meet Sergio Leone?

CARLO SIMI: I knew of him long before *A Fistful of Dollars*, indirectly, but not as a personal acquaintance. He had helped to write *Romulus and Remus* – where I was on the credits as Giancarlo Simi – but I never met him on that. *Romulus and Remus* was directed by Sergio Corbucci, and it was he who introduced me to the Western, with a project called *Minnesota Clay*. I did some research on the look of the West, especially illustrations from books of architecture, for Corbucci's film, which was the story of a blind pistolero and his fight for justice. We were very excited by the idea of an *Italian*-style Western. Then one day Sergio Corbucci phoned me and told me that the film had become impossible. There was not enough money. Oh well, I was still a qualified architect, even after Corbucci called me! Then one evening I went to pick up a friend in Rome, and I met him in his office. He was Franco Palaggi, an executive producer involved with Jolly Film, and we were going to have dinner together. Sergio Leone was there in the office and, worried that I might be interrupting a meeting, I asked if I should perhaps wait outside. "No, you might as well stay," they said. So I did. And while they continued talking, I saw on a table a few drawings that looked elaborate and professional and finished – but I said aloud some terrible thing like, "Are you *really* intending to make a film with things like these?" The architect in me

judged them to be unacceptable; plus by this time I knew a bit about the architecture of the American West. My friend had no patience with this outburst, but Sergio Leone turned around and said to me, "I'm interested in what you say – what do you do?" "Well, I am a qualified architect." "Could you give me a detailed opinion of these drawings?" "No, I'm sorry, because if I did I would have to say some dreadful things about them." He looked at me very seriously and asked, "Well, have you got something to show what *you* can do – how long will it take?" I said, "Twenty minutes; I will be back soon." So I went home to the studio and picked up a few sketches I'd prepared for *Minnesota Clay*. Sergio examined them and then looked me straight in the eye and said, "You will do the film with me." The film was called at that stage *The Magnificent Stranger*. Sergio went straight to his producer, Arrigo Colombo, on the next floor up, and said that he no longer wanted the designer who had been appointed – he wanted me. He said this in a very dominant way! "What an idiot that designer was!" he said. That is how I met Sergio Leone.

Colombo struck quite a hard bargain, though.

Yes, he insisted that if I was to work on *The Magnificent Stranger*, I had to work on the designs and costumes for *Pistols Don't Argue*, directed by Mario Caiano, as well. They were being made back-to-back by Jolly Film. So I was plunged into a completely new experience for myself. When I was at university, studying architecture, I had never even considered getting involved in cinema: The optional subjects I chose in the early 1950s were to do with stage design (for the theater) rather than film design. In Italy, most people come to art direction through stage direction rather than architecture. I majored in architecture. But for now I had a lot of work to do in Italy. Sergio was always a real devotee of the script. After we'd made the contract, he assigned me the script

Opposite: **Original design for Joe's costume in *A Fistful of Dollars*, by Carlo Simi**

of *The Magnificent Stranger* and by making comments on it would draw out the things he determined were significant. He wanted to communicate visually the hate between the two families within the script. The film had to be built upon that feeling of violence. And then it was announced that *Minnesota Clay* had the go-ahead. They had found a Spanish coproducer. So I was working on all of them.

Was Sergio fascinated by details, even at that early stage?

I remember at the beginning, after he told me I was also doing the costumes, I said it would be a good idea to dirty the hats, to make people "feel" the sweat. He was enchanted. "I couldn't agree more, these are the sorts of things I love – make the audience feel the 'truth' of the situation: the desert, the wind, the dust." That was when a real dialogue began between us two – a meeting of minds. I hated things that were false, inauthentic, and so did he. We wanted to know why things looked the way they did. And to achieve this, we needed books and books on the subject of Western clothes and streets and buildings in America. They are all in the films somewhere. They weren't invented. Where research

was concerned, Sergio became pitiless: He would accept no excuses!

What about the famous poncho, worn by the Clint Eastwood character?

To be honest, this costume came out of the original script. What seems to be an inspired idea had a story justification. The character begins by crossing the Rio Grande and arrives in northern Mexico. He is dressed like a deserter from the Confederate army. He then gets rid of half his uniform and, finding a Mexican person asleep or something, steals his poncho. In this way he becomes half a soldier and the other half with a poncho. This was cut out, which made the costume seem like just an inspired idea. But for the costumes I had to be versatile – architect and costume designer. It was all part of the decor. I had to add costumes for the Mexican peons while they were shooting, when [second unit director] Franco Giraldi arrived in Spain.

Which sets were specially built for *A Fistful of Dollars*, which were ready-made?

There was already the "Western village" at Hojo de Manzanares in Colmenar Viejo, north of Madrid, which

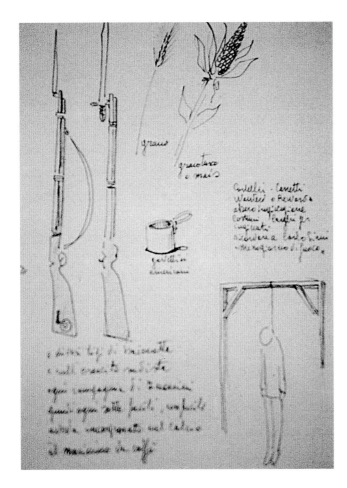

had been used before, and there was the "Casa de Campo" – a permanent museum of Spanish rural life with all the fixtures and fittings, where they wanted to film in order to save as much money as possible. I designed some parts of the rich Baxter family house, with its ornate furnishings, and a new frontage for the Rojo house; and I redesigned the refuge of the mine where Clint Eastwood cuts his breastplate. And some other things. But there wasn't much money for that film. I mean, at the same time as Sergio left for Spain, Mario Caiano came back to Italy to shoot interiors for his film. I think Caiano had the bigger budget! And when *A Fistful of Dollars* was released, Sergio went under the name of Bob Robertson: "Bob, son of Robert." My name was Charlie Simmons or something like that. I can hardly remember. We used American names because at that time we didn't think an Italian film on that subject could be successful. But this first film turned out to be enormously successful, which in some ways surprised Sergio as much as everyone else. He knew he had said something, but not whether it would catch the

Opposite: **Original design for Langstone Bridge in** *The Good, the Bad and the Ugly,* **by Carlo Simi**
Above: **Carlo Leva prop drawing for** *The Good, the Bad and the Ugly*

public's imagination. Major incomes now meant more major possibilities.

So on *For a Few Dollars More*, you had many more resources to work with.
Yes, Sergio asked me for "the finest Western town in the world." We were originally going to build it near Madrid, but it snowed while we were there, and so we moved further south to Almería, where there was much more sun. Almería resembled Arizona or New Mexico, and it had a useful geological feature that is thousands of years old – dried-up riverbeds, which the Spanish call *ramblas*. These ramblas are very useful from the cinematographic point of view, because they are lower than their surroundings. The camera has 360 degrees of free movement, while above you the trucks and cars can easily move about. The Western town was built at Tabernas. In Sergio's imagination, it was a cast of characters in its own right! The bank was one of the main characters. Since the town was El Paso, I wanted to get away from the traditional bank in the main street with its front door and barred windows, and instead I designed an old Spanish fortress with parts of the building destroyed. It looked like a prison, a treasure-house, and a fortress all at the same time. My "town" of El Paso – which is still there – was where much of *For a Few Dollars More* was filmed, with the Sierras in the background. We also used an abandoned monastery called Cortijo de Fraile and a deconsecrated church in the hills above Tabernas, which was enhanced with various Spanish-baroque elements – with help from a painter. We put in angels and cherubs and twisted columns like in St. Peter's Basilica in Rome.

The climax of *For a Few Dollars More* was the first of Sergio Leone's famous "circular" duels.
It was filmed in a little Spanish village called Los Albaricoques ["The Apricots"]. For some reason, Sergio had a particular weakness for duels in a round arena made up of stones. I was always too discreet to ask exactly

Above: **Carlo Leva reference drawing of Sad Hill Cemetery, for the climax of *The Good, the Bad and the Ugly***

why this meant so much to him. It was as if it reminded him of something. I was never able to bring myself to ask him, "Sergio, why do you always want an arena?" He would simply say, "Look, Carlo, make me a round stone arena like this." His mind was made up. When *The Good, the Bad and the Ugly* was filmed, the same thing happened with the scene in the military cemetery: "Carlo, can you make an arena for me, with the stones positioned around it in a circle? It must be a circle." I had previously had a little experience of psychoanalysis, and I got the impression that this particular thing was beyond the reach of that! So I felt it best to hold back and never asked Sergio, "What does this circle represent to you?" It must have represented *something*, because it was always associated with the death of someone. The cemetery in *The Good, the*

Bad and the Ugly was specially built for the film, when we found a valley that was suitable for it. Each grave looked like a pile of earth after a battle, with a wooden cross stuck into it. Because Sergio wanted this cemetery to have great presence, I decided to locate it within a civilian cemetery – with more noble columns or crosses or tombs here and there. And because he was difficult to please, the seven hundred graves soon became four thousand, five thousand!

How did you go about selecting the locations in Almería?
It depended. If he had already been there, he might say to me, "Listen, Carlo, I have found some beautiful places: Come and see them." Sergio was always respectful about the functions and skills each of us had. Or we would look for locations together. Or perhaps I would find something and would ask him to see it. He would then, not necessarily on the spot but after a few days, say very politely and carefully: "Carlo, I have thought about what you showed me and I really like it."

It sounds from your description as if Sergio could sometimes be prickly to work with.
He could be very kind, but he was obsessed with his work. It could be difficult, and it could be very easy. He went through various phases when working with people. First, an inquiring period around the person, during which he would decide what the person was capable of and whether there could be trust. Then, when he'd made up his mind that the other person would not disappoint him, a door would be opened. If the person failed the test, Sergio would be unreachable. And with each new film there were new challenges. Each new film – the second, third, fourth, fifth – seemed in a way to be the fourth or fifth version of the first one. Each time a new Sergio, a "wider" Sergio, was revealed – as if the fluctuation of a magnifying lens caused its field to become wider and wider, and on the contrary caused its field to shrink more and more, catching the detail of things. There was never any *déjà vu* – always more

magic, to completely engulf the spectator. Sergio was a very special man.

The Good, the Bad and the Ugly had an even bigger budget.
In the first film, there was one main character. Then there were two, and with *The Good, the Bad and the Ugly* they became three. We used a wider variety of locations this time. For example, the first time Tuco was "hanged" was at the Western town built at Elios Studio in Rome. My Western town at Tabernas was where Tuco arrives after he has crossed the desert. Then there was a real village near Los Albaricoques and a real farm near San José. We went into the desert for the arrival of the stagecoach full of corpses. We adapted an existing Western set at Colmenar Viejo, near Madrid, for the town that had been shelled in the war. The railway station was at La Calahorra, just outside Guadix. The battle scene was filmed in a new location further north – with more greenery – at the river Arlanza in a place called Covarrubias, south of Burgos. Since the river was almost dry at the time we were filming, we had to build a barrage to fill it up again!

For the battle, the details of the firearms and weapons were extraordinary.
Yes, we took a lot of trouble to find them or to have them made. We discovered some of them in museums – in the military museum of Madrid or in other museums. If they didn't exist we would have them made. Sergio knew everything about firearms and how they worked. He knew that the sights of a Colt at one particular time were a bit crooked here or there. That the handle was made in that particular way. We had books and books on armaments. There was trouble if I brought him the wrong weapon! What would he say when he got angry? He said things I would have a hard time repeating to you. One way and another, we collected quite an archive in Rome.

Details like those seem to have been important to him as a storyteller.

Our relationship on a particular film would begin with Sergio calling me: "Carlo, could you come to my office or shall we meet at a restaurant?" He would then tell me the entire film with great detail and drama. He would see if I was excited by the same moments of the story as he was, if we had an agreement of sympathy. After this, his toy – because it was his toy – would gradually become your toy as well. He would issue a warning, though: "Hey, be sure you don't spoil it; don't make mistakes; don't spoil the magic." From then on, I knew I was completely accepted.

The "Carlo Simi style" becomes really apparent in *The Good, the Bad and the Ugly* from the first sequence onward.

There was a very funny story about that opening sequence, when Tuco is introduced to us. I had arrived in Spain just as Sergio left. I had asked Sergio, "What kind of a location do you want?" and he had replied, "Nothing. An empty plain with nothing, just infinity. That's what I would like from you." So, I arrived in Spain with the Spanish driver, and I started giving instructions. I asked, "Sergio has already been here?" "Yes, he has already been here and has chosen some locations." "Would you show me the one for the introduction of Tuco?" He led me to a small place, a small road on one side, a ditch on the other, and two small hills. I said, "Is this it? It cannot be, it cannot be. I want a plain that reaches all the way to the horizon." Well, we looked and looked, and he finally drove me to the highlands of Almería – a place that gave me the shivers when I saw it. It was windy, and I said, "This is the right place." I constructed the village there, a wonderful site, entirely built with old wood. I then departed and went to Guadix to build another set. When Sergio came back, he told the crew that they would be shooting the introduction of Tuco the following morning. At the last moment he was told: "The architect has chosen a different location, up high," and that they would have had to travel along all these hairpin bends to get there. The whole procession of cars and trucks and other huge things set out on its way to the top. On the way, the road

collapsed, stopping this procession of a thousand people in their tracks. At this point Sergio said, "Where is that madman?" "He is at Guadix," they replied. "Go and call for that madman and bring him here to me." The car arrived at Guadix: "Senor Simi, Senor Sergio is very angry. Because the road collapsed." "Why, I don't understand. I have been working here for a month, and you haven't even built the roads? Couldn't you have built them?" "We were waiting for you." So I got into this car and arrived where he was. From far away, Sergio looked like Napoleon on St. Helena. He stood on the edge of the curve, with his coat and hat, allowing me to see from a long way off that he was angry. When he saw the small dot that was my car in the distance, he began making gestures . . . The scary Sergio. The only thing left for me to do was to pretend I knew nothing. When I arrived I said, "Sergio, is something wrong?" "What do you mean, is something wrong? Can't you see the car over here, or that other one, which has fallen over there? It's like a landslide. Everyone just follows the madman. Where the hell are we going?" "Hold on a minute, it was you that wanted an infinite plain." "True." "Well, one car has managed to get through to the top, or we could continue to the top by foot." He then asked me, "Where on earth is this village?" "It's over there." "But I can't see anything." "Exactly. You told me it had to be an empty plain." We finally sat in the car and on the way he said, "Why is it, that the moment I leave you alone here in Spain, these things happen? Everyone is watching us." "What did I do wrong? Wait till you see the village." Eventually we arrived at the village. It was windy; rags were flying about and the big boards of old wood were slamming. There was a creepy sense of death. He began to say, "And you have led me all this way . . . Wow, look at what you have done . . . Holy Mary!" I understood this was the right moment and said, "Excuse me, Sergio, didn't I come here to build villages?" "Yes." "Is this not a village? What have I got to do with production problems? They knew I was working here, and they knew that you would be arriving. They should have sorted things out. What

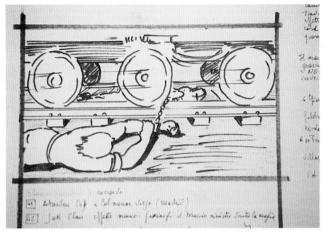

have I got to do with that?" By this stage, he was on my side. "True," he said. "What has he got to do with that?" When he got back to the crew, he gave them a good shouting: "This poor guy is doing his job, doing things, and you haven't even repaired the roads!"

The opening sequence of *Once Upon a Time in The West* is another classic example of the "Simi style" – with that station platform made out of railway sleepers.

That was another funny story. I said, "Listen, Sergio! I've seen some old abandoned wagons covered in dust and sand – with pots and pans still under the canvas – in some American books I've been looking at. Instead of making a station that looks like a station, why not let's have a station that looks like an old abandoned wagon?" His usual answer to suggestions like this was "What on earth are you thinking about, you must be crazy." Then on reflection

Top: **Carlo Leva prop drawing of weaponry for *The Good, the Bad and the Ugly***
Bottom: **Carlo Leva reference drawing for *The Good, the Bad and the Ugly***

he would say, "What were you saying yesterday?" and I would say, "We could have an abandoned wagon there, and then imagine that a person living here would have thought of building a tent to store things here, and there's a water tank over here, and maybe something else over here." That's how the station evolved. Not the cliché little station made of neat planks of wood – I had recently come back from Arizona, and I knew they didn't exist – but a "nonconstruction," which just grew and grew over time. We built it at La Calahorra on the railway line linking Almería with the rest of Spain. It was the same process with the *posada* in the desert where Claudia Cardinale arrives with Paolo Stoppa on the buggy. We started from the cliché idea of a saloon with a shiny counter and lots of polished brass. And I said to Sergio, "I've explored the American West, and I've never seen a single one of those shiny counters: Everything is so dirty up there in the mountains. Why don't we have a place where men and horses live together, where the horse is given more consideration than the men; with dust, and wood that has been ruined by the sun?" Again, after reflection he called me at six o'clock in the morning: "Listen, Carlo. What was that you were saying about the horses?" "Well . . ." "Let's do it that way." Sergio was the sort of person who would never be stubborn about ideas because they happened not to come from himself. That was one of the nice things about him. Where was the posada filmed? Well, the exterior was built in Monument Valley and the interior was filmed in Rome.

Was it difficult to match the footage shot in Monument Valley with the footage shot in Spain?

It was a question of matching the colors. The same with the Indian village in the mountains, near Monument Valley – with the houses built into the red rocks. This is Frank's Indian hideout in the film. The exterior was filmed in Arizona, the interior in Rome – with that wooden Indian bed hanging on ropes made of hide. There was the famous story of Sergio asking me, "Are you certain you remember the exact color?" "Of course, I am certain." "But wouldn't it be better, to be absolutely certain, that you go back there and bring back a sample of that earth and dust?" "Sergio, you're crazy! How on earth could I get away now?" "You are quite right. Don't leave the studio. Send someone else!" And the next day he really did send someone else all the way to the United States to collect a sample of that earth!

The McBain house at Sweetwater is an extraordinary construction: a huge chalet made of logs.
Sergio originally wanted it to be built in America – the house of a seeming madman, who knows that it will be justified one day when the railroad has to come by. Because he has access to water. He wanted an isolated house that was near a lot of water. Almost as if it was in Louisiana, surrounded by water and swampland. We traveled all around America until in Nevada – near Las Vegas – we found a valley close to some rivers. By means of water-supply systems, we could have flooded the valley. But it still wasn't quite what we wanted. So we built it in Spain, near where we had built El Paso for *For a Few Dollars More*, and abandoned the idea of flooding the valley – which would in any case have been a colossal undertaking. The location in Almería allowed us to have a hill that blocked the horizon, so the train could arrive as a surprise. For four or five months, excavators dug into the hill, creating a small canyon. Rails were then bought, put into the ground, and then hidden. After that, the locomotives and the flat wagons were transported there and put on the short lengths of rails. I wanted the McBain house to be solid, and it certainly was. It will still be there in one hundred years!

And then there was the town of Flagstone, which apparently cost as much to build as the entire budget of *A Fistful of Dollars*.
Not much of that town has survived, unlike Sweetwater. Sergio liked it a lot. It was my basic idea. Historically, the Western town was characterized by the passage of human beings through time: a track where humans,

instead of animals, passed through. So as time proceeds, a saloon appears, then a bank, then a prison. This is usually called Main Street. I studied the process, with architectural knowledge and historical research. My basic idea, instead, was to have the saloon as the center of gravity – so in effect you have *two* main streets, one on this side, one on the other. This also served the plot of the film. When shooting from the window, the hero, Charles Bronson, must be able to hit different targets from the same position. Because the site had to be developed in the future, I had also created potentially two towns – one here and the other there. The station was positioned on the Almería-Madrid line, again in the valley of La Calahorra. What Sergio wanted was to be able to follow Claudia Cardinale from the coaches, lead her up to the station entrance, and then see the inside of it . . . and after all this, the surprise of the town. He would lift upwards, revealing the whole town. When he had finished the shot, I remember being seated beneath him. He leaned out and said, "Have you seen what I have done? I've shown the whole town." He had a special Chapman crane brought in from Madrid for this vertical panorama, which cost a fortune. But it was a fantastic scene – the same location, by the way, was used for *The Genius*, directed by Damiano Damiani. But we had very little time to prepare it that time and not much money.

I must ask about the duster coats. Sergio Leone told me they are historically accurate, but they also have a movie history . . .
The dusters were a mania of his, and they became a mania of the time as well. We went to look at costumes at Western Costume in California, and we happened to find these beautiful dusters, which were dustcoats for riding. They had also been shown in the film by John Ford, *The Man Who Shot Liberty Valance*, in the flashback. They were white, so we changed them to chocolate brown. Before we changed them, they looked like they were worn by ice-cream vendors.

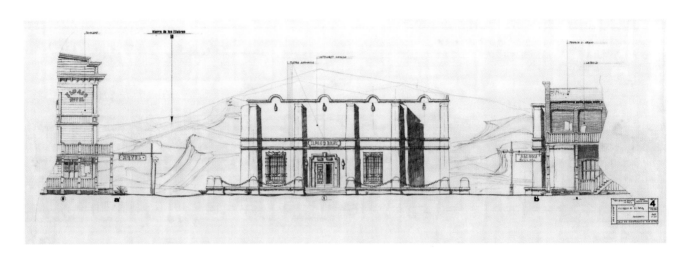

And where did you find that large American locomotive?

We didn't. I redecorated an existing Spanish locomotive with various elements that looked more elegant. The design work was done in Rome, and the elements were transported to the railway set at La Calahorra.

Were you sorry that you were unavailable for *Duck, You Sucker/A Fistful of Dynamite*?

I was too busy, working on other film projects and on architectural work for Alberto Grimaldi – a big commission at that time. Sergio begged me as a friend and as a director to do his film, but I had to say no. I remember him saying, "Carlo, from this day onward I appreciate you even more because you were able to say no. Knowing that you would not be able to work hard on it, you preferred to say no." Isn't that nice? In the finished film, I thought the firing squad in the rain and the shootings in the trenches by the station were magnificent. I would have designed some scenes differently – a question of different sensibilities.

Above: **Original design for the El Paso bank, in *For a Few Dollars More*, by Carlo Simi**

With your design work on the Italian Westerns *Django* and *The Big Gundown*, and above all with your close collaboration with Sergio Leone on his Westerns, the contribution you've made to the look of popular cinema has been enormous – and still very underrated. You earlier mentioned that Almería resembled the American Southwest. I think it is fairer to say that you turned it into the "Southwest Carlo Simi." Your design contribution – and Ennio Morricone's music – are among the most distinctive aspects of the Italian Western.

You are too kind.

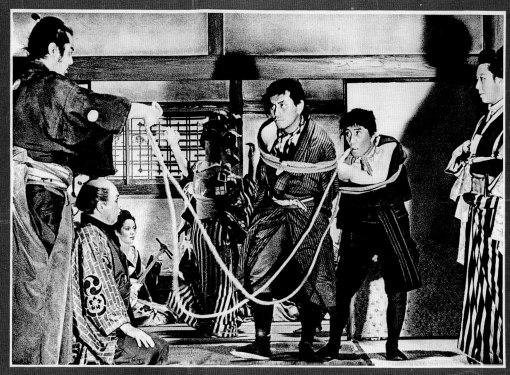

PRESENTA
UN FILM DI

AKIRA KUROSAWA

PER L'INTERPRETAZIONE DI

TOSHIRO MIFUNE

COPPA VOLPI PER L'INTERPRETAZIONE - VENEZIA

CON

SEIZABURO KAWAZU
ISUZU YAMADA - EIJIRO TONO
KYU SAZANKA - DAISUKE KATO
TATSUYA NAKADAI - KAMATARI
FUJIWARA - TAKASHI SHIMURA
IKIO SAWAMURA - YOKO TSUKASA

UNA PRODUZIONE
TOHO CO. LTD.
ESCLUSIVITA' SERENA FILM

LA SFIDA DEL SAMURAI
(yojimbo)

TONINO DELLI COLLI

DIRECTOR OF PHOTOGRAPHY:
The Good, the Bad and the Ugly
Once Upon a Time in the West

This conversation with the veteran cinematographer occurred in two places – in France at the Montpellier Festival of Mediterranean Cinema, on October 24, 1998, during a symposium and exhibition devoted to Sergio Leone and Carlo Simi; and at the Taormina Film Festival, in Sicily, on July 13, 2002. Tonino has a terrific, down-to-earth sense of humor, but he is well known in the business for being touchy about critics.

CHRISTOPHER FRAYLING: You had known Sergio Leone for a very long time.

TONINO DELLI COLLI: I met Sergio when he was still thin, when he did not have much money, and when he was starting from scratch in the industry. These days all filmmakers are instant heroes from the beginning, but it wasn't like that then. I met him when I was working with Mario Bonnard on films such as *Il Voto* (1950) and *Tradita* (1954), and Sergio was a good assistant director – preparing scenes, choosing some of the secondary actors, etc. Bonnard had been an actor in the days of silent films and had moved on to film direction. Sergio was like a son to him – in those days he was thin, with a big personality. He already had a passion for cinema. His father had been involved in the industry, and his mother, too. The whole family. After Sergio had completed *The Last Days of Pompeii* (1959) for Bonnard, when Bonnard was taken sick, he made *The Colossus of Rhodes* as a director in his own right, and then he did the second unit for Robert Aldrich with *Sodom and Gomorrah*. We met again when Sergio had the idea of making a kind of *Magnificent Seven* set in ancient Rome, and he came to Spain when I was there to try and attract a Spanish producer – without success. It was the wrong moment.

Do you know why he then decided to make a Western, *A Fistful of Dollars*?

Sergio had a passion for the Western film and could recall whole scenes. He had Lee Van Cleef already in his head when he cast him in *For a Few Dollars More*. I think he knew *Stagecoach* from start to finish, by heart. And he knew all the landscapes of the Western as well. When we

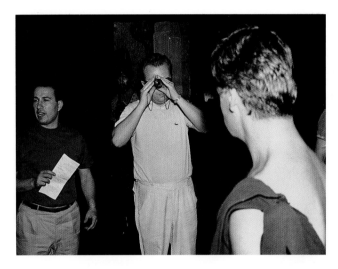

went to recce Monument Valley for *Once Upon a Time in the West*, Sergio kept recalling the sequences of John Ford that had been shot there: "This is the angle he filmed the landscape from; oh, and he placed the camera there for this or that other shot . . . ," etc. He had all these shots in his head. Here is *Stagecoach*. Here is *The Searchers*. We were doing a recce of Monument Valley for just two minutes of screen time. But with the carriage and the music and the colors of the land, the two minutes were very beautiful! Sergio loved American films with a passion, and he had a strange love/hate relationship with America. He didn't speak English, you know.

Do you know how Sergio communicated with Clint Eastwood?

He got by somehow because he was smart. When they spoke together, if Clint looked serious, Sergio would be serious. If Clint smiled rarely, Sergio, too, would smile rarely. If Clint looked sad, Sergio would look sad – to make Clint think he understood. But he didn't really understand anything! I would ask, "Sergio, what did you

Opposite: **Italian *fotobusta* for Akira Kurosawa's *Yojimbo***
Above: **Leone got his start as a fully fledged director on a sword and sandal picture, *The Colossus of Rhodes*.**

understand?" and he would say, "Mind your own business." It was the same with Lee Van Cleef and Henry Fonda and Charles Bronson, but they all queued up to work with him – even the superstars – even though he would shoot a scene up to thirty times. Sergio would perfect a take as he went along and used a lot of film.

How did the specific opportunity to make his first Western arise?

Well, I arranged Sergio's introduction to the producer, Arrigo Colombo. Colombo was one of my wife's cousins. Sergio had contacted me after *The Eagles of Rome* and asked me to go and see a Japanese film with him that was showing in Rome. It was Kurosawa's *Yojimbo*. And we both agreed it would make a terrific Western. Which is why we were looking for the right producer. Sergio never concealed the fact that his idea was inspired by another film. Attempts to contact Tokyo – and the office of the Japanese company in Rome – did not result in any replies, so they all agreed to go ahead anyway. Italian Westerns were not of much importance at that time, and personally I did not believe in them. It was me who suggested to Arrigo Colombo: "This film has to be made in Spain, where there are two Western-town sets already standing," and, in fact, at the beginning we started a company together – I had a financial interest in the film. But I pulled out because, as I say, I did not believe in it, and I moved on to what I thought was a more important project in Yugoslavia. I liked to work with bigger budgets than *A Fistful of Dollars*. I was sorry about this afterwards, because I would have made a lot of money if I'd stayed in. But even Sergio wasn't paid very much for that one. It was my idea that he take a percentage of the film – which he did; he kept kicking me under the table when we talked money with the producers – but somehow, although the film was a huge success, the profits for him were scanty. And he'd put his signature on a contract with Papi and Colombo, committing himself to making at least three more films for them – including, I think, something about *Diamonds A-Go-Go* in South Africa. Evidently he hadn't foreseen the success of *Fistful* either! Anyway,

there was much legal activity and he took them to court; he only won the case a couple of years before he died. He was awarded as compensation the Mexican rights to the film. Unfortunately, *Fistful* had never been sold to Mexico, because the Mexicans were the bad guys in the story! So the Mexican rights weren't worth a whole lot. Sergio did not even sign this film. When it came out, he was Bob Robertson – a reference to his father, Roberto Roberti. But after the row with Papi and Colombo, Sergio began to work with a new producer, Alberto Grimaldi. The arrangement this time was 50 percent for him, plus fifty million lire as a director's salary. This was when Sergio Leone began to make some money, from *For a Few Dollars More* onward.

Then you worked together on *The Good, the Bad and the Ugly*. Were there a lot of discussions with Sergio about the visual aspects of the project?

You know, a critic once asked me about the sequence at the Indian cliffside village in *Once Upon a Time in the West* and the sunset lighting. He asked if I got inspiration from a painter for this. "What, the sunset?" I'm afraid my answer was short and mean, and he never spoke to me again! The thing was, with *The Good, the Bad and the Ugly*, that you can't have too many colors in a Western: red, brown, beige, off-white. A lot of dust, constructions made of wood, sand-colored tones. There wasn't really much to talk about. We shared the same point of departure: not too many colors. Carlo Simi was a fantastic colleague, a great help. Together with Sergio, they had studied a lot of books on the American West, and in the Almería scenes of *For a Few Dollars More* they had created a setting, for the first time, exactly the way Sergio wanted it. Sergio and I understood each other very well indeed. There was never any need for much discussion.

But didn't Sergio Leone use paintings as reference points for the visuals? Giorgio De Chirico, for example?

While we were actually working, we didn't refer to paintings. Sometimes we referred to them during the preparation stage as a kind of shorthand for costumes and sets, but that's about it. For documentation rather than composition. Maybe for lighting, sometimes. We certainly looked at photographs of the period – that library of American books collected by Sergio and Carlo Simi. But, look, whatever Vittorio Storaro [another great Italian cinematographer] says, we are not making poetry. We turn the lights on, and we switch them off. That's what we do. I don't remember De Chirico. The resemblance could be by accident.

Sergio was famously meticulous about his work, a real perfectionist. Did this create difficulties?
The one problem about working with him was that he would never leave the set until he had completely finished what he was doing. We worked sometimes for fourteen to fifteen hours a day. Each day was filled to the brim! In America, those extra hours would have been well paid, but not with us. There were sometimes discussions about the long working hours. They consisted of Sergio saying, "Bugger off – we'll continue till *I* am ready." He would start the day with a wide lens and finish with a big close-up; the close-ups were often in the evening. In Spain there was daylight till nine-thirty, so we worked from first thing in the morning till late. I would try and hide the camera, shut it away at the end of the day, and he would remember that there was another close-up to do. I would tell him, "We can shoot it tomorrow," because it could be done at any moment since you couldn't see anything else in the shot *apart* from the extreme close-up.

He seems to have known a lot about the technology of filmmaking and enjoyed it too.
He put a lot of work into the script – a lot of people would work on it; he contributed but there were also screenwriters. Because he was never happy and made a lot of changes . . . then he would closely follow this detailed script. Technically, he was perfect; technically, he was a great director. Sometimes he would ask for a small dolly of twenty centimeters, and I would say, "Why a dolly?" but when it was edited, you could notice those twenty centimeters. The public didn't realize about things like this at a technical level, but felt them psychologically. His films were very carefully shot, and it paid off with audiences.

The logistics on his Westerns became more and more complicated.
Well, in *The Good, the Bad and the Ugly*, there were a thousand soldiers – a thousand Spanish soldiers – for the battle-of-the-bridge scene: the famous bridge that blew up before we filmed it. We had about twelve cameras installed for the explosion of the bridge, in all possible positions! At a certain moment, around about noon, we were waiting for everything to be ready to give the signal for the explosion. I was looking up at a cloud and saying, "Sergio, let's wait a little." Every morning, we would go past a monastery, about three kilometers from the set, and the artificer who had organized the explosion would always say, "I'm worried about the monastery" – it dated from the Renaissance – "and whether it will be affected by the explosion." But I said to him, "Are you crazy? This monastery is three kilometers away from the set." And he was worried about the camera crew, and I said, "We'll be twenty to fifty meters from the explosion." "Well, I'm not sure, you know . . ." Anyway, to be absolutely certain, I took a camera a hundred meters away with a telephoto lens. Sergio asked, "Which camera will *you* be with?" "I'll be with the camera up there." "Well, I'll be there, too." I had made a wall out of bits of wood to encase the camera, with a small hole lined up. And so anyway, Sergio was standing right next to me; I said, "Wait a little before giving the signal," then I heard and felt a "*pouf*" – not a huge bang – and I turned to see the bridge in pieces, pieces whizzing through the air. I said, "Sergio, what's going on?" "I've no idea." "And what do we do now?" "Let's go and eat," he said.

What happened then?
It all worked out fine. I've mentioned that many soldiers were collaborating with us. Which is why the bridge exploded – because the Italian artificer had been assisted

by a Spanish officer to mine the bridge. Our man had explosives, but they were not so good, and the officer had more effective explosives for the job. So he gave the officer the honor of issuing the command to make the bridge blow up, but the officer didn't quite understand, and at a certain moment he triggered the explosion when the cameras weren't turning. So his soldiers helped to reconstruct the bridge – which had taken us a month and a half to build – and with the army's help it was rebuilt in a week, ready for us to shoot the scene.

Were the scenes at the cemetery – the end of *The Good, the Bad and the Ugly* – a particular challenge?
When we filmed Eli Wallach running around the cemetery, I had the idea that in order to cut the close-up and the long-shot together, I'd put a pole on the tripod and put a camera at each end of it – at one end a camera with a 25mm lens and at the other a camera with a 75mm lens. The cameras turned together, so if the actor was framed with the 75mm lens, the 25mm would automatically be okay as well. It took half the time to shoot it, and it was better for the editing as well. In this way, we made a lot of circles all at the same time, while Eli Wallach did a lot of running. That's how that was done.

Sergio liked to use music on the set, didn't he?
Morricone made a guide track of some music, a track that would be elaborated on and improved later. Sergio wanted music from the beginning of the project, before starting to shoot. He usually had it playing in the studio for the interiors, which used to irritate me because I couldn't talk to the electricians. He liked to work with a musical soundtrack. But when we actually went for a take, he cut the music so we'd have good production sound.

You've mentioned the recce to Monument Valley for *Once Upon a Time in the West* . . .
Yes, we were in Arizona, looking for a place to build the exterior of the posada, the place in the desert where Claudia Cardinale and Paolo Stoppa arrive. In the end, we found a good place with a small building, a hut, on it. We called to see whether anyone was at home, and we met the owner. You won't believe this, but when we arrived he was making pasta – and doing it by the book. "First I have to finish this, and then we can talk." He was measuring fettucine with a ruler! Anyway, Sergio said to him, "You don't do it like that, you do it like this" – and Sergio taught this man how to make Italian pasta! The man simply couldn't believe it . . . A pasta lesson in the Arizona desert!

And then to Almería, making it match the Arizona desert.
In Almería, Sergio even had two kilometers of railway built and arranged for the locomotive and wagons to be transported to the mountains. When he had made up his mind about something like that, it was impossible to change it. We argued a lot about things over the years, but he was, above all, a good friend.

Why didn't you photograph *Duck, You Sucker/A Fistful of Dynamite*?
Because I was not free. I was working on another film at the time. So Ruzzolini, who had worked with me, did it instead.

I get the feeling that you are not too comfortable talking about some of these things – that you share the philosophy of Tuco in the bathtub in *The Good, the Bad and the Ugly*: "If you're going to shoot, shoot; don't talk!"
Well, I get a bit cross with some of the critics and the questions they ask. At the time, Sergio's films did not interest the critics, though the films were huge commercial successes. Now, after the fact, things are being put right. Critics in general I don't have much time for. They confuse films with Picasso paintings.

Opposite: **Jason Robards starred as the bandit Cheyenne, as shown on this Italian poster for *Once Upon a Time in the West*.**

EURO INTERNATIONAL FILMS PRESENTA

CLAUDIA CARDINALE

HENRY FONDA   JASON ROBARDS

IN

"C'ERA UNA VOLTA IL WEST"

C'ERA UNA VOLTA IL WEST

CON CHARLES BRONSON NEL RUOLO DI ARMONICA · GABRIELE FERZETTI · PAOLO STOPPA

E IN ORDINE ALFABETICO

JACK ELAM · LIONEL STANDER · WOODY STRODE · FRANK WOLFF · KEENAN WYNN

REGIA DI   PRODOTTO DA   PRODUTTORE ESECUTIVO

SERGIO LEONE · BINO CICOGNA · FULVIO MORSELLA

UNA PRODUZIONE RAFRAN - S. MARCO

TECHNICOLOR® TECHNISCOPE®

THE WRITERS
LUCIANO VINCENZONI

CO-SCRIPTWRITER:
For a Few Dollars More
The Good, the Bad and the Ugly (also story)
Duck, You Sucker

This conversation took place in two parts, both of them in Luciano Vincenzoni's apartment in Rome. The first was in spring 1999, in preparation for my biography of Sergio Leone; the second a year later in March 2000 for my BBC World Service radio series, How the West Was Shot. *On both occasions, we were surrounded by Luciano's archive, including letters from Billy Wilder (they worked together on the script of* Avanti! *in 1972) and a well-thumbed copy of Louis-Ferdinand Céline's novel* Journey to the End of the Night *– a key influence on his scripts for both* The Great War *and* The Good, the Bad and the Ugly.

CHRISTOPHER FRAYLING: **You first met Sergio Leone when he was an assistant director in the 1950s.**
LUCIANO VINCENZONI: I knew him from 1953. I used to go to a restaurant that was very fashionable at the time, called Gigi Fazi. And there would be this young assistant director sitting at the table. He was a very tiny, skinny, timid, shy, introverted guy, and he was always with the people who could give him a job. He never talked, never said anything, but he was a very good assistant director, and he listened carefully. And at this moment, there was also this old gentleman by the name of Mario Bonnard, a director, who was a friend of Sergio's father – a kind of father figure to Sergio. Sergio was his assistant. And there was another old man, the great Italian actor Aldo Fabrizi. Maybe Sergio was slightly bored by the company of these older people, and by running errands for them, but he was shy, and he never said anything. That was his job. At that time I had sold Bonnard a story – *They've Stolen a Tram* – it was my first movie and they went to shoot it in Bologna, with Aldo Fabrizi. And during the shooting, Bonnard became sick, and so Sergio Leone for the first time in his life became a director, and he finished the movie. And after that he went his way, and I went my way.

Was Sergio a good assistant director?
The best. He was the assistant of everybody. Also the American directors that came to Rome. Very professional. And after his start with the "sandal movies," as we call them, he had this great idea to make his first Western.

Did you see him, in the meantime?
No, never. I glimpsed him one day when I went to see *A Fistful of Dollars* because when I came out, I saw him in the middle of the crowd, looking at the audience coming out and trying to understand if they liked the movie. Then I was here in this apartment, in 1964, and I was a little depressed because I'd fought with my *maestro* and friend, the director Petro Germi, after ten years working together – because I have a bad, bad temper – after three movies together that had won all the festivals in the world. And there was a knock at the door. I opened, and it was Sergio Leone. But I hadn't seen him for ten years, and he was three times the size he had been! And he said, "Dottore Vincenzoni, may I come in?" And I said, "Listen – you call me 'Dottore' now? We are friends. Come in . . ." And he entered and told me, "You saw my picture, *A Fistful of Dollars*?" "Of course, I saw the picture; I enjoyed it a lot." "You . . . you would like to write a sequel of this Western?" He was still very shy and humble, like he thought that maybe I'd refuse, because in his mind I was maybe a little sophisticated – I'd had a big movie in the film festivals in Venice, Cannes, Berlin, and so on. He didn't know that I was flat broke. I had been so unhappy when I fought with Germi that I went to the casino in Venice, the only place in which I didn't think about my problem, and lost everything. I gambled every single dime I had in the bank. So I said, "Why not?"

Was the treatment of *For a Few Dollars More* already written?
Yes, he gave me a treatment he had written with his brother-in-law, Fulvio Morsella, and it was called *Boots Hill*. After, I changed the title. It was not a particularly good treatment. And then he started to act the main scenes, playing like he had a Colt in his hands, you know.

Opposite: **Original Italian large-scale poster of *For a Few Dollars More***

Above: **British quad poster for** *For a Few Dollars More*
Opposite: **Spanish poster for** *For a Few Dollars More* (known as *Death Has a Price*)

"Watch me." He was a cowboy, he was a killer, he was Clint Eastwood, he was everything. I was scared! I remember the first scene he told me about was the duel between Clint Eastwood and Lee Van Cleef, when they kick each other and pull each other's hair – somebody with one big hat hurts another person in another big hat. And it sounded to me a little infantile. I couldn't imagine John Wayne and Henry Fonda doing this. But he explained to me: "You see, Luciano, you know the *real* Roman people, the people who live in that beautiful quarter of Rome that is Trastevere. They are very arrogant, and they provoke each other. They say, 'I put one finger in front of your nose – if you are a man, do something about it.' What is the difference between the cowboy – macho, arrogant –and the people that live

in the quarter of Rome where I grew up?" Because in Trastevere there is the macho culture, you know. And he said, "You see, when I was a kid, there would be two guys in a little alley. And they'd stop one in front of the other and one would say, 'Let me pass by,' and the other would answer, 'And if I don't?' 'If you don't, then . . .'" You understand. This is the spirit he suggested in the scene where Clint Eastwood and Lee Van Cleef are like children – when they shot all the hats. One thing Sergio had was a great sense of humor – he was a fantastic storyteller – he made me laugh when he told me the story about these sorts of guys, and he convinced me. He said, "I think that if we put into the Western this kind of irony, we are winners." In a way, he transferred his childhood memories into the Western. His feelings about his history, his youth, all those kinds of things. And this Romanesque spirit, the Roman soul. It was the irony that struck people the most in America.

Also, his memories of seeing Westerns when he was a child?

Absolutely. He mentioned the four or five movies he liked and that he'd memorized – because he had an incredible visual memory. He'd seen them dozens of times. And he remembered frame by frame entire scenes. That was very helpful to him when he was shooting. It was the classics of John Ford – especially *Stagecoach* and *The Searchers*. Another one was *Warlock* with Henry Fonda, Richard Widmark, and Anthony Quinn. That was his favorite. He had it printed in his head: Sergio had an incredible culture about movies and he had a great memory. When he saw something in a movie that impressed him, it went straight into his head. But he had one credo like if you swear on the Bible: "Never one Indian in his movies." He hated Indian scenes in Westerns. But I'm certain he'd had inside himself, from the time he was an assistant, this desire to make a Western. One day he would make one

himself . . . His dream was to make a film around all the best sequences in the best American films – but with a big difference: "In all the American Westerns," he said, "the story begins slowly, with an explanation of the characters, a love story, etc., all leading up an hour and a half later to the final duel. What I want is a duel every ten minutes." It was a new approach to dramatic structure: no longer the classic American structure of three acts leading to a single resolution.

How did you work together, turning the treatment into a screenplay?

Very simple. I read the treatment, and the following day I agreed. After I'd signed the deal with the producer, Alberto Grimaldo, I wrote the first draft. And Sergio came here – I read the first draft to him, and because he was acting to me, I started acting with him. And he was very pleased with the screenplay. Asked me two or three things to change, add or cut something, and they went to shoot.

With *For a Few Dollars More*, the "Leone style" comes through really for the first time: the humor, the irony, the design, the flamboyant approach to storytelling . . .

Well, it was a kind of cocktail. After the big success of the first one – that was a little naive, more than the others, and not too much sense of humor – after that he felt more secure. And the relationship with me helped him bring out the irony he had inside; now he started to have the courage to do things. It was a nice combination. Because I was a bit snobbish about this Western at first, I treated it like a kind of game. I couldn't take myself seriously with a Western. So I wrote it in nine days, with my left hand, so to speak. And I'd had a lot of success with comedies *all' italiana*. Research? I didn't need to because, like Sergio Leone and like everyone, I saw all the American Westerns on television and I liked them – *Stagecoach* and *My Darling Clementine* – so I knew. I didn't have them in my head like Sergio. He had a pictorial view. I was following always the plot, not the

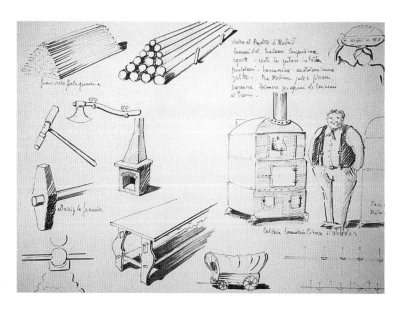

vision – the lines they said, the timing. That was maybe a good combination.

Why do you think Westerns became so popular in Italy at this time?

Because the Western was always a popular show in Italy, and because in the industry they needed to eat. The film industry was collapsing, only a few directors were working, and Sergio Leone had this idea to make a Western in Spain with fake cowboys, fake horses – I think everything was fake – and it worked. It was an enormous success. And now everybody started to make Westerns – lousy Westerns that cost nothing – they made about 845 in six years! With incredible titles, because they did not understand. I remember one producer made a Western with the title *Star Silver* – he wanted *Silver Star*, but he didn't know that in English you put the color before. Everyone went to see *Star Silver*! *Boots Hill*, or *The Hill of Boots*, was the original title of the treatment Sergio Leone brought me. I asked him, "What is this hill of boots?" and he said, "Because in the cemetery, they used to bury the people and put the boots over the grave. Okay?" I chose the title *For a Few Dollars More* exactly because the audience went to see *A Fistful of Dollars*. Eighty-hundred-forty-five Westerns were made after Sergio's success! Naturally, we remember now only the three of Sergio Leone. But the others made a fortune for the industry. The producers became millionaires. Still today they are showing on television. *For a Few Dollars More* was a fantastic success at the time.

The next film, *The Good, the Bad and the Ugly*, seems to have originated in a viewing of *For a Few Dollars More* in Rome.

Well, I was a close friend of all the people at United Artists, and when I realized the kind of success the movie was having with the audience, I called Ilya Lopert – the vice president of United Artists – who was in Paris, and I said, "Ilya, you have to come to Rome because the movie I've done with Sergio Leone is making a fortune." And Ilya

Lopert said, "I don't want to buy that movie – because I bought *Yojimbo* in Japan and they stole it from me!" I said, "Ilya – this is in the past. Please come to Rome and try to buy the movie, because if you don't come, I am obliged to call Warner Bros. or Paramount" – I was personally involved in sales abroad – "and if somebody, not you, buys the movie and if it is a big hit in the United States, you will be fired. I don't want that!" And Ilya flew to Rome, with all the senior staff of UA. Instead of taking these people to a private screening room – which are always cold – I decided to take them to the Supercinema, the biggest theater in Rome, where three thousand people were yelling and laughing and applauding. Breaking all weekly box-office records three times over. And I called the manager of the theater and said, "Please, I need six seats – use the police, use a machine gun, but I must have six seats." When the movie ended, at the door of this theater, the UA people said, "How much?" I said, "One million dollars minimum guarantee, excluding Italy, France, Spain, and Germany because the producer has a coproduction." They said, "It's a deal – let's go to the Grand Hotel to sign the contract." This was three times higher than the most optimistic forecasts of the producer, Grimaldi. As usual with Hollywood, the first thing they said when they signed the contract was, "What next? Because we want to cross-collateralize – to compensate profits and losses with the *next* film. What *is* the next film?" And Sergio turned to me and said, "Yes, what *is* the next film?" "What . . . who?" So with the tacit agreement of Leone and Grimaldi, I began to invent things on the spot. "It is a film about three rogues who are looking for two hundred thousand dollars in gold during the American Civil War. They don't care about the South and the North,

Above: **Carlo Leva prop drawing for *Once Upon a Time in the West***

they just want the money. It has the same spirit as my script for *The Great War/The Best of Enemies*. In that one, you'll remember, a comedy about the First World War, you see the two characters – Gassman and Sordi – two lousy people who don't want to fight; they are only interested in saving their own skins." By the way, *that* story I took from Guy de Maupassant's *Deux Amis*, three pages set in the war between France and Germany in 1871. This gave me the basic idea. "Well, imagine *The Great War*, only in the American Civil War . . ." And they immediately said, "Good – it's a deal. How much?" I said to Grimaldi, "How much?" He said, "How much what?" "The story I've just finished telling!" "What do you think, eight hundred thousand dollars?" I said, "One million one hundred thousand, and it's a deal." And they signed. Without any story having been written.

After I came home, I started to write. And after that came the idea of *The Good, the Bad and the Ugly*. It was originally called *Two Magnificent Rogues*. One night I was in bed, dreaming. And suddenly I saw a poster – Clint, Eli Wallach, and Lee – and I saw the words in Italian *Il Buono, Il Bruto, Il Cattivo*. "My God, this is the title!" Why? Because it is a title like in a fairy tale for babies. The concept is so simple and direct. You know that is the only one of Leone's titles never to change anywhere, even in Japan. So I jumped up and ran to the office and said to somebody that was very close to Sergio, "Listen, *Two Magnificent Rogues* was mine – it doesn't work – tell him that the right title will be this!" And this guy went to Sergio. An hour later, Sergio called me and said, "Luciano, what do you think about the title *The Good, the Bad and the Ugly*?" I said, "Well, I think it's very good, because it was I who told him." "Well, I think it's good too."

Then what happened?
After that, I worked with the scriptwriters Age and Scarpelli, but Sergio wasn't so happy, and they don't work really for this brand of movie, so after that I worked by myself, and I made a couple of rewritings. The Padre Ramirez sequence I wrote after we'd finished the screenplay. When Sergio went for editing, he had the chance to hire my friend Sergio Donati as well.

You have said that when you looked at the finished film, you sometimes asked yourself, "Did I really write that?"
Yes. In *The Good, the Bad and the Ugly*, there's an exchange of jokes between the two heroes, who are sitting round a fire. Sergio wasn't happy with this scene until the assistants had found him a place on a mountain pass with a majestic view, which gave a huge boost to the dialogue. You see, when you write a scene for Sergio Leone you say something like, "You and I, here in this corner of the room, talking." Then Sergio goes and shoots the scene – from the top of St. Peter's church with all Rome in the background. I mean, the scene becomes something incredible. And when I wrote with Sergio Donati the third movie I did for Sergio – *Once Upon a Time, the Revolution*, or *Giù La Testa* – there's a scene we wrote in which Coburn and Steiger after a little fight say, "Let's sit down and have a bite and talk," and they were supposed to be sitting on two stones, eating and chatting. Sergio Leone pushed the art director to find a place in the high mountains of Almería where there were two stones, but when the camera pulled back there was all Spain as well – all Spain, including Portugal in the background! Because this is the gigantic point of view of the man. If you see the movie, it is a little scene – just two guys, no shooting, just two guys having a talk and eating something. And the camera frames on them, they start to talk, the camera pulls back, *piano*, *piano*, you see – my God! – all Spain, Madrid, Francisco Franco, everything. Everything was gigantic. This was the talent of Sergio.

With the bigger budget, Sergio Leone could also indulge his fascination with details and textures.
He loved objects, and he collected furniture and paintings and eighteenth-century Roman silverware. Also jewels. He had a great sense of antiques and a great visual education. When we had our meetings, he used sometimes to put on

a gunbelt and turn the pistol around on his finger like a cowboy. The love with which he touched those weapons! It had to be seen to be believed.

You've mentioned the opening sequence of *Once Upon a Time in the West* as a good example of his use of texture.

Yes, you've got Leone's memory of *High Noon*, with the three killers who are passing the time, bored, at the station. And he wanted the set to be constructed of planking with thousands of railway sleepers that were brought specially – the planking where Bronson comes face-to-face with the three killers. A forest of railway sleepers. This is such a great *plastic* idea, isn't it? Another director might have said, "There's some stones, there's some grass, doesn't that amount to the same thing?" But not Leone. He wasn't worried about credibility. What was important was to make an effect on the audience and give the scene depth. Sometimes, his great art director, Carlo Simi, would say, "My God, he asked me something impossible: 'Make that platform – over a hundred yards long, with tons and tons and tons of wood – an esplanade of trees.' " It was very expensive, but Sergio said, "I must have that, because that will give me at the beginning the attention of the audience. Their attention must be captured – even by the materials that are lying around." And he was right. Carlo Simi was very good at this – only with Sergio Leone, only because Sergio Leone completely trusted him.

He always had to go one step further than what was expected.

We always talk about when two men confront each other in a duel. Okay. Sergio made this the *triello* with *three* people on the ground shooting at each other. Always three. In Italian he invented the word *triello* instead of *duello*. And this was his attitude – in *The Good, the Bad and the Ugly*, in the cemetery. He wanted to push as far as he could all the possibilities of this confrontation – with the music, the long shots, and the long close-ups on the characters'

faces, the stretching of time. I think actually the power we felt – Sergio and I – in front of the movie, was that we saw things with the point of view of the child that plays cowboys. This is the reason for the impact we had on the audience. When Eastwood meets Van Cleef, there are babies under the house who are watching. Because – and this is Sergio – he told me that he used to do this kind of provocation with his friends when he was growing up in Trastevere. He transferred his soul into the West, and naturally that was funny. Instead of the John Wayne type, you had someone who was a little self-interested and a little deep, also. You wouldn't buy a used car from them! No way. This philosophy, or this style, was 100 percent from Sergio Leone. I interpreted it and sometimes made bigger what was in his mind, in his soul, in his education.

You get this unusual combination of exaggerated spectacle and dirty realism.

It was very strange, you know. When we went to the United States to scout locations and costumes for *The Good, the Bad and the Ugly*, United Artists arranged for a limousine to take us from New York to Washington. And I went to the Library of Congress, where there are a lot of documents about the West and the Civil War in Texas, and I found some things. And after, we went around North Carolina. But Sergio was interested in these things because he *already* had in his mind the movie. He spent time on research – he wanted to have costumes, uniforms that had to be stinky. But he already had the movie in mind. Though I spent hours at the Library of Congress, he spent weeks at Western Costume – a big building in Hollywood where you find all the costumes from old movies. He was really into material, color, texture.

The interpretation of the Civil War in *The Good, the Bad and the Ugly* is cynical – troops sent to the slaughter, a drunken officer, gray uniforms that turn out to be blue when dusted . . .

Yes, we were a little cynical. But mainly there is an interesting thing Sergio Leone told me, one of the first

Above: **Australian daybill for *The Good, the Bad and the Ugly***

things he said – maybe that day when he came and proposed the first movie we did. He said, "What are the American Westerns you like best?" And I mentioned three or four titles. "I like the same ones. One thing, though: In the American Westerns, mainly you have a violent scene at the beginning and after that you wait all the movie until the end to see the showdown. Luciano, if we want to win, every ten minutes we have to have a showdown one after the other. Because I remember that when I went to see the American movies, I enjoyed them a lot, but the thrill, the big moment was at the end when they shoot at each other – *bang, bang, bang*. Now these things we will put every ten minutes."

And he had a kind of obsession for the circle. The last duel in *For a Few Dollars More* is round – a round circle behind a farm, like an arena; the last duel in *The Good, the Bad and the Ugly* in the cemetery . . . He goes running, running, running to the music, and it is a circle. Maybe the circle came from the movies we call "the big sandals." He had this vision . . . Scenes like these were when the direction came up. He liked – and I liked – dry dialogue, very few words. But when you have a scene like this one – with no dialogue – you write: "Cemetery – the Good goes there – the Ugly runs around looking for the tombstone – the Bad comes – and suddenly they stop, watch each other, and shoot." You write six lines, and Sergio Leone makes twenty minutes, and they are lyrical. This is the director. Because he was a great director. I'll tell you another thing: I only started to understand the greatness of Sergio Leone when I stopped working with him. When I was close to him, I misevaluated his power. He was greater than I imagined. It is too late now.

Sergio Leone didn't ask you to write his next film *Once Upon a Time in the West*.

Because we fought. We fought about the length of *The Good, the Bad and the Ugly*, because United Artists gave me the responsibility. I was like a representative . . . "Luciano, we don't want the movie to be more than two hours." And we started to fight. And so then he made another movie,

Once Upon a Time in the West. That was a good movie. Sergio Donati sent me the screenplay – very detailed, very long, very big. Everyone – even big names – forgets that only Sergio Donati wrote that screenplay. I say this not because he is a friend – we made twenty-five movies together – but because I read his screenplay. And then Sergio Leone had to make *Once Upon a Time, the Revolution* or *Fistful of Dynamite.*

Originally, Sergio wasn't going to direct this film.
I'll tell you something. The meeting between Peter Bogdanovich and Sergio Leone happened in this room, on this couch. Sergio was there, I was here, Peter was there, and we started to chat about *Once Upon a Time, the Revolution.* From the first moment, it wasn't going to work – with Peter Bogdanovich directing and Sergio Leone producing. Because Sergio was arrogant and ignorant, and Boganovich was arrogant and cultivated. The problem was, I was in the middle. Besides, I think a director should never be the producer of another director – especially a guy like Peter, who was growing at that time. He had done only one movie, *Targets,* but UA trusted him . . . And I was trying to be the peacemaker. Sergio didn't speak more than one word of English. My English was poor, but anyway . . . They started to fight. "Now you have two big green eyes." "I don't use two perforations – I use 1:85 ratio . . . and I am the director, Sergio." "No, because . . ." They fight and they fight, and then they parted. At one point, Sergio Leone suggested *me* to direct the film. And for a moment I was tempted, but after I said, "No, no way." He would have jumped onto my shoulders; and besides I knew my temper.

Did you feel that Sergio Leone himself was "growing" with each film?
Following his career, I now understand that he was growing, movie after movie, in style. Because at the beginning, the style was a little rough. Successful, yes, but rough. Even *For a Few Dollars More. The Good, the Bad and the Ugly* was better. With *Once Upon a Time in the West* he already had a lyrical sense of cinematography . . .

Giù La Testa was one of a number of Italian films at the time that were about the Mexican Revolution. Some of them were quite left wing.
I wrote *A Professional Gun* from a treatment by Franco Solinas. I remember the last line in the movie. The bandit is going away, he stops the horse, he turns and says to the cynical Franco Nero character, "In your life, you never had a dream." But I was absolutely not political. A left-wing Western? It just came out like that! It wasn't in my mind. People tried to find some connection with the political situation at that time. I guarantee that with Sergio Leone we never talked about, thought about, politics. He didn't know if Italy was a monarchy or a republic! We were intrigued about the characters – no? Rod Steiger a lousy bandit, a second-rate bandit, and a guy who comes from Ireland and has a dream. Two characters that if you put them together you have a good cocktail. And part of the cocktail was the music.

That's another thing about Sergio Leone – very important. He had a sense of the lyric of the music, a lyric soul; he had one of the greatest musicians in the world, that is Ennio Morricone, and melodrama needs music. Sergio had something inside; he was a musician in his mind, he chose the right tune and made Morricone develop the tune with the right kind of orchestra – so many brass, so many violins; and after, when he was editing the movie he used the music as the fourth very important element: direction, writing, photography, music. I remember when they were doing the score for *A Few Dollars More,* naively I went to the recording studio where Morricone and Sergio Leone were, and I took with me a Miles Davis record, *Sketches of Spain.* I said, "Why don't

Above: **Leone and Rod Steiger (Juan) before filming a firing squad scene of *Duck, You Sucker***

you use something like that." Five minutes later they threw the record out of the window and said, "Get out of here!"

You don't mention the acting among your elements!
No [*laughs*]. The part of the bandit was destined for Eli Wallach, but they didn't make a deal. Rod Steiger and Sergio Leone fought a lot. Steiger did his best to be a good Sergio Leone character, not a Rod Steiger character. This is the only movie in which Rod Steiger is not Rod Steiger – he is Sergio Leone! I remember one day there were four or five crews shooting in Almería, and in this big hotel there was an enormous restaurant where in one corner was Sergio Leone's crew and myself. Now entered Rod Steiger, who went with some people to a table – thirty yards from our table. "Sergio, I want to talk with you!" he shouted across the room. I watched Sergio, and I said, "Don't move." And he said, "Luciano, if one day you are a director and you know the relationship between a director and an actor – an actor can blackmail you any time he wants. I have to finish the movie." He stood up, and he went. And I remember that broke my heart. And after talking about the scene with Rod Steiger at the actor's table, he came back and sat down. At that moment I said, "If you want, I'll wait outside the hotel and punch him on the nose." "Forget it – let's finish the movie."

Were there any autobiographical elements in *Giù La Testa* from Sergio's early life?
Well, Sergio Leone once described to me the first scene in his early script about his childhood, called *Viale Glorioso*. And I'll tell you the scene. There are a bunch of kids – eleven, twelve, thirteen – on the top of some steps, a public stone staircase above Trastevere. And they bet on who is the champion at peeing. They pee, and the one who goes farthest down the steps is the winner. That was to be the first scene of *Viale Glorioso*. And it is the opening of *Giù La Testa*, when Steiger pees over the colony of ants on the tree. Same scene.

I was thinking more about the many references to Rome in wartime, 1943–45.

I don't remember. They just came up, you know. Me or Sergio Donati or Sergio . . . Sergio wanted to get away from the Stetson and the Colt Navy.

After Steiger urinates against the tree, that incredibly luxurious stagecoach arrives . . .
That was so typical of Sergio. "You want a stagecoach? I'll give you the biggest, the most luxurious you've ever seen." It was a masterpiece of carpentry – with original Louis Vuitton suitcases from the end of the nineteenth century and a lavatory like in the old Pullman carriages. Sergio Leone wanted to lay it on, to increase the idea of the humiliation of the illiterate peasant. And they built the carriage, even though it cost a fortune. Originally, he wanted it to be pulled by twelve horses, but no one can possibly drive twelve horses . . . and then the thing would not move! He had a vision in his mind's eye, and he could not accept any less. Always creating an effect.

In the 1970s, after the Italian Western boom was over, you wrote a sequel to *The Good, the Bad and the Ugly*.
It was in 1977 or 1978, and it is a very good story. I went to see Eli Wallach and Lee Van Cleef, who were crazy about it. Clint Eastwood would not want to have a part, but maybe he would give us his voice. The director was supposed to be Joe Dante. He liked the treatment, and we were going to make a screenplay together. It started one stormy day, in an isolated village. A very tired, starving horse arrives with a very tired man in the saddle. They stop in front of the saloon. The wind whistles. Nobody's around. The man entering the saloon is Eli Wallach – twenty-five years older, with white hair. He arrives at the bar. "Give me a scotch." And the bartender says, "Money!" "I need a drink desperately." "No – money!" "Forget it. Listen to me. Have you by any chance seen around a guy – he's tall, blond, with green eyes, he smokes a cigar, and he's an incredible son of a bitch." And the bartender says, "No – I haven't seen this man." Okay. He goes out, and the horse is there dying on the ground. He says, "Please don't

die now," and he tries to pick up the horse, but the horse won't get up. He is tired. Eventually, the horse gets up; he jumps on and disappears into the night with the wind. The wind whistles. Now the camera goes around a corner, and there is Lee Van Cleef – the twin brother of the other Lee Van Cleef – who is watching this man. And the wind blows this piece of newspaper under the boot of Lee Van Cleef. He picks it up. And there is a picture of Clint Eastwood, smiling, with a wide Stetson: "On Sunday our mayor will be married to Miss Rosemary Whoever." We discover now the face of Lee Van Cleef, the twin brother. Now the Bad knows where he is going. He jumps on the horse and rides after the Ugly. The second scene is Eli Wallach with the horse that just arrived at a little town – and died because it was too tired. And all over this little town are posters with the picture of Clint Eastwood and saying: "Our beloved mayor, who died because somebody shot him," etc. So we don't need Clint Eastwood in the movie! Eli Wallach has found him, but too late. Now he goes to the cemetery, because he knows he's buried in it, and there is a tombstone: a cross with the famous poncho, the hat of Clint, even with the cigar – which is smoking. It is a little piece of iron in the cross, and there's this cigar with smoke. Now he hears somebody coming. He hides himself behind a tree, and a young kid – blond, good-looking – arrives, changes the cigar, and lights it. He says, "Daddy," – or "Uncle," or whatever – "I have done what you suggested. I converted all our property into cash money, and I went East and invested it all in the railroads. I will return, I hope, once a year to visit you. Pardon me, your cigar has gone out." He lights his cigar. *Puff*. "Goodbye for now." And as the young fellow turns to go, Eli Wallach comes out from behind the tree, and from the tombstone we hear the voice of Clint Eastwood say to the boy, "Be careful, son, because the world is full of sons of bitches and they are always on your back." Now the young guy disappears. Eli Wallach follows him, and from behind another tree comes out the twin of Lee Van Cleef. This is the beginning of the movie. I wrote it over twenty years ago, and now Eli is eighty years old. I suppose it is unlikely to be produced now. Anyway . . .

Looking back, what do you think is the significance of Sergio Leone's Westerns?
They saved the industry in Italy, because everybody was working at that moment. And they stand out from the hundreds of other Westerns made in that six to seven years. They are in another category. I don't want to go into philosophy or compare them with the classics of Bergman or Renoir or Fellini or Antonioni – but they have something, something more. I don't know if there exists in English the word *artigiano* – "artisan-craftsmanlike" – but Sergio Leone was a sublime craftsman. Fellini was an artistic dreamer; Sergio Leone was a sublime craft-worker – that's for sure. He used to say, "cinema cinema." Twice the word. Not about reality but cinema. I was surprised at the success the movies had all over the world but also in the U.S.A. They are still cult movies. If you watch a Sergio Leone movie, you'll see that he tried hard to be precise in the costumes, the kinds of horses, even the color of the hair. In Italy, most men are short and dark. Cowboys in the movies are normally tall and blond. And he chose one by one the extras, and the guns had to be exactly right. The other 845 movies, they were incredible – a Texan, with one yard of saddle, dark hair, a Neapolitan way of looking, dressed like a performing monkey, with a gun from Germany – not a Colt or a Smith & Wesson but a Walther. Sergio Leone lived movies, he wanted to make movies, and he wanted to make them better and better . . . It seems like when he was an infant, his mother gave him one tit milk and the other tit film!

Opposite: **Leone films the aftermath of the Battle of the Langstone Bridge in *The Good, the Bad and the Ugly*.**

$ 10,000 REWARD

for
EL INDIO

DEAD OR ALIVE

CON LEE VAN CLEEF
GIAN MARIA VOLONTE'

MARA KRUP - LUIGI PISTILLI
KLAUS KINSKI - JOSEF EGGER
PANOS PAPADOPULOS - BENITO STEFANELLI
ROBERT CAMARDIEL - ALDO SAMBRELL
LUIS RODRIGUEZ e MARIO BREGA

musiche di ENNIO MORRICONE
sceneggiatura e dialoghi di LUCIANO VINCENZONI

TECHNICOLOR
TECHNISCOPE

RA presenta CLINT EASTWOOD in un film di SERGIO LEONE

PER QUALCHE DOLLARO IN PIU'

THE WRITERS
SERGIO DONATI

SCRIPT DOCTOR:

For a Few Dollars More
The Good, the Bad and the Ugly

CO-SCRIPTWRITER:

Once Upon a Time in the West
Duck, You Sucker (also story)

This conversation also happened in two parts, both of them at Sergio Donati's house in Fregene, Italy – about an hour's drive from Rome. The first was on May 23, 1998, and the second on March 19, 2000. As our discussion reveals, Sergio Donati still feels very strongly about his writer/director relationship with Sergio Leone. At one point, he picked the original script of Once Upon a Time in the West *from a shelf of bound scripts and took me through it, scene by scene.*

CHRISTOPHER FRAYLING: When did you first meet Sergio Leone?

SERGIO DONATI: We met in 1956. I had begun as a writer of detective novels, and my first work for the cinema was on a screenplay with director Riccardo Freda. And around that time I met this young, very keen guy with a large nose: You can see him in *The Bicycle Thief* and also in the film with Aldo Frabrizi, *They've Stolen a Tram.* He was a very keen, hungry-looking assistant director who used to drive around in an old Fiat Seicento. In those days, he seemed to be surrounded by older people. I think he developed in himself some kind of bitterness, because Mario Bonnard and Aldo Fabrizi, these cynical old men, sent him off to buy cigarettes and to find girls. He had some bitterness about that . . . They tell me that he really filmed many of the things in Bonnard's movies. Then he made a lot of second-unit work also with big American directors. Later, Sergio was very sure of himself and behaved like he was one of the Lumière Brothers, but he was the same when he was nobody. When I met him as an assistant director, he was already the inventor of the movies. Explain that!

What was your first involvement in Italian Westerns?

It's a long story between Sergio Leone and me. My books were successful, but I still couldn't make a living from them, so when I had finished my studies in law I went to Milan, the Madison Avenue of Italian advertising and stayed there for some years. In the meantime, Sergio would phone me from Rome, with unlikely offers. I was working in Milan and he was trying to get me to Rome . . . One day Leone phoned me and asked me to go and see

Yojimbo, because he wanted to make a Western out of it. You must remember that the Western was in Italy the B movie, the C movie. And the movie he then went on to make was a *B-B-B* movie. So I didn't trust him about this, and I said, "You're crazy – I don't believe in that B Western Italian movie." I didn't even go and see *Yojimbo*, which is why I didn't get to write *A Fistful of Dollars.* Then it was a success. And he kept calling me. And then there were lawsuits with the producers Papi and Colombo and so on, because he broke the contract that would have made him do ten movies in a row for a ridiculously small sum of money. But the first Western I wrote: I was in Milan and it was a Spanish director called Joaquín Romero Marchent who came, and it was called *One Hundred Thousand Dollars for Lassiter.* And I came to Rome and made some ghostwriting for Sergio – *For a Few Dollars More* – and then I wrote two good Westerns for Sergio Sollima – *The Big Gundown* and *Face to Face.*

What did you add to Luciano Vincenzoni's script of *For a Few Dollars More*?

Sergio was not particularly happy with it. Luciano didn't know who was the guy who put his pen to that script. And Sergio asked me, "Come to Rome, because I want you to write something." And I stayed three hundred meters from Vincenzoni's house, and I rewrote some things on the movie. Particularly, I made a big work on the dialogues. This I'm very proud of. For instance, I wrote the line "This train will stop at Tucumcari," and a scene of mine is the one with the old man and the train. And the thing that I'm most proud of in my career is at the end of the movie. It was too flat in the script. Clint Eastwood was saying the names of the bandits at the end – "Johnson, Smith" – and I said, "No, Sergio, it would be funny if this bounty killer adds up the money instead – thirteen dollars, eighteen dollars, twenty-five." And then the Colonel says, "Having trouble, boy?" He says, "No, old man, thought I was having trouble with my adding." This was a joke that provoked

Opposite: **Italian *fotobusta* for *For a Few Dollars More***

the most amazing applause. I remember the time the movie was shown at the Supercinema in Rome and there were football stadium cheers: "Hurrah!" So I did this work, paid but uncredited. And Alberto Grimaldi convinced me to leave advertising and move to Rome.

Why in the mid-1960s did Westerns suddenly catch on in Italy?

You know, we Italians had the chance – such a chance – in Sergio's generation, my generation – I was a little younger, but I'm almost the same generation – in 1945/46, we had the chance to see fifteen years of American movies all together – fifteen years of American literature all together, so we were filled up; we *lived* in that myth. And it was not only Westerns; there was the phenomenon of remaking with a little money and a lot of imagination all the genres: horror; science fiction (not the musical – we did not have the money for that); everything that could be done even in the bathroom, like the Antonio Margheriti science-fiction movies – he made them in his bathroom with nylon rope.

Hollywood had stopped making so many Westerns, and Europe spotted a market niche.

Well, in a sense we digested the American Western, and then we recycled it in a more Italian – I would say Roman – way: more cynical, ironic, like the *commedia all' italiana*. And then when the Americans tried to do Westerns Italian-style – in the sense of *Silverado*, for instance – it was not good, because they had not the craziness. The director who was nearer to the Italian Western, maybe, for his foolishness, was Sam Peckinpah. This was the director Leone felt most as a rival. In fact, he buried him in a movie: You remember in the cemetery in *My Name Is Nobody*? Peckinpah's name is on the grave.

Did Sergio, when he talked about the script, consciously ask you to write dialogue "in the Roman style"?

Yes, absolutely. All the time. He told me, "Think of the dialogue like in a Roman *osteria*, a saloon." The irony, the boldness, the machismo – these are Roman.

You were involved in *The Good, the Bad and the Ugly* during post-production, the editing stage.

Sergio said – he'd just shot *The Good, the Bad and the Ugly* – he said, "Now you are with the editing, because you have to stay every day with Nino Baragli [the film editor] and Ennio Morricone, to know perfectly how I shoot things, because you will be *my writer*. You have to know everything about me. From the next movie you will be my writer. We must have the capacity to think the same things, understand everything." I was almost divorced. I was about eight months in the editing, during which time we dubbed it, mixed it, edited it, and put in the music. And something happened to Sergio Leone in that period. In the autumn of that year, when we were finishing the editing – we were supposed to have the movie ready for Christmas 1966 – and at the end, you can ask Morricone or Baragli, something happened in his mind. Maybe he was insecure, I don't know. On his previous films, he'd worked with great happiness and enjoyed inventing things, but he looked like he didn't want this movie to be finished, to be released. Maybe it was the fear of not living up to his reputation. Morricone had made the music of the *triello*. At half past five in the morning, the twentieth remake; Sergio was never satisfied. It looked like he didn't want to meet the deadline, you know? He killed us. He said, "So you are my writer," and I was happy. I gave him my life. We slept in the dubbing room on benches next to the Moviola machine the last week – Baragli, Morricone, and I – five o'clock, the twenty-third of December, there was that spirit of "We did it!" We could get the first copy out the next day. Fifteen reels; no, twenty-one reels. And the last mix. Up, down. And there was the owner of the establishment ready with champagne – it was Christmas – champagne and cakes. Everybody else was moved. And exhausted. And at the end, Sergio just brushed the owner aside and said, "Okay, good night." And he went away. To the people who gave their blood! "Okay, good night." That was it. I gave him eight months of my life, and I expected that Sergio would

Opposite: **French large-scale poster for *The Good, the Bad and the Ugly***

at least have said to me, "Sergio, I put your name on the end titles." Nothing.

Part of your job was to help cut down *The Good, the Bad and the Ugly* and make the dialogue continue to make sense . . .
Sergio's movies were always long. But this was really *too* long. And we had to cut more or less twenty to twenty-five minutes of the movie after it had been shot. And I was in the Moviola with Nino Baragli, and we took a not-very-important scene when Lee Van Cleef meets the soldier with no legs, the "half soldier," and I adapted the dialogue in this scene to make a résumé of what we had cut. In fact, if you see the movie and look at the expressions – not only the lips but the expressions – you'll see they are serious when they should be roaring with laughter. That was the material we worked with. I wrote a dialogue, with the concentration on what we cut: "Baker is gone and this one has moved." These details are what is missing. In one line, he explains all of this. Sergio never committed the common mistake of abbreviating a sequence and spoiling the rhythm of the film. He preferred to take out entire blocks of story. He was right about that.

Above: **Leone admiring a firearm**

One great advantage of postsynchronization is that you can reinvent the story at the editing stage.
Yes. We used to rewrite everything, and I remember when I was with Sergio in New York on Broadway and we came to visit the dubbing studios, and Sergio was not very good in English, but I discovered they were translating absolutely crazy things just to get the lips matching. Because it was a high-cost movie, the American audience would have to think it was direct sound. Well, it wasn't – it was people who were just saying numbers like in a Fellini movie. So, taking the Italians who talk Italian, the Spanish who talk Spanish, and Mario Brega, who was *romanesco*, we changed everything, and it was a problem. It cost me almost two months staying in New York and following the dubbing, until a freezing December. The Americans were fixated on invisible dubbing, and to create lip synchronization they were just changing the dialogue! It was a kind of disaster at first. And then there was a big showdown between Sergio and Clint Eastwood, because they were in that particular situation when everybody thinks "If it was not for me, you would be nobody." Clint was now a star, and Sergio thought he'd wanted too much money for *The Good, the Bad and the Ugly*. And the vice president in charge of this movie at UA called Clint in Los Angeles and said, "Monday, nine o'clock, can you be in New York?" And Clint said, "No, I can't make

Monday – but I can come next week." And then he received the classic Hollywood phone call: "If you want to work in this town," etc. And so he arrived. I remember I was talking with Sergio and Eli Wallach, who is a charming guy, and Clint came in like in a Clint Eastwood movie . . . There was a negotiation, and in the end, of course, he dubbed it.

It sounds like a scene in an Italian Western, the way you tell it . . .

Absolutely. Clint is a guy who in real life is absolutely like in his movies. You never know what he thinks. He talks slowly . . .

And then, after all your hard work on *The Good, the Bad and the Ugly*, you were promised the script of the next movie.

Because I was in the editing. Because he said, "Now you are my writer." He used to say that: "My writer." And he said, "You have to know how I work." And I said, "Okay." And then I waited for months by the phone. I refused every offer. And I waited. January, February, March, watching the phone. I was his writer. And then I understood that he was working with Dario Argento and Bernardo Bertolucci. Not a word. And then at the end of April, he said, "Now the two intellectuals have abandoned work. Come and let's make a movie."

You were upset?

I was hurt, you know, because Sergio was a fantastic guy to work with, but as a human being he was not so fantastic. He had no idea of friendship – maybe that is the reason friendship is mythical in his movies. But in professional life he used people . . . This nice book came out recently, the story of Cesare Zavattini and Vittorio De Sica. The relationship between the writer and the director is always the same. The writer is Penelope: He stays at home, he cooks, he's loyal, he thinks only of his director. The director meanwhile is Ulysses: He's disloyal, goes around, looks always for new experiences, takes all the credit – "*I* did, *I* thought, *I* wrote, *I* said, *I* do . . . *I, I, I*."

Having directed the three *Dollars* films one after the other, *Once Upon a Time in the West* represented a change for Sergio Leone.

He wanted to make this *the ultimate film*, which is maybe why he forgot his promise to me. I think the contribution of Bertolucci to the conception of the story was very important. But I wasn't there. In a sense, from my personal background – cultural background – I "got" the hint from Bertolucci. I tried to widen also this thing, the idea of the capitalist with no legs, whose legs are the money, and the railroad – this idea is mine, for instance. And the character of Cheyenne, the romantic hero played by Jason Robards – who is like Sean Mallory in *Giù La Testa* – he is my favorite character. The first character in my first novel was that kind, too. I like the idea of the unlucky hero. Mallory is my kind of character. And in that movie there was to be a Leone character and my character put together.

You have said: "I wrote the whole script in twenty days, the second draft without even getting up from my seat."

That's right, but I was two weeks together with Sergio, too, telling me the movie. In fact, I never met Bertolucci and Argento at that time. Their treatment was not so gigantic. It was about eighty pages. All their intentions were in the treatment, for sure, but it was slow and rhetorical – Sergio was unsatisfied with that. It was not Sergio Leone. There were very good intentions, but no substance. The main contribution I gave, because I'm a romantic, was the characters like Cheyenne . . . And the best thing I did, I guess, is to give a *meaning* to the story. I mean, this railroad that unites one ocean to the other is the end of the frontier, the end of adventure, the end of the lonely hero, and so on. This was much of me. And I invented the man with no legs, this Mr. Morton, who wants to make it to the other ocean. Mine is the concept of "This is the end of the West."

So you began with Sergio telling you the story . . .

We stayed two weeks together to make a skeleton, the outline, to talk to each other about the scenes very clearly, and then I wrote the script in twenty days, I think.

Working like hell. And I had to rewrite just two things. If you read the official shooting script, it says: "From a story by . . ." Everything was shot in this movie exactly like it was in my script.

Sergio said he wanted to distance himself from the popular Italian film industry; to make a quasi-American epic.

Sure. It was the first time Sergio shot in the United States – the desert of Monument Valley and so on. He was conscious of making an ultimate Western; and we wanted to do that. It was the end of the adventure, the end of the West – when the railroad meets two sides of the ocean.

Are you yourself a fan of the Western?

Yes. Not maniacal like Leone, though. Sergio was omnivorous. He was a real film buff. He could remember whole scenes. He almost didn't read any books, but he had a fantastic visual culture – also for paintings.

The design of the sound became even more important in this film.

We had, I think, nineteen soundtracks at the mixing table, and all the ducks and the dogs and the cicadas and – Jesus Christ, the crickets! He said, "Don't up the sound – down . . . down" or "up . . . up." He covered every single centimeter of film with sound. He couldn't understand silence. Sometimes I say to myself: If Sergio were living today with computer editing, he'd go absolutely crazy! He would make Baragli go crazy too, but he would be so happy. He loved editing. More than shooting. For him, the movie started when he got into the Moviola. "Show me the details, show me the cuts"; he had a room full of takes. I remember on the earlier films he and Morricone seated at a Moviola, and Morricone had a school notepad – that kids use – and wrote down everything. Sergio would say, "He goes on . . . he goes on . . . stop there!" "It's just an empty road." "Yes, we put here birds crying and all the noises à la Sergio!" And I remember, on *For a Few Dollars More*, when Sergio said – about the scene of Volonté in the church, and the duel – "I want here something

religious." And Morricone said, "J. S. Bach, huh?" "But also with the *deguello* on the trumpet!" Sergio enjoyed so much playing around with the sound. He really hated silence. For instance, the revolvers are Winchesters; the Winchesters are little cannons. They sent a man to a valley near Rome where there are sounds of nature, no roads or distracting noises. He sent this man, who came back with the *ping pong pung*. The guns were recorded in the nature, because he wanted air and atmosphere. He was concerned with every detail.

He didn't storyboard in advance, did he?

No, it was no use to storyboard. Not with his style.

Luciano Vincenzoni has said that when he saw a finished Leone film, he sometimes found himself saying, "Did I really write that?" Did you ever experience this?

Absolutely not. I have here the shooting script. And you can see here "*from* a story by Bernardo Bertolucci and Dario Argento," not "story by . . ." And it is 420 pages long. And I used to make a workshop for young scriptwriters, and I would put on the cassette of the finished sequences, and I [would] read from this, and it is almost identical to the shooting. It is so descriptive, the feeling of Jill as she goes among the men and maybe somebody touches her ass. Sergio asked to have everything written down; he liked that. Long descriptions, indirect dialogue, long biographies of the characters, lots of suggestions on how to direct the scene. Many different possibilities. Hundreds and hundreds of stage directions, with just one line of dialogue. The first sequence – there is the fly, the water, the knuckles, everything. The first line is on page thirty, I think. Here, the old man asking for the money for the tickets. Then nothing, nothing, nothing. It is exactly what you see on the screen – the [still on the] cover of your biography of Sergio Leone. The small station of Cattle Corner, exterior, day. Camera finds detail of gun in holster. It was shot just as it was written. We're introduced to the three bad guys waiting at the station – more and more stage directions. We're on page eleven already – no words yet. Pages seventeen to twenty – no words except the notice board, which says "delays"; whereas in *High Noon* the train is on time for sure. And then page twenty-nine, the stationmaster, the old man, says, "For the tickets, you have to pay . . ." All the sound effects are written down, too. The *plop* of water – that's Woody Strode standing there with the water dropping on his head. The insect – zzzzz. That, Leone loved. The cicadas. Here's the fly, everything.

Did some of this detail come out of your conversations with Sergio?
With Sergio you sat down and you imagined the scenes together. It was a very fast work. He said that, and it's true. But he also says, "*We* wrote it." He never wrote even a postcard. But that's typical for a director. I wrote, but we worked together. He used to imagine the scenes. I remember Sergio before even Luciano Vincenzoni wrote a line, he would narrate you *For a Few Dollars More* scene by scene because he had it all in his mind. For *Once Upon a Time in the West*, we sat around the table for fifteen days, and I didn't take many notes. He used to say to other people, "Oh, he remembers everything." It was a surprise to him, because what I believe in I don't need to jot down. And if I take notes, they are no use. I can write only when I have the script clear in my mind. And so I came home, and in three weeks I wrote this 420 pages, and I rewrote just two or three scenes, no more than that.

I can imagine Sergio really taking his time, while he told the story of the opening sequence.
He had in mind also the actors Woody Strode and Jack Elam, and the third one – the unfortunate one who killed himself – Al Muloch. Jack Elam and the fly was written long before the movie – the crossing eyes and the fly. And all of that was in the script. Because we imagined the scene beforehand and just wrote it. Leone didn't like to improvise on the set. He shot every angle, every close-up, of every character – he shot a lot of material. But he was

not very creative on the set. He always asked me to have the opportunity in the script to have a cut before a cut, to cut in two or three ways to the next scene. "Give me lots of possibilities."

This time, Ennio Morricone's music was written and recorded in advance. Did you play the tape while you were writing?
While I was writing, no. I first heard the music on the set in Almería. I was there to cut the movie, and I saw when they shot the scene where Jill comes to the McBain farm and the corpses are laid out on the table – and they played this theme, and the grips were in tears. It was sunset. Only Claudia Cardinale was concentrating, to get to her mark. She had a responsibility to stop on her mark. But the toughest grips were crying. Everybody on the set was crying except Claudia.

You say you were on set "to cut the movie." What happened there?
We knew the script was too long. A 420-page Italian-style script is a good 300 pages of an American script, and it would be four hours. Absolutely. But Sergio said, "No, this time I want to give it a new rhythm." And then he phoned me from Spain. Sergio stopped the movie for a couple of days – with the insurance; he was officially ill – and he was very humble at that time. I felt him to be in a crisis. He said, "Sergio, I cannot do it. I am just starting to shoot the McBain sequence – McBain father and son – with my rhythm and my timing – I was convinced I could give it a different rhythm – I've tried and I can't. We don't want to do it like in *The Good, the Bad and the Ugly* – so come here, we have to cut at least twenty to twenty-five minutes." So I came in a car with my wife and son and a babysitter and stayed for three weeks to cut the script during the shooting.

Sergio still didn't speak very good English . . .
He made himself understood. He was absolutely not able to act. Every time he tried – in different movies with

other directors and also on TV shows – he was blocked, he was shy. But when he showed to the actors the scene, he acted like a great actor. And so, like Italians are – he showed the scene to Henry Fonda and explained himself with mime. And with Eli Wallach on *The Good, the Bad and the Ugly*, this made the character more Roman as they went along. Eli stole the movie from Clint! Sergio let him do it because he was so great. And I wrote *Giù La Testa* for Eli.

At that time, there was a brief craze in Italy for making movies set in the Mexican Revolution, with the bandit-revolutionary as the hero.
Sergio had the script of *Viva Villa!* by Ben Hecht – which is a fantastic script – and he thought for a time about making a remake. I read the script, which was exceptional. But that didn't happen.

When you were on the set of *Once Upon a Time in the West*, you were already working on *Giù La Testa*?
They'd acquired a treatment called *Mexico*. I came to Almería with some thoughts on a new story, but Sergio's mind was on other things. He said, "Okay, okay," and I came back and wrote a draft script. The part of the Mexican was written for Eli Wallach, and for the Irishman I wanted Jason Robards. Robards read it and said, "Mallory is the part of my life – I want to do it – I love you – Yes, it's my part." He was very emotional, and he was drinking like crazy. I remember once he drank the entire hotel canteen dry, but the next day he was on the set half an hour late and he apologized to everyone – not only Leone, not only the actors – he said, "Excuse me, excuse me" to everyone.

At the heart of *Giù La Testa* is the relationship between the cynical revolutionary and the peasant who becomes a reluctant hero.
Like Charlie Chaplin with the red flag in *Modern Times*, he doesn't know there is this crowd behind him. You have to remember this was right after 1968 – the Italian *Viva la Revolución* before the big illusion. I was very excited about it. Sergio didn't care at all.

Giù La Testa seems cynical. Unlike in the other Mexican Revolution films, no one believes in anything at the end . . .
Not cynical. It is the story of a man who is completely disillusioned because he believed in something, and he finds a man who has the quality of a leader. This man doesn't know he has that quality. He moves only when they kill his family. He doesn't understand that his larger family is the Mexican people. I don't think this is so cynical. I think it is even noble. Mallory doesn't believe in revolution anymore, but he believes a man like Juan can lead something. There's a great line in *Viva Villa!* when Wallace Beery dies and he is with his friend the newspaperman. Villa says, "Well, what will you write about me?" He replies, "Pancho Villa – this man who did such good and such bad for Mexico!" "What did I do bad?" says Wallace Beery. It is the best line!

Then you had a row with Sergio, and Luciano Vincenzoni took over the scripting.
I did the first draft of the script, which was discussed on a Sunday at Sergio's house with a whole load of people, and he seemed to be agreeing with *everyone*. He wasn't into the movie yet. So I took my script and spent five days making a second draft with every stupid thing that had been suggested – with Sergio not supporting me, not saying anything – every single modification. And Sergio read it and said, "What did you do?" I said, "I did exactly what they all suggested, since you didn't say anything." And he got offended, and we didn't see each other for six months. Then, as you say, Luciano entered, then Bogdanovich, and they didn't get on at all. Finally, six months later, I agreed to come back, and I stayed in a room with Sergio for a few days, then I wrote what is the final shooting script, and then we argued again. It was very tiring. At the end, you see, he was unsatisfied, like with Bertolucci, and so he called me back. And he knew I was the guy, but he never was clever enough to understand that I needed him just to say "Bravo!" Never once.

Above: **Spanish lobby card for _Once Upon a Time in the West_**

What did you think of the finished film?

You know, it is much too long. Luciano and I were shown the final cut in a private screening, and we wrote together a ten-page letter to Sergio suggesting cuts and things. Sergio was very offended, but we were absolutely sincere. There was too much in there. And personally, I hated the quotation from Mao Tse-tung that opens the film. We didn't know about that in advance. It was the first we'd seen of it. That _was_ very cynical of Sergio. It was such a provocation. Because he was absolutely the least politically involved guy. I found that really cynical. It was exploiting feelings that were around in that period.

And there was Steiger's big speech, "Don't talk to me about the revolution," which was Sergio's idea.

We contributed. I was Mallory, he was Juan! Sergio was absolutely uninterested in politics. He was what we call _qualunquista_ – not interested, doesn't give a damn. I really don't like _Giù La Testa_.

So then you went your separate ways?

Wait a second. After that, I worked on the first project of

My Name Is Nobody. It was an idea – I wrote a treatment – the first idea was to do Homer, the famous phrase: "My name is nobody," and the Cyclops. It was the story of Ulysses – with a Southerner who is in a Yankee concentration camp. We had Circe, the pigs, the Cyclops, all the incidents. The idea was to make the _Odyssey_ as a Western. It was Ulysses who is a captain of the Southern army, in a concentration camp. He escapes, and they meet all these adventures. And then he comes back home, and there's Penelope with the bad guys: _bang, bang, bang, bang_! The dog, everything. And I did go to New Mexico, looking for locations. Then I was out of it doing other things.

Looking back, how do you rate Sergio Leone as a filmmaker?

He was a great filmmaker. I think that internationally speaking he was one of the best, absolutely. I think he's as good as Luchino Visconti, for instance – who is a little overrated, in my modest opinion. I think the best Italian director after the Second World War was De Sica. And then maybe Rossellini. Visconti has something in common with Leone. They were very different, but there was the richness, the nostalgia, the mannerism – in Leone's case with the Western. Was Sergio Leone just a craftsman? What is an artist anyway? Yes, he was fascinated by technical things. As I say, if he were alive today, he would be absolutely crazy with the choices. I remember he was fascinated by the use of Steadicams. The gyroscope on helicopters – he was always trying to make a shot from a helicopter, and he went crazy because it was jumping. He loved the Chapman crane. When he used a big Chapman for the first time on the famous scene where Claudia Cardinale arrives at the station . . . _ahhh_ . . . it was a toy!

That's a big operatic moment, with the crane moving in time with Morricone's crescendo.

Yes, an Italian critic wrote once, maybe about this movie: "It looks like at any moment they will start to sing a _romanza_."

PARAMOUNT
présente

Un film de
SERGIO LEONE
CLAUDIA CARDINALE
HENRY FONDA - JASON ROBARDS
CHARLES BRONSON
dans

IL ETAIT UNE FOIS
DANS L'OUEST
avec

GABRIELE FERZETTI - Woody STRODE

et la participation de (par ordre alphabétique)
JACK ELAM - LIONEL STANDER - PAOLO STOPPA
FRANK WOLFF - KEENAN WYNN

Réalisé par SERGIO LEONE - Produit par FULVIO MORSELLA - Producteur exécutif BINO CICOGNA - Une production RAFRAN-SAN MARCO

TECHNISCOPE® TECHNICOLOR®
C'est un film PARAMOUNT

CLAUDIA CARDINALE   HENRY FONDA   JASON ROBARDS   CHARLES BRONSON

Visa de Censure n° 3282

BERNARDO BERTOLUCCI

COWRITER, STORY:
Once Upon a Time in the West

This conversation took place over lunch at the Institute of Contemporary Arts, in London, on February 25, 1988, just after the launch of the book Bertolucci by Bertolucci *by Enzo Ungari and Don Ranvaud. I had previously had the opportunity to discuss* Once Upon a Time in the West *with Bernardo Bertolucci at London's National Film Theatre in January 1980, when he seemed surprised that Leone's films were being taken seriously. So was the audience.*

CHRISTOPHER FRAYLING: **How did it happen that you worked on *Once Upon a Time in the West*?**
BERNARDO BERTOLUCCI: Well, I went to see *The Good, the Bad and the Ugly*, on the early afternoon show of the first day of its run in Rome, at three o'clock in the afternoon. Sergio Leone was in the projection booth, supervising the projection, and he recognized me. So our first meeting took place in a cinema! He telephoned me at home the next day, to ask if I had liked the film. I told him that I liked it a lot. "Why did you like my film?" "Because of the way you shoot the horses' asses. Most directors shoot them in profile or from the front, but you have this wonderful line of asses, a chorus of asses. Very few directors shoot the back, which is less rhetorical and romantic. One of them is John Ford." He went quiet and then said, "We must make a film together some time."

As a New Wave Italian director, how highly did you rate Sergio Leone?
He was the only one, apart from the four great *maestri* of Italian cinema – Rossellini, Antonioni, Visconti, De Sica – who was doing something different. He was brilliant – vulgar and very sophisticated both at the same time – which was something that hadn't happened before in Italian popular film. Maybe *vulgar* isn't quite the right word: He grabbed ideas directly from life. Actually, in 1967 the only one of the Italian maestri I really liked was Rossellini.

Opposite: **French poster for *Once Upon a Time in the West***

Were you fond of Westerns, when you were growing up near Parma?
As a child, some of the films I loved best were full of cowboys and Indians. I used to reenact them with my friends in the countryside around our house a few kilometers from Parma. I'd see the films at the Orpheus Cinema and act out the stories for my friends who hadn't seen them. One film I loved was *Stagecoach* by John Ford, and I tried to imitate John Wayne with his walk and his half smile. I identified completely with John Wayne between the ages of seven and ten. The relationship of a child to the movies is all about this kind of identification, and it is a great loss when it goes.

How did the treatment of *Once Upon a Time in the West* come about?
I needed work desperately at that time – I'd spent three years since *Before the Revolution* without succeeding in making a film – and in the first place I got involved because I did not have any lire. Also because I was very excited at the prospect of collaborating with a director like Leone on a popular film. He hired me and Dario Argento, who was then a critic, to write the treatment – at a time when Leone was working on *Once Upon a Time in America* and *Once Upon a Time in the West*, both at the same time.

What were your working methods?
Leone has a double nature. On the one hand, he wants to be a kind of Luchino Visconti, part of an elegant aristocratic world that is visually rich. Those soldiers in the desert in *The Good, the Bad and the Ugly*, covered in white dust, are like the dusty ancestors in *The Leopard*. So he shot a Western like Visconti. On the other hand, his basic ideology is a childlike vision of life. The world is divided into two kinds of people: the ones in front of a gun and the ones behind, with those long close-ups of men looking at each other for millions of minutes! When I was with him, at his house in Rome, he spent quite a lot of time asking me, "When you were a child, how did you like to shoot? Like that [*arm's length*], or like that [*waist level*]

or like that [*fanning*]?" So this man of the West was like a child who has access to the dynamics of the imagination. Anyway, I started work with Dario, and we wrote a long treatment together, a treatment that had hardly any dialogue in it. The process began with Sergio telling us the beginning of the story. He loved telling stories, like the stories of childhood. My plan was to fill up the treatment with quotations and places and moments from favorite films, from the Westerns I love. Moments of magic. I was a great cinéphile, and there was a cult of using cinematic quotations at the time. I warned Leone about this. But I didn't always tell Leone where the quotes came from. My dream was to create a situation where a great director would quote a film in innocence, without being aware of it. The quotations would just happen. In a couple of them, I think I was successful in making him do this.

Can you remember where these quotations came from?
There was the name Brett McBain, which was made up from the writers Ed McBain and Brett Halliday. We had many obscure references like that, not just to Westerns but to American cinema in general. I took Sergio to a special screening of *Johnny Guitar*. He may have seen it before, I don't know. But that was one of the explicit references in the film; *The Searchers* for the scene where McBain is waiting for Claudia Cardinale to arrive; *The Man Who Shot Liberty Valance* for the duster coats; *Stagecoach* for Monument Valley. Sweetwater? No, the name didn't come from Victor Sjostrom's *The Wind*, which I hadn't seen, but we just looked at a map of the area for a name we could give this part of the country, and I liked Sweetwater very much. There was also *The Iron Horse*, of course, and all those films about the building of the railroad. And *3:10 to Yuma* for the train that is going to Yuma.

So *Once Upon a Time in the West* was really a modernist project – film about film, quotations, revisiting old moments in new ways.
[*Laughs.*] It was more postmodernist. The first and only postmodernist Western!

What do you think was your distinctive contribution to it?
I'm proud of the fact that I convinced Leone to have the character of a woman for the first time – to accept that character, a character to be taken seriously. I worked a lot on that. We made great efforts to persuade him. He tended to avoid the possibility of sexual relationships in his films! . . . But in our discussions, he did have an astonishing way of visualizing the things he imagined. I remember that the treatment said Claudia Cardinale appears for the first time when she gets down from the train, and she's wearing the latest fashions from New Orleans. Leone added: "The door of the carriage opens, focus on the steps leading up to it, you see the feet come into view, then the camera gets covered by her skirt and we realize that she hasn't got any knickers on!" That was a beautiful idea. Leone never tired of trying out ideas. He was a real perfectionist that way.

Did the finished film resemble your treatment?
The first twenty minutes or so, the beginning and the massacre of the family. The part where they are waiting for Claudia Cardinale to arrive was very close. I had described in detail the sounds of the cicadas interrupted by those worrying silences, then the duster coats and desert clouds of the bandits emerging from the cornfields. I wrote the word *cornfields* because I remembered them from the Emilian countryside of my childhood.

You never contributed to the screenplay, though.
Dario and I wrote the long treatment, Sergio intervened, and everyone was happy with the result. Then I had the chance to make a short half-hour film with the Living Theater Group – *Agony*, part of the film *Love and Anger*. So I never wrote the screenplay. Someone else came in. I wanted to direct something of my own. But *Once Upon a Time in the West* was a great experience.

Opposite: **Italian poster for *Once Upon a Time in the West***

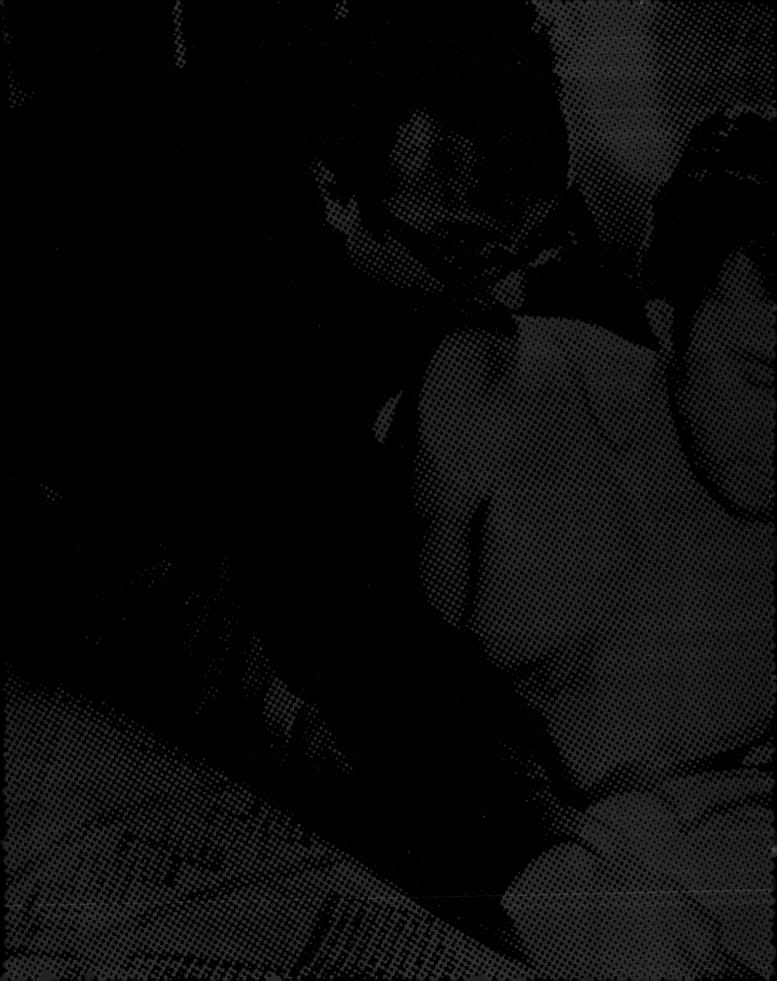

TO JOHN FORD FROM ONE OF HIS PUPILS, WITH LOVE

BY SERGIO LEONE

Translated by Christopher Frayling

This article was originally published in the Italian newspaper Corriere della Sera, *on August 20, 1983. It ran under the headline: "Ten Years After the Death of the Master Filmmaker, 31 August, 1973, the Director of* A Fistful of Dollars *Recalls a Great Lesson in Cinema."*

Among other trophies collected during a long cinematographic safari, I keep on my office wall the framed photograph that my friend John Ford gave me some time before he died [at left]. The great director appears in the photograph, in a suit that is too big for him – as if he had been shrunk by old age. He has a cigar in his mouth and a wrinkly grimace on his face like a sergeant-major – a grimace that is like a glorious regimental flag. On the photograph, in small, dense, handwriting, there is a beautiful inscription: "To Sergio Leoni. In admiration. John Ford." Not Leone, but Leoni – which is how the director of *Stagecoach* and *My Darling Clementine* must have pronounced my name. John Ford, the Homer of the Seventh Cavalry and of friendships between men, had multiplied me times two. That was much too generous, of course, though I must confess I do keep that inscribed photograph where I can see it. I'm as fond of it as a little boy who has won at a fairground shooting range every single one of the stuffed dolls, the plastic penguins, and even the clay pipes. I am susceptible to compliments just like the next man. But the admiration of John Ford, in my profession, honors me more than any other possible token of esteem or friendship. The old Irishman is one of the very few directors who deserves the title of Master – in a world of cinema where the drumbeats of publicity and the shouts of impressionable critics seem to be heralding a miracle, for all the wrong reasons, at least three times a week. Ford earned this title for serving in the celluloid civil war and in sad Hollywood bivouacs, just like the soldier in his films who earns promotion and medals for his conduct under fire. His cinema, so clean and direct and naive, so human and dignified, has left an indelible mark on the cinema that has followed it.

To start with mine. I like to think that the glacial Henry Fonda in *Once Upon a Time in the West* is the legitimate son, even if he's the diabolic and monstrous son, of the intuition that John Ford brought to *Fort Apache*: an unpleasant, authoritarian colonel who violates moral codes and treaties with the Indians, to the point of leading his men to destruction in the Valley of Death. "The best kind of cinema," said John Ford, "is the one where action is long and dialogue short." For collectors of similarities who are reading this: I think the same way.

From the beginning of the 1930s onward, John Ford refused to shoot in a studio, preferring to place his camera under open skies. He transformed his Western scripts from little edifying tales into grand parables. And in so doing, he became one of the real pioneers of modern cinematographic realism. Another reason why I call myself his pupil.

Opposite: **Leone's prized possession, an autographed photo of John Ford**

Above: **Leone buys a ticket to see a movie in Paris in the 1970s.**

He shot films that were full of truth, at a time when realism – with the exception of some rare episodes in the silent era – was a lost art. For example, we would never even have heard of Monument Valley – that perfect mountain setting for epic cinema, still used in *Easy Rider* and even good for Steven Spielberg's U.F.O. – if John Ford hadn't discovered it, with an eye that saw distant horizons, during the legendary time he spent on Indian reservations. And he was the first to reveal to us that the real cowboys of the American West didn't go around dressed in black on milk-white horses, strumming a guitar and fluttering their gigolo eyelashes, like Tom Mix and Hopalong Cassidy in the pathetic serials of those years.

The stiff, dirty overcoats of the Earp Brothers at the beginning of *My Darling Clementine*; the clouds of dust behind the horses of his soldiers in blue; the weather-beaten John Wayne, stopping the stagecoach in *Stagecoach*; his Indian encampments that look nothing like picture postcards: These are all points of no return for the Western, and indeed for cinema in general, which at that time ran the risk of fading away in the antiseptic comfort of Californian studios, clean as hospital wards. It is quite extraordinary that this revolution in the use of cinematographic equipment was the work, not of a sophisticated intellectual or a genius craftsman but of a simple man a thousand miles away from any hint of formalism. Another John Ford maxim – "I love making films but hate talking about them" – applies to me, too. All the same, I can guarantee that the characters who register strongly in front of distant horizons in my Westerns – Westerns that are in many respects more cruel and definitely less innocent and enchanted than his – owe a great deal to his lessons in cinematic form, even if the debt is involuntary. I could never have shot *Once Upon a Time in the West* or even *The Good, the Bad and the Ugly*, if John Ford hadn't shown me, when I was a boy, the Arizona desert with its baking wooden towns bathed in an intense, astonishing kind of light.

One thing is for sure: The images and stories of his films will never grow old. And in ten years' time, we will *not* be gathering together to weep over their death. I say this without rhetoric. The images and stories are still alive and bright, transparent and real, unlike so many artificial, untruthful films of all those years ago where you can *still* spot a con trick. You just have to compare *The Grapes of Wrath* with *Gone With the Wind* to see what I mean. You can't mistake the difference. Careful, though! Ford's realism wasn't absolute as the naturalism of the gangster film was – or tried to be.

In fact, that Irish immigrant was a poet, not a journalist. The real strength of his films was in their powerful nostalgia for a frontier world forever lost, as well as in his vision of America that breathed out of every frame. "I'm a peasant," he once said. "My parents were farmers. They came here and received an education. They deserved this country. I love America." The America he was talking about wasn't the America of ghettos, of inner-city misery, or of trade union struggles: It was a fabulous America that had opened wide the gates of Hollywood for his directorial debut when he was nineteen, after he'd worked for a short time as an actor in Griffith's films. Like Frank Capra, another great immigrant who was immediately adopted by the cinema, John Ford regarded America as a land of opportunity where, a long time before, the promise of liberty, peace, adventure, and bread had been made – a promise that was not going to be forgotten. As far as he was concerned, the promise had undoubtedly been kept.

If you think about it, Fordian heroes are never individualists or solitary riders. Instead, they are men who are always deeply rooted in their community, exactly like Irish immigrants who are happy with their new life. The director of *The Grapes of Wrath* and *Wagonmaster*, riding ahead of his splendid company of actors, of characters, many of them Irish and closely bonded together, would never have been able to shoot *High Noon* or *A Fistful of Dollars*. The characters most like him are not the soldiers in blue, but those who – like John Wayne in *The Quiet Man* or James Stewart in *The Man Who Shot Liberty Valance* – are simply looking for a roof over their heads, where they can live in peace, protected by the law, with good neighbors for a chat and a pint after Mass. His America was a utopian land, but it was an Irish utopia! In other words, deeply Catholic, full of pietàs and camaraderie with a lot of humor but without irony – and, more important, without cruelty. I know that my vision of America is very different and that in my films I have always looked at the wrong side of the dollar, the hidden side rather than the face. I also know that the sunny and humane West of John Ford led the way into the arid prairies of my cinema, right up to the last slate of *Giù La Testa*.

Now, examining again his inscribed photograph, prominently on view in my office among my other trophies, I see the old director look at me with such innocence and candor that I am *almost* ashamed – I stress "almost" – to have lifted all the rocks of the desert, certain to see scorpions and rattlesnakes beneath. Because if John Ford admired "Leoni," "Leone" will never tire of looking on him with respect, envy, and even reverence. And for "Leoni," as for John Ford, "shooting a Western was always like a hobby. Yes. I go away with the crew for weeks and weeks, and I don't give a damn about anything anymore!"

This
short cigar
belongs to
a man with
no name.

This
long gun
belongs to
a man with
no name.

This
poncho
belongs to
a man with
no name.

He's going to trigger a whole new style in adventure.

THE LEONE LEGACY

One of Sergio Leone's favorite after-dinner stories was about the typical circumstances in which low-budget Italian Westerns tended to be made in Italy and Spain in the heyday of the mid-to-late 1960s. Following the runaway box-office success in Italy of his *A Fistful of Dollars* in 1964, he liked to say, "There was a terrifying gold rush – based on sand rather than rock."

"A film was being financed week by week. They'd show the first week's rushes to the investors, who would then decide whether to pay for the second week, and so on. Everyone was expecting to be fired at any moment. Well, during the last of these tense weeks, the leading man walked out because he hadn't been paid. Since they were about to shoot the final sequence, the director was in serious trouble. The sequence was to be about the leading man riding into an Indian encampment, either to make peace or to have a showdown. Which would it be? Well, the director was told the bad news of the leading man's departure: 'Give me half an hour,' he said to the producer. 'I'll come up with something.' Half an hour later he returned. 'You know the old man who cleans the floor of the studio? Well, put him in a cowboy costume, quick as you can.' In the revised script, which they began shooting immediately, the old man drives in a buggy to the Indian encampment and says, 'My son couldn't come, so he sent me instead.' That's what it was like in the heyday of the Italian Western."

It was a time in Italian film history when actors answered to the pseudonyms of Clint Westwood, Charles Southwood, George Eastman, and Montgomery Wood – one director even called himself John W. Fordson. In 1964, about twenty-seven Westerns had been produced in Italy: *A Fistful of Dollars* was number twenty-five. In 1965, the year of Sergio Leone's follow-up *For a Few Dollars More,* there were thirty Westerns, and in 1966 there were about forty. By 1968, when Leone started preparing *Once Upon a Time in the West* – his farewell to the assembly-line world of popular Italian filmmaking – a staggering seventy-four other Italian Westerns, or Italian-Spanish coproductions were either in preproduction or being filmed. This at a time when the numbers of Hollywood Westerns were in steady decline, from 150, or 34 percent of all North American releases, in 1950, to 11, or 9 percent of all North American releases, in 1963.

Critic Pauline Kael had pointed out in 1963 that those American Westerns that were being produced staked their appeal less in the vitality of the stories than in the veteran movie actors wheeled out to embody them. On the whole, she said, cinemagoers appeared to turn out for Westerns only to reassure themselves that James Stewart and John Wayne could still manage to struggle onto a horse. As Kael added in her review of the Kurosawa samurai film *Yojimbo,* American audiences had become saddlesore, bored with

Opposite: **A teaser for the U.S. release of *A Fistful of Dollars***

Above: **French Ennio Morricone soundtrack recording of *A Fistful of Dollars*, coupled with another Italian Western, *A Pistol for Ringo***

a played-out Hollywood genre that had about as much relevance to modern life as the Elizabethan pastoral.

Kael concluded that a filmmaker such as Kurosawa, operating from outside the Hollywood myth factory, was in an excellent position to exploit the conventions of the Western genre while debunking its morality. By the same token, he was also in an excellent position to reenergize the American Western. It was time to make the aging stories "click" with audiences again. Kurosawa himself had conceded that his *Yojimbo* was originally born, in part, out of a love for the Hollywood Western, and particularly for *Shane* – an incredibly popular film in Japan and an unusually self-conscious piece of mythmaking seen from the point of view of a child: "Westerns have been made over and over again," he said, "and in the process a kind of grammar has evolved. I have learned from this grammar of the Western." But, he had added, he had no intention of making any kind of a "pastiche" of George Stevens's movie. After all, the 1950s Western had become a global text: the one enthusiasm that Joseph Stalin, Ludwig Wittgenstein, and Winston Churchill all had in common. Westerns belonged to everyone now. The energy to revitalize them could well come from outside America.

Over in Italy – particularly Southern Italy – Westerns remained as popular as ever. One of the reasons why Italian and Spanish Westerns began to be produced in the early 1960s was precisely *because* Hollywood wasn't delivering the goods. If *Hollywouldn't,* then Cinecittà and other Italian studios would. And the Italian product would feature more youthful, stylish heroes; more action; a soundtrack that sounded like a mixture of Duane Eddy, the slow movement of Rodrigo's guitar concierto, and Puccini recorded in a bathroom; dusty Andalusian locations; and high-stepping horses. Also Italian and Spanish actors hiding under American pseudonyms – not to fool the Americans, but to reassure the Southern Italians.

Alberto Moravia wittily suggested that the Western gold rush – and the big success on the domestic market of at least some of these films – had something to do with an unconscious fear, on the part of Italian audiences, of overpopulation: The solution was more and more massacres. Others wrote of the increasingly urban sophistication of rural Italians. From the late 1950s to the early 1960s, the popular genre of choice had been "sword and sandal" epics featuring an assortment of American (or sometimes Italian pretending to be American) bodybuilders who photographed like heavy cruisers and who played characters called Hercules or Maciste or Ursus or Goliath or Samson; these muscular heroes sorted out their problems by superhuman demonstrations of physical strength. The Westerns, on the other hand, involved much more technology (and a gloating, closeup emphasis on the intricacies of firearms),

Opposite: **Italian** *fotobusta, **A Fistful of Dollars***

Above: **Sergio Leone in the late 1960s**

and its heroes, who went by the name of Django or Ringo or Rojo or Joe or Indio or Gringo or Diablo or even Clint the Solitary, sorted out their problems by demonstrations of cunning, guile, and sleight of hand. Harlequin the trickster had taken over from Hercules, partly thanks to the international success of James Bond.

Early in 1967, Moravia wrote a perceptive article about this Italian Western phenomenon:

"The entrepreneurial filmmakers who have acclimatized the Western to Italy have been faced with a problem of expression which is quite different from their American counterparts. There's no West in Italy, no cowboys and bandits on the frontier; no frontier for that matter, no gold mines or Indians or pioneers. The Italian Western was born not from ancestral memory but from the herd instinct of filmmakers who, when young, were head over heels in love with the American Western. In other words, the Hollywood Western was born from a myth; the Italian one is born from a myth about a myth . . . The dominant theme is no longer the struggle between the lone, intrepid individual and the negative forces of nature and society: The dominant theme is the scramble for money. The main characters are everyday delinquents who were in the background of American films but who, in Italian ones, have invaded the foreground and become the protagonists . . . These misanthropes, this scramble for money, this guile contrasts radically with the grand settings and epic tone of the Western genre. So you find yourself asking this question, and often: 'After all these stories – then what? Just a fistful of dollars? Or is there more?'"

Was there more? Well, Sergio Leone certainly believed that such films could contain much more. He had grown up among filmmakers and technicians who worked at the popular end of the movie spectrum, and they believed in what they were doing – even if critics tended to be scornful of them. And the immediate impact of *A Fistful of Dollars* and its follow-up *For a Few Dollars More* was felt within this popular end of the Italian industry. Since the beginning of the 1950s, Italian cinema had depended for its economic well-being on a series of hit-and-run film cycles – such as the opera film with big stars dubbed by opera singers (1946–56); the *commedia all'italiana* (1955–61); the "sword and sandal" epic; and the horror film, Hammer-style. A windfall success would prompt an avalanche of cheaply made films, financed either by guarantees from distributors or by coproduction help from abroad. Then, just as suddenly, the assembly line would retool for a different attention-grabbing product, triggered by another hit that was thought to be repeatable. This approach did not lead to stability: Every four or five years, Italian newspapers would write of a "crisis" or "slump" in the industry. But it did lead to the production of a lot of films – often pitched toward regions of Italy that did not yet have television. These

¡EMOCIONES A RAUDALES EN UNA HISTORIA ALUCINANTE DEL LEJANO OESTE!

LUTECIA FILMS
presenta:

¡EL PRIMER Y AUTENTICO "WESTERN" EUROPEO!

POR UN PUÑADO DE DOLARES

(PER UN PUGNO DI DOLLARI)

con CLINT EASTWOOD, MARIANNE KOCH,
JOSEPH EGGER, WOLFGANG LUKSCHY, JOHN WELLS
DANIEL MARTIN, CAROL BROWN y BENNY REEVES.
Dirección: BOB ROBERTSON

TECHNISCOPE-TECHNICOLOR

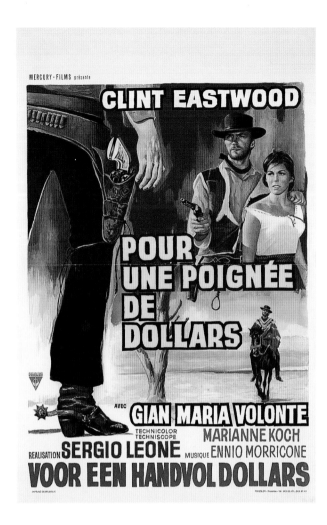

films seemed less like freestanding productions than episodes in a long-running serial. The windfall success of 1958 had been Pietro Francisci's *Hercules*, starring ex-Mr. Universe Steve Reeves, and it had stimulated the production of around 170 sword and sandals, including Leone's *The Colossus of Rhodes.* Such muscleman epics accounted for two-thirds of the revenues of all Italian films in the 1962–63 season.

When these sword and sandals ran out of puff – and following the financial disasters of *Sodom and Gomorrah* and *Cleopatra* – the Italian film industry went through its worst postwar slump in living memory. In 1963, annual ticket sales fell fast: about 680 million in 1963/64, as compared with 820 million in the mid-1950s. There were too many cinemas, not enough product to keep them going, an almost complete lack of stimulus at the lower end of the market, and a crisis of confidence from the banks. It was *A Fistful of Dollars* that reenergized the entire industry, in time-honored fashion. The new, younger Western hero – with stylish clothes, hat brim pulled over his eyes, cigarillo, superhuman expertise with a gun, and ironic sense of "cool" – seemed to be everywhere. As one critic famously said, in the old days the hero used to be the quickest on the draw; now, suddenly, the quickest on the draw was the hero.

While Leone was making his second and third Westerns, there was, as he put it, "pressure from all sides to reveal the exact location of a second gold mine." The pressure initially came from the many rival attractions rushed into preproduction the moment *Fistful* began making serious money – an army of

Italian gunfighters, bounty hunters, avengers, parodists, and comedians. Over the next few years, Clint Eastwood's "Joe," Franco Nero's "Django" – the second most popular Italian Western hero, named after the wild gypsy guitarist Django Reinhardt, who had shown American jazz bands that he could do it, too, but in a European all-string style – Giuliano Gemma's "Ringo," Tony Anthony's "Stranger," and Gianni Garko's "Sartana" competed with other lone gunmen whose names featured prominently in the titles. There were sixteen Djangos, fourteen Ringos, fourteen Sartanas. In the days before intellectual property was protected from trespassers, these big names became public domain. There was even a Ringo cookie.

All these gunman-heroes combined the resilience of Hercules with the ingenuity of James Bond in a style that was all designer-Italian. The standard plot involved this loner riding into an isolated Southwestern shantytown – ruled by warring factions or clans (usually one Mexican, one gringo, divided by interests rather than values) – being seriously beaten up by one or both before defeating the strongest villain in a ritualized "settling of accounts." The gunman-trickster was distinctively dressed, he posed a lot, and he had distinctive weapons as well. Soon, there were so many gunmen it was necessary to develop even more noticeable brands to help them stand out from the herd. So there were one-armed gunmen, handless gunmen, gunslinger priests, blind gunmen, mute gunmen, epileptic gunmen, a ghost gunman, and on one celebrated occasion, gay gunmen dressed in black uniforms led by a Mexican psychopath called – what else? – Zorro.

Leone was keen to distance himself from the astonishing craze for noisy and attention-grabbing films, which he had inspired. As he recalled to me in 1982: "When they tell me that I am the father of the Italian Western, I have to ask, 'How many sons of bitches do you think I've spawned?' There was a terrifying gold rush after the commercial success of *A Fistful of Dollars,* and I felt – and continue to feel – a great responsibility for this phenomenon . . . A stampede!"

Not quite four hundred, in fact. The peak years of Italian Western production were 1966 (forty), 1967 (seventy-four), 1968 (seventy-seven), 1969 (thirty-one), 1970 (thirty-five), 1971 (forty-seven), and 1972 (forty-eight). That is 352 in total, and not all of them were derivations from *Fistful.* By then, though, the Italian film industry had become, after the American film industry, the world's second-largest exporter of feature films. The Westerns came to be known in Italy as *Western all'italiana.* In America, the term *spaghetti Western* was preferred – sometimes as an insult (associating the genre with cheap Italian food and stereotypes of Italian behavior), sometimes as a term of endearment. Today, the more neutral phrase *Euro-Western*

SERGIO LEONE:

"Several great directors of Westerns came from Europe: Ford is Irish; Zinnemann Austrian; Wyler is from Alsace; Tourneur, French. I don't see why an Italian should not be added to the bunch."

has become fashionable. And of all these, Leone's films were by far the most influential.

The new characteristics of the Western, Italian-style, included an obsession with American currency (which, even in inflationary times, seemed a little over the top); a hero whose main ambition was to exploit the injustices he saw all around him (rather than to "do what a man's gotta do" or to say "there are some things a man can't ride around"); an emphasis on Mediterranean *machismo* and *style* rather than on American toughness; and an energetic and increasingly brutal action climax every ten minutes to hold the audience's attention. Also essential were jokes at the expense of minor officials or corrupt sheriffs; a "rhetorical" use of the camera, which tended to linger on, and extend, the visual clichés of the Hollywood Western as if they were part of the liturgy; a setting in the borderlands of the American Southwest rather than on the Midwestern frontier; and a memorable up-tempo musical score with unusual orchestrations, echo effects, choral interludes, a Fender Stratocaster guitar, a catchy melody, and amplified natural sounds. Gunfights, or rather gun*downs,* were usually preceded by solemn trumpet *deguellos* or stately boleros on Spanish guitars held very close to the microphone.

The even greater success of *For a Few Dollars More* added two new elements: the relationship between an older gunman and a younger one (which led to countless imitations, often costarring a Hollywood veteran such as Lee Van Cleef playing opposite an Italian youth), and a plot involving revenge. The latter sometimes led in turn to an increasing emphasis on moral values of a sort – usually involving family honor – and paved the way for the "Mexican Revolution" phase involving a central character, a peon, who has to decide whether to become a bandit or a revolutionary, and a charismatic foreigner who is even more cynical and ruthless than the peon. They play cat-and-mouse games with each other, until the peon sees the error of his ways and becomes a revolutionary. This phase began with Damiano Damiani's *A Bullet for the General* (1966) and turned into a stampede with Sergio Corbucci's *A Professional Gun* (1968) and *Compañeros!* (1970), Sergio Sollima's *The Big Gundown* (1966) and *Face to Face* (1967) – both set in the American Southwest, and Giulio Petroni's *Tepepa* (1968). Many of these films were written or suggested by left-wing author Franco Solinas; some included veiled references to the directors' experiences as partisans during the Resistance of 1943–45; and a few had rude things to say about Leone-style bounty hunters.

By now, the *Western all'italiana* had also diversified into the "horror Western," "thriller Western," "musical Western," and in the final phase – stimulated by the huge success of the double act of Terence Hill (guile) and Bud Spencer (strength), and first appearing in 1967– the "comedy Western,"

Ein neuer Meister-Western - noch härter - noch spannender!

Für ein paar Dollar mehr

CLINT EASTWOOD
LEE VAN CLEEF

Klaus Kinski

Josef Egger · Gian Maria-Volonté
Panos Papadopulos · Werner Abrolat
Kurt Zips · Mario Brega u.v.a.

Regie:
SERGIO LEONE
EIN FARBFILM
der PEA/CONSTANTIN/GONZALES-FILM
im Verleih

Constantin-Film

CONSTANTIN Constantin-Film 21271 · B · 0288 · 28 · FP-DRUCK HEIDELBERG

led by Enzo Barboni's *They Call Me Trinity* (1970) and *Trinity Is Still My Name* (1971), and the "circus Western," led by Gianfranco Parolini's *Sabata* and Giuseppe Colizzi's *Boot Hill* (1969). Terence Hill's real name, incidentally, was Mario Girotti (he was Venetian), and Bud Spencer's was Carlo Pedersoli (he was Neapolitan). The whole cycle came to a spectacular end with Tonino Valerii's 1973 film *My Name Is Nobody* (billed as "presented by Sergio Leone"), which took as its theme a meditation on the relationship between Hollywood – or maybe Leone – Westerns (represented by Henry Fonda) and their Italian cousins (represented by a hyperactive Terence Hill) and Enzo G. Castellari's antiracist *Keoma* (1976), structured like a ballad and exploring the dark side of the Western genre.

Sergio Leone was not too fond of the *Trinity* films, or of comedy Westerns in general. As he once admitted to me: "Along came a film where pistol duels were replaced by slaps in the face! The audience felt liberated. It was a form of retaliation. They were delighted to see the bad guys from all these earlier films having their ears boxed and their hats forced down over their ears. And the second *Trinity* was a colossal success . . . It was released at a very precise moment of exasperation with a genre that had run out of breath."

These films encouraged audiences to laugh at the Italian Western, rather than with it. They made Leone's own contributions since *Fistful* seem superficial – a set of clichés about clichés that were all too easy to mock. Leone did not have much time for the "Mexican Revolution" phase either. "Of the so-called political – or was it just intelligent? – Italian Westerns, I think I only saw one, *The Big Gundown,* which owed its original title, *La Resa Dei Conti,* to me, having taken it from a musical theme by Ennio Morricone [written for *For a Few Dollars More*] . . ." For Leone, these "eulogies to revolution" – in which the focus of audience identification had shifted from the cool superhero to the wretched of the earth – seemed "old and formulaic like the prayer of a medieval mystic." But he had to admit that they were the not-so-distant relations of his own first Western. The Italian Westerns between the mid-1960s and early 1970s had, in short, amounted to a changing form of Leone's "cinema cinema" that functioned as a commentary on Hollywood – partly celebratory, partly critical. They also "created jobs for ten thousand people in ten years," as screenwriter Luciano Vincenzoni recalled, and developed a volition of their own.

The commercial success of Leone's *Dollars* Westerns in the United States – where they were released almost back-to-back as a single package in February 1967, July 1967, and January 1968 – meant that, following their influence in Italy, their immediate impact overseas was on the American Western. Sergio Leone reckoned that this first manifested itself in the

Opposite: **U.S. lobby card** for *For a Few Dollars More*

Above: **Italian poster** for *For a Few Dollars More*

TONINO VALERII:

"*My Name Is Nobody* is the synthesis of the two modes of making Westerns: the American and the Italian Western. But we have also to remember that the Italian Westerns came from the other side of the ocean and that they were about developments within the *Italian* Westerns as well. *My Name Is Nobody* was born to demonstrate that the Sergio Leone Westerns were superior to the Westerns of Enzo Barboni. And to do this, a John Ford character was to be contrasted with Trinity. After that, and after the scene with the Wild Bunch and the Valkyries, there was nowhere left for the Western to go. It was the end of the Italian Western. There was in us the consciousness of something that was over. The fairy tale time had ended."

Opposite: **U.S. poster for one of the many reissues of *Fistful* and *Few Dollars More***

post-1967 Westerns of Sam Peckinpah: "In retrospect, I can see that *A Fistful of Dollars* heralded the beginnings of a new cinema . . . Sam Peckinpah would have hesitated before shedding so much blood. He told me himself, 'Without you, I would never have thought of making the films I have made.'" Director Sergio Corbucci added "Peckinpah made *The Wild Bunch* after thinking about the films of Leone and Corbucci." It wasn't that Peckinpah's twilight romantic heroes owed anything to the anarchic Italian bounty hunters – they were literally worlds apart – but that the success of Leone's Westerns helped Peckinpah to interest producers in a big-budget film with a story about bandits on the run, Mexican bandit/revolutionaries, nasty children, and – yes – bounty hunters, set on the Southwestern frontier.

Reviewers at the time saw similarities in the two directors' approaches to violence, which was missing the point. True, both approaches were highly stylized. But Leone was interested in the rituals preceding violent confrontations; Peckinpah in the impact of a bullet as the gun was fired. The similarities between the two directors were more general, more to do with "the beginnings of a new cinema." In pre-Leone days, Peckinpah had unsuccessfully tried to persuade his producers to release *Major Dundee* uncut. Yet the biographies of Sam Peckinpah all fail to mention the Italian Westerns – an omission that has been shared by a lot of American critics and film historians who have simply treated these films as a backwater of the Hollywood product. Sometimes they have even treated them as American Westerns filmed in strange places.

Leone himself came to realize that, longer-term, an equally significant impact was on the American films of Clint Eastwood, which explored and enriched the image that the pair had first created in the *Dollars* films. In the four years after Eastwood returned to the states – and spent a little time finding properties and directors to customize that image – his most interesting work resulted from collaborations with director Don Siegel. Many of the films they made together were explicitly intended to repackage the Man With No Name for American audiences. In interviews, Siegel often expressed his appreciation of Leone's directorial style, and the opening scenes of *Coogan's Bluff* (1968) and *Two Mules for Sister Sara* (1969) both contain explicit references to the equivalent scenes in Leone's *For a Few Dollars More*. Siegel, in fact, screened the three *Dollars* films before agreeing to direct *Coogan's Bluff*. He said of them: "Great fun, magnificently photographed, very well directed, and no question that a new star was born – Clint Eastwood!" The interpretation of the American Civil War that runs through *The Beguiled* (1971) owes much to *The Good, the Bad and the Ugly*: The Union soldier (Clint Eastwood) is utterly cynical about his role in the war and spends the

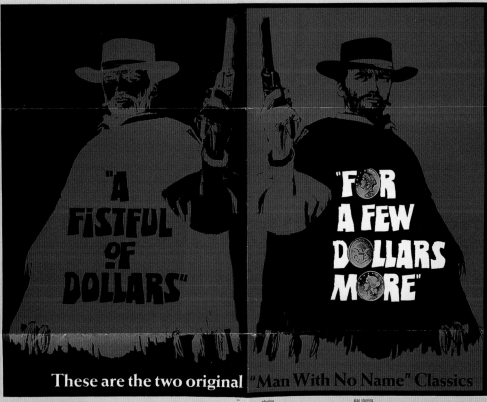

entire movie hiding from Confederate scavengers who might drag him off to the Andersonville internment camp.

Clint Eastwood's own early films as a director continued the domestication of the image – giving the character a concern with justice and with righting society's wrongs, albeit in a vigilante manner – and helping him to develop relationships with other people. In the first of these, *Play Misty for Me,* Eastwood cast Don Siegel as a friendly neighborhood barman. His first Western, *High Plains Drifter,* was an attempt – literally – to exorcise the enigmatic character of the Man With No Name. The early sequences of *Drifter* – Eastwood's entry into Lago and "welcome" by the inhabitants – closely resemble Leone's treatment of the stranger's arrival in San Miguel (*A Fistful of Dollars*) and Agua Caliente (*For a Few Dollars More*); the explanatory flashbacks are like El Indio's fantasies (also in *For a Few Dollars More*). Eastwood later said of his protagonist, Jim Duncan, "I had been familiar with that character for a long time." But, as *High Plains Drifter* progresses, it becomes more like a medieval morality play, with each of the townsfolk representing one of the seven deadly sins, and Duncan as a vengeful god.

A press still from *Drifter* shows the stranger (Eastwood) standing by Verna Bloom, near two gravestones: the inscriptions simply read LEONE and DONALD SIEGEL. Actually, Leone was not too fond of this film: He thought the central character lacked irony, and he added that the morality of the story – supernatural avenger reminds society of its responsibilities – was for him a little hard to stomach. The basic idea of *Drifter,* incidentally, resembled that of another Italian Western, *Django the Bastard* (1969, directed by Sergio Garrone), in which the avenger – who keeps mysteriously appearing and disappearing – turns out to be a ghost.

The Outlaw Josey Wales represented a different kind of exorcism of the Man With No Name. Josey Wales rides through Kansas and Missouri just after the American Civil War, bent on personal revenge ("I don't want *nobody* belonging to me"). But he is constantly being deflected from his quest by various marginal people (an elderly Comanche, a "hippie" girl, an old lady from Kansas) who refuse to take his machismo image seriously. Even a dog he picks up on the way seems to "see through" his tough exterior: Josey Wales spits a wad of tobacco in the direction of the dog (hitting it right between the eyes), but the dog simply growls, then comes back for more, wagging its tail. Eventually, the lone avenger is persuaded by these perceptive characters to give up his quest, to choose "the word of life" and to settle down in a little log cabin on the prairie. The interpretation of the Civil War in *Josey Wales* is cynical (a ferryman sings "Dixie" or "The Battle Hymn of the Republic," according to whether he is ferrying Confederate or Union troops), but the conclusion to the film is decidedly not: There is hope for the postwar generation after all. The society of 1865 is presented as full of drifters and uprooted people: bounty hunters ("There's no other way to make a living"), carpetbaggers, con men, Redlegs, vigilantes, unemployed saloon folk; and the style occasionally tips its hat to Sergio Leone. But the main themes of *Josey Wales* are by now a lot further away from the world of the early Italian Westerns. A tree grows by the graveside; "I guess we all died a little in that damn war."

When Sergio Leone died, on April 30, 1989, Clint Eastwood sent a cable from California: "Sergio Leone had a great influence on my career. I learned a lot from him as an actor and as a director. And he was an extraordinary human being. His loss is one of the saddest of my life." Subsequently, at the Venice Film Festival, Eastwood turned to the Italian audience and said he owed the start of his career as a major movie star to Sergio Leone. Three years after Leone's death, he dedicated his *Unforgiven* "for Sergio and Don," in memory of Leone and Don Siegel. *Unforgiven* was Eastwood's final exorcism – in a Western – of the Man With No Name. This time, instead of being an avenger who is deflected from his quest, he is William Munny – a retired gunman turned pig farmer who needs a lot of persuading to join the quest in the first place. The violence is messy and always has human consequences. The weapons are inaccurate. The kid who wants to become a superhero (he names himself the Schofield Kid, after the model of pistol he prefers) immediately regrets it when he actually has to shoot someone: "It don't seem real, how he ain't gonna never breathe again, ever . . ."/"It's a hell of a thing, killing a man." The sunny plains

ROD STEIGER:
"Sergio Leone was huge, but he was a big baby. He adored the West, but I don't think the West was grand enough for him, so he created his own West – everything was a bit bigger; everything was a bit louder. But he was also very proud of being authentic."

of Spain have become a dark night of the soul. Eastwood's career as a director of Westerns represents a series of increasingly sophisticated variations on a theme – a theme first articulated in 1964 with *A Fistful of Dollars* and one that Eastwood has managed successfully to reconfigure for changing, more grown-up, sensibilities.

If these Westerns by Peckinpah, Siegel, and Eastwood revealed in their very different ways the resonance of Leone's films in Hollywood from the late 1960s onward, there were more general symptoms as well. The commercial success of Leone's Westerns helped to lead a resurgence of the Hollywood product, not a resurgence in numbers (they averaged about twenty a year) but a resurgence through fresh themes and styles. The frontier shifted to the arid Southwest, even in Westerns not shot in Spain. Desolate "Leone towns" – a saloon (where bored and irritable gunmen get out of the sun and pass the time), maybe a bank, and certainly a muddy main street, with Spanish-style outskirts – turned up all over the place. More and more American Western film crews used locations in Almería or Alicante. Unshaven heroes who were less heroic than they used to be, long duster coats, cigars, corrupt posses, amplified sound effects, cacti, crucifixes, and – in the less thoughtful ones – expendable Mexicans who took over from expendable Native Americans became more and more the order of the day. Marlon Brando wore a poncho. Where the action was concerned, it was a case of "chili con carnage" – to the point where veteran director Anthony Mann, who had made several films in the 1950s about the nastiness of "professional assassins," complained that "The shootouts every five minutes reveal the director's fear that the audiences get bored . . . [In] a tale you may not put more than five or six minutes of 'suspense': the diagram of the emotions should be ascending, and not a kind of electrocardiogram. . . ."

Critic Andrew Sarris noted with characteristic asperity that "the spaghetti Western . . . is slithering into Hollywood Westerns as well" and cited in evidence some imitators rather than innovators: Henry Hathaway's *Five Card Stud* ("Killings have been replaced by murders, the vanity of villainy by an insane deviousness"), and Ted Post's *Hang 'Em High,* the first Western made in Hollywood to cash in on Eastwood's *Dollars* image ("Catering to the lowest instincts"). "We may be in for a long siege of stranglers with ten-gallon hats," Sarris concluded, bemoaning the fact that post-Leone Westerns "here and abroad" carry the message "Every man for himself."

He was certainly right about the influence at the level of story. The gun-in-the-bathtub gag from *The Good, the Bad and the Ugly* reappears in, of all unlikely places, the John Wayne vehicle *Big Jake* (George Sherman, 1971). An extremely unpleasant bounty hunter named Dan Nodeen (even the bad guys call him "meaner than a gutshot grizzly") spits his way through Andrew V. McLaglen's

Opposite: **Spanish poster for *The Good, the Bad and the Ugly*, foregrounding the Eli Wallach character**

Above: **Leone lines up an extreme close-up of Henry Fonda for the final duel sequence of *Once Upon a Time in the West*, June 1968.**

Chisum (1970) before he leaves town, when there's no one left to pay him –
he resembles Clint Eastwood, and John Wayne does not like him at all.
The jokey, relaxed, episodic quality of Burt Kennedy's scripts and direction in
such films as *The War Wagon* (1967), *Support Your Local Sheriff* (1968), *The Good
Guys and the Bad Guys* (1969), and *Support Your Local Gunfighter* (1971) – far
removed from the celebrations of the traditional Western hero that Kennedy
scripted for Budd Boetticher between 1956 and 1960 – owes much to the *Dollars*
trilogy and in particular to Leone's lighthearted takes on the clichés associated
with the Hollywood Western. *Support Your Local Gunfighter* closes on a shot
of Jack Elam (who plays a retired gunslinger) taking a train out of town, and
telling the audience that he can always earn a living in the Italian Westerns.
In William Graham and Blake Edwards's *Waterhole #3* (1967), antihero James
Coburn seems to be doing just that: In true Colonel Mortimer style, he fights
a duel by waiting until his opponent is out of pistol range and then shooting
him down with a rifle – but in all other respects, this antihero had very
traditional ol' boy attitudes.

By 1972, Carl Foreman, who had written *High Noon* twenty years earlier,
was writing a magazine parody of the new style of Westerns – dedicated to
"S. L." – called *High Noon Revisited.* In it, all the traditional ingredients (such
as cattle drives and crusading heroes) are missing, having been replaced by
a dog-eat-dog society and a marshal who smokes an opium pipe. Ten years
later, at the Santa Fe Festival of the Western, there was a heated debate about
whether the Italians had killed off the Western completely – or saved it.
Katy Jurado, the actress from *High Noon,* announced that a great tradition had
fallen victim to the Italian Western's "lack of respect." James Coburn was not
so sure: "Well, Serge! Serge has his own ideas." Some delegates supported the
motion "Let's hear it for irreverence." The consensus was that Westerns since
the Italians came on the scene were more aware of their own history than
Westerns had ever been before. And that it had become impossible to make a
successful Western that simply reproduced the old certainties.

Already in 1967, Larry McMurtry – author, then, of *Horseman,
Ride By* (filmed as *Hud*) and *The Last Picture Show* – had published an essay
titled "Cowboys, Movies, Myths, and Cadillacs," in which he noted that the
lone Western hero, as a figure of high romance and myth, was in the process
of changing his role and function:

"Indeed, a certain change has already taken place . . . [If] one can apply
to the Western the terminology [literary critic] Northrop Frye develops in his
essay on fictional modes, we might say that in the fifties the Western began
working its way down from the levels of myth and romance towards the ironic
level which it has only recently reached . . . No doubt high mimetic Westerns

MICHAEL MADSEN:
"One of my early mentors was
Sergio Leone. He gave me
some great encouragement
when I was starting out.
He said I had a quality
about me that he liked, and
said that I reminded him
of Henry Fonda. He said
there was remoteness about
me, something unreachable.
I'm not exactly sure I
understand what he meant.
But something tells me he
was right."

will continue to be made as long as John Wayne is acting – he wouldn't fit in any other mode – but in number they are declining, and the figure of 'the Westerner' is gradually being challenged by more modern figures."

So, the Western hero was on a long journey from the world of romance to the world of irony, with various stages in between. But the latest incarnation, concluded McMurtry, was a hero who succeeded in being both mythic *and* ironic – "the Italian-made Clint Eastwood films mark the reappearance of the archetype." So here was a paradox. A larger-than-life mythic hero had emerged, from within a series of stories that were clever and ironic. An icon who was also an iconoclast. Putting this in other ways, some critics – including the filmmaker Paul Schrader – argued that *all* the important American Westerns made after the mid-1960s were at some level parodies of the traditional Western and its old certainties. These would include *True Grit* (1970), with its self-consciously naive patchwork-quilty style (yes, John Wayne *could* engage in self-parody after all); *The Wild Bunch* (1969) with its over-the-top inflation of the gunfighter Western to Wagnerian proportions; and *Butch Cassidy and the Sundance Kid* (1969) with its Beverly Hills dialogue and hip references to other Westerns. So, yes, let's hear it for irreverence. Critic Scott Simmons put this well: "Eventually Westerns started to *look* like they were no longer preaching to the converted and could hear the rude noises from the side aisle." Part of the legacy of Leone's Westerns was a strong sense that the old fairy tales had to keep up with or even keep ahead of 1960s audiences – especially young audiences.

From these young audiences came the up-and-coming generation of American filmmakers later to be dubbed by critics "the movie brats" or "the new Hollywood" (John Milius, George Lucas, Steven Spielberg, Francis Ford Coppola, John Carpenter, and Martin Scorsese), who studied film at precisely this time. Milius has recalled that as part of their studies they "took apart all Leone's films, shot by shot," and that they admired Leone's Westerns even as they were immersing themselves in the traditional Hollywood versions as well: They shared Leone's admiration for the old masters and for samurai films, plus his disappointment with the seeming inability of contemporary Hollywood to create magic as it used to. Most of them were "baby boomers," born after a war that Leone had lived firsthand. But they still identified with his use of film language – especially the final scenes of *The Good, the Bad and the Ugly* and the opening sequence of *Once Upon a Time in the West* – and his unfashionably firm belief in the possibilities of cinema. Milius's scripts for *The Life and Times of Judge Roy Bean* and *Jeremiah Johnson,* he added, were "certainly influenced by the cynicism in the Leone movies"; *Roy Bean* would have improved if it had been shot in Almería on a lower budget with less of a "soft and cute" atmosphere.

Opposite: **Italian reissue poster for** *For a Few Dollars More*

QUENTIN TARANTINO:

"His films have some of the funniest gallows humor – in particular, *The Good, the Bad and the Ugly* is just so funny. Almost whenever they open their mouths, you get some of the funniest lines I have heard in my life. To think it was written in Italian and then we hear the translated version and it is still that funny – it just blows me away. It is this whole world he created. There have only been a few filmmakers who have done this with an old genre – as old as you can possibly get – and he did it, with the spaghetti Westerns."

John Carpenter gave the "something to do with death" line from *Once Upon a Time in the West* to one of his characters in *Assault on Precinct 13* (1976); he declared that *West* was "one of the classics of all time, a movie that states the essence of the Western, and the essence of mythology, and maybe finished off the genre." Carpenter even had its music played at his first wedding. Of this new generation of filmmakers, who took Hollywood by storm as the old studio system crumbled around them, Leone was to observe: "They watched *Once Upon a Time in the West* on a Moviola in college, to discover its secrets." One of its secrets was that films could be about other films, rather than necessarily about the real world. Recapturing the excitement of childhood visits to the cinema could be both inspiring as well as challenging and rewarding.

Sergio Leone reckoned there were other "debts of love" paid to his work, among the leading lights of the "new Hollywood" generation:

"When I saw the opening sequence of Spielberg's *Close Encounters,* I thought 'That was made by Sergio Leone.' You know, the dust, the wind, the desert, the planes, the sudden chord on the soundtrack . . . George Lucas has told me how he kept referring to the music and images of *Once Upon a Time in the West* when he cut *Star Wars,* which was really a Western – series B – set in space. All these younger Hollywood directors – George Lucas, Steven Spielberg, Martin Scorsese, John Carpenter – they've all said how much they owe to [my work] . . . But none of them has ever been tempted to make a Western which is actually a *Western.*"

His films, he added, had had an immediate impact on the Hollywood Western and had even fueled a revival of maybe a decade. But it had become increasingly difficult to find the right tone for a big audience – even with the old-timers in the saddle. Henry Fonda's last Western had been the Italian *My Name Is Nobody,* while John Wayne's final film, *The Shootist,* was produced by Dino De Laurentiis: Both were melancholy farewells. The mid-1960s generation of filmmakers had learned many lessons from the Western, but they had used them in other ways.

As would the "video brats" of twenty years later – directors Quentin Tarantino and Robert Rodriguez. In 1983, Tarantino got his job at Video Archives on Sepulveda Boulevard by talking incessantly to the owner about Sergio Leone. *Reservoir Dogs* and *Pulp Fiction* both end with a "Mexican standoff," and the characteristic advice Tarantino gave to actor Samuel L. Jackson before shooting a scene in *Fiction* was, "We're gonna start with the opening shot of *Casablanca,* then go into something Sergio Leone did in *The Good, the Bad and the Ugly,* and finish up with a kind of Wile E. Coyote thing." He would request extreme close-ups with the words, "Give me a Sergio Leone." The triangular shootout in *The Good* was, for Tarantino, "one of the

Above: **Sergio Leone**
(in white pants)
overseeing *My*
***Name Is Nobody*,**
as producer, on
location near Guadix,
Spain, with Henry
Fonda (on ground)
and Terence Hill
(standing), June 1973

best action sequences of all time"; the film is now his "favorite movie of all."
Of the black suits, black ties, and shades in *Reservoir Dogs,* he has said, "My
genre characters are in suits of armor . . . like Sergio Leone's dusters he'd have
his characters wearing." *Kill Bill* fused the Italian Westerns (not just Leone's)
with the Hong Kong martial-arts movies – which succeeded them in the late
1960s – to a soundtrack that is a sampler of both. When I first saw *Kill Bill:
Volume One,* I was convinced someone had raided my record collection!

    Meanwhile, Robert Rodriguez's *El Mariachi* and its bigger-budget remake,
Desperado, seemed to be transposing *A Fistful of Dollars* to modern-day Mexico;
this time the Man With No Name (Antonio Banderas) was armed with
automatic weapons hidden inside his guitar case. Surprisingly, Rodriguez did
not take a close look at the Italian Westerns until *after* he'd finished
El Mariachi: "I was inspired by guys like George Miller who did the *Road
Warrior* movies. He was really inspired by the Leone pictures, so I got it
at one remove." Then, following the success of *Desperado,* Rodriguez revived the
Banderas character in *Once Upon a Time in Mexico.* When he was postproducing
Desperado, his friend Tarantino had suggested this third film: "He said to
me, 'You've got to make the third one now. This is your *Dollars* trilogy. You've
got to make it epic and call it *Once Upon a Time in Mexico.*'" Which is what he
proceeded to do, with a film that included a blind CIA agent (Johnny Depp)
who has a prosthetic arm and does a lot of shooting on the Day of the Dead.

    It is interesting that Rodriguez cites George Miller's Australian
Road Warrior films. The influence of Leone's work has extended well beyond
Hollywood, and it has become so thoroughly absorbed – as critic Geoffrey
Macnab has written – that "you can be influenced by it without even
knowing where your influence came from." Taking a global perspective, the
shadow of Leone has fallen on films ranging from Nils Gaup's *Pathfinder*
(1987, Norway) – "a reindeer Western," as described by its director, the
opening sequence of which was inspired by the McBain family massacre

in *Once Upon a Time in the West* – to Richard Stanley's *Dust Devil* (1993, GB/South Africa) – which features a supernatural Eastwood–look-alike hitchhiker in a long duster – to Perry Henzell's *The Harder They Come* (1972, Jamaica) – a celebration of the impact of the Italian Westerns on a Rasta rude boy. Ramesh Sippy's astonishingly successful *Sholay* (1975, India) is a modern Hindi-speaking Western which, according to a recent book by Anupama Chopra, was greatly influenced "in both material and attitude . . . by Sergio Leone's spaghetti Westerns and, of course, by the mother of the mercenary movie, Akira Kurosawa's *Seven Samurai*." Ales Verbic's *Once Upon a Time* (1989, Yugoslavia) treats life as a train journey and is "dedicated to Sergio Leone who once traveled on this train." Bruce Lee's kung fu films and the complete thrillers of John Woo, from *The Killer* (1989) to *Broken Arrow* (1996) were strongly influenced, as were the Jackie Chan East-meets-West send-up *Shanghai Noon* (2002), with its Marshal Nathan Van Cleef of Carson City; Jean-Jacques Annaud's *Enemy at the Gates* (France, 2001) – with its ritualized duels in Stalingrad between a Russian sniper (Jude Law) and his Nazi challenger (Ed Harris); and Tsui Hark's martial-arts epic *Once Upon a Time in China* (1993), followed by two sequels. Not to mention Guy Ritchie's *Lock, Stock and Two Smoking Barrels* (Great Britain, 1998), which transposes Leone-style shootouts to contemporary gangster London; and of course, George Miller's *Mad Max* (1979, Australia). When Miller's sequel to *Mad Max* was poised for release in America, the director sought a new title because the first film had not done great business there. Since the plot was about gasoline as a form of currency in a postnuclear desert, the present writer suggested (on BBC radio) the title *For a Few Gallons More*. They chose *Road Warrior* instead. They were right.

And this brisk global roundup does not include popular music – from Jamaican ska to gangsta rap, from "found" pieces of Ennio Morricone's Leone soundtracks on digital remixes to Mike Oldfield and Jean-Michel Jarre. Leone himself enjoyed spotting references to his films all over the place, even in television advertisements. He tended to be defensive about the fact that critics first time around had been dismissive of his work as "violent, noisy, naive, pretentious, and astonishingly popular" – and yet he was pleased that filmmakers had been quicker to see their merits. Above all, he liked to say, his Westerns had introduced "a new style of hero," a hero who did all the stuff John Wayne would never do. In his book *Cult Heroes,* design critic Deyan Sudjic outlines the distinctive characteristics of this figure:

"The qualities of the new cult heroes have very little in common with the virtues attributed to heroes in the past. Chivalry and modesty are conspicuous by their absence. But then the new breed are rarely presented as role models

Opposite top: **The Wild Bunch ride, *My Name Is Nobody***

Opposite bottom: **Spanish lobby card highlighting the iconic image of Frank's gang garbed in dusters, *Once Upon a Time in the West***

in the way that heroes once were. Today's cult hero is seen by the audience as a focus for the projection of their dreams, more than as a model for emulation."

I would argue that this transformation – from role model to style statement, from chivalry to efficiency, from warmth to cool, from affection to affectlessness, from life experience to lifestyle, from home to traveling alone – began with the Man With No Name in Italy in 1964. The character of James Bond has sometimes been given the credit. But James Bond, in the end, was fighting for queen and country, for the goodies versus the baddies, at the time of the Cold War. The hero as style warrior had no such ties.

Post-1960s blockbuster action heroes from Eastwood to Bronson to Stallone to Schwarzenegger to Willis to Van Damme and beyond have all belonged to this modern "cult hero" club at one time or another. They have substituted one-liners, technical skill, and antiheroics for the honor and glory of their pre-*Fistful* antecedents. Their mixture of irony and sadism started life with Leone's hero, intended to be viewed in contrast to more traditional movie heroes who stood for something on the other side of the Atlantic. The irony made sense if audiences had "chivalry and modesty" on their collective minds. And it made sense if, as in the Civil War sequences of *The Good, the Bad and the Ugly,* the sadistic behavior of the heroes was further contrasted with the bloodletting of official wars sanctioned by politicians. "I've never seen so many men wasted so badly," says Eastwood. Today, the hero of Leone's *Dollars* films remains center stage, but he has lost his sense of irony in the meantime. There is no traditional hero to provide a contrast. He is sometimes even seen fighting those official wars.

When Sergio Leone was asked about his legacy – as he often was toward the end of his life – he sometimes cited Hollywood Westerns, sometimes the early work of the movie brats, more often "a new style of hero" in film. But he was equally likely to sidestep the question in a playful way:

"Without doubt, I do occupy a place in cinema history. I come right after the letter *K* in the director's dictionary, in fact . . . right after Alexander Korda, Stanley Kubrick, and Akira Kurosawa . . . That's my place in cinema history. Down there between the *K*s and *M*s, generally to be found somewhere between pages 250 and 320 of any good filmmakers' dictionary under *L*. If I'd been named 'Antelope' instead of 'Leone,' I would have been number one. But I prefer 'Leone': I'm a hunter by nature, not a prey."

Ironically – and he would have enjoyed this thought – Sergio Leone's films are as highly rated in today's Hollywood as those of Akira Kurosawa, and yet *A Fistful of Dollars* would never have existed if Leone had not gone to see *Yojimbo* in Rome in the autumn of 1963. The modern action hero, appropriately enough, owes his existence to an act of theft that had far-reaching and surprisingly productive consequences.

Opposite: **Sergio Leone with vintage camera in Almería, Spain, on location**

There were three … her life. One to take her...
one to lo… one to kill her.
PARAMOUNT PICTURES PRESENTS
A SERGIO LEONE FILM
CLAUDIA CARDINALE
HENRY FONDA
JASON ROBARDS
CHARLES BRONSON
IN
ONCE UPON A TIME IN THE WEST
WITH
GABRIELE FERZETTI · WOODY STRODE · GUEST STARS (IN ALPHABETICAL ORDER) JACK ELAM · LIONEL STANDER · PAOLO STOPPA · FRANK WOLFF · KEENAN WYNN · DIRECTED BY SERGIO LEONE · PRODUCED BY FULVIO MORSELLA · EXECUTIVE PRODUCER BINO CICOGNA · MUSIC BY ENNIO MORRICONE · A RAFRAN-SAN MARCO PRODUCTION · TECHNISCOPE® TECHNICOLOR® · A PARAMOUNT PICTURE
M Suggested for MATURE audiences (parental discretion advised)
Copyright © 1968 by Euro International Films, S.p.A. and Rafran Cinematografica, S.p.A. All Rights Reserved.

AFTERWORD
A CONVERSATION WITH MARTIN SCORSESE ABOUT SERGIO LEONE

CHRISTOPHER FRAYLING: When did you first see a Sergio Leone film, and how did you react – as an Italian American?

MARTIN SCORSESE: The first Leone film I saw was in Amsterdam, and it was *The Good, the Bad and the Ugly*. I think it was in the early part of 1968. And I hadn't seen the *Dollars* trilogy, so it was very surprising to see a movie like this. I had a very strange reaction to it. There was something in me that had loved the American Westerns so much, and the American Westerns had such a way of taking me out of my daily existence when I was living down on the Lower East Side, with asthma, and I'd go to a movie theater and love seeing color Westerns and even black-and-white Westerns and the idea of watching these extraordinary images – wide landscape that was open and free, and beautiful horses –it was the perfect fantasy for me. It was a place to retreat to. So that I was very fully immersed in the American Western, and I reacted totally against *The Good, the Bad and the Ugly*. I saw what was happening in the framing of the scenes, the extraordinary storyboard effects, almost like a cartoon – not a cartoon, but like the best of comic-book art, in a way. But it was not really a Western, and I didn't know what it was. The music to me sounded very tricky. I didn't understand the slowness of the pace, I couldn't understand it at all, and so I reacted against it. There was this Mediterranean atmosphere in *The Good, the Bad and the Ugly*, and maybe that was what I was reacting against because I knew the American Western as American. And I didn't think these films were going to go anywhere.

Later that same year, in New York, I saw *Once Upon a Time in the West*, and again I saw it at a press screening, and again I found it to be very slow; I certainly couldn't get into the way the film played out. I had no idea what it was about, and I had no interest in it.

The next thing that happened was that a few years later, 1972, I began to notice *Once Upon a Time in the West* on television. When I saw it on television, I remembered the images were very strong, so I tried to look at those images again from time to time. I usually had the television on when I was doing other work, so the images of *Once Upon a Time in the West* would come and go – even pan and scan, they were quite interesting. And what they would do with the film would be to play it over a three-hour period with commercials, and I remember it being on television a number of times in the early seventies, and by 1972 – I was working on *Boxcar Bertha* – when the film was on television and I was doing storyboards, I began to understand the picture. I began to be swept up in the images and especially the music. I began to realize that it was not a Western, in a way – that it was an Italian film: that it was more in the Italian theatrical tradition, which is opera.

It is a combination of images, which are framed impeccably, slowness of pace, and choreography of camera – to music. In another way, I also began to understand the humor of the piece, the tongue-in-cheek attitude of the way the people were behaving, because in a sense he brought Italian *commedia dell'arte* and opera to the Western. A lot has been written about *A Fistful of Dollars* and how it was a Western version of Kurosawa's *Yojimbo* of 1961, which in its turn was based on Budd Boetticher's *Buchanan Rides Alone* of 1958; also Kurosawa had been inspired by a 1929 novel, *Red Harvest*, by Dashiell Hammett. Leone's inspiration, besides *Yojimbo*, was apparently Carlo Goldoni's *Harlequin – Servant of Two Masters*.

The Italians had *masks* in the *commedia dell'arte* tradition for these different characters and types – Harlequin, Pulchinello, different figures – and each character represented something, a certain trait in humanity you can have fun with. And they had different masks. But what is interesting is that Leone created new masks for the Western, and he set new archetypes for a genre that needed fresh influences . . . it was like the revision of a genre in a way – or more like an evolution of a genre, because the Western genre was getting old at that time. They were simple masks he placed in there but also

Opposite: **Poster for *Once Upon a Time in the West***

very complex ones. A mask on a character could hide many others underneath – it was like a Chinese box that really fascinated him; he kept taking off these layers of these characters. Ultimately, in *Once Upon a Time in America*, the whole movie is constructed like a Chinese box.

But what I found so fascinating, and how *Once Upon a Time in the West* became such a favorite film of mine – such an obsession – was that I began to understand more and more the combination of commedia dell'arte with operatic tradition and the *framing*; the framing, which was not simply comic-book art – which is very strong and very visual, it's very cinematic – but also baroque art, the faces of the characters like landscapes, explored in close-ups and in even tighter close-ups, extreme close-ups; the extraordinary manipulation of the editing, slowing down time – first in the opening sequence of *Once Upon a Time in the West* before the titles – slowing

down time or accelerating time; and the choreography of Ennio Morricone's music was the overall cue. I began to understand that this is opera, this is commedia dell'arte, this is Italian, it's not an American Western, this is an evolution of the Western – this is a whole new genre and *that's* what made it so important . . . It was these Italian elements rather than the Hollywood ones that finally took hold, and maybe, as an Italian American, I responded to the music first, the repetition of the music, when this film *Once Upon a Time in the West* was shown on television. It was shown so many times, and I had it on so many times, for some reason, and maybe the music made me see the images in a clearer way and understand what he was doing.

Although *Once Upon a Time in the West* – in its cut-down version – was not a box-office success in the United States, it seems to have made a big impact on the late-1960s/1970s generation of filmmakers. There's no doubt that *Once Upon a Time in the West* influenced the 1970s generation of filmmakers – Spielberg, Lucas, Milius, particularly John Carpenter with *Assault on Precinct 13* – but speaking for myself, I relate most to the

Above left: **Publicity photo of Claudia Cardinale (Jill) and Henry Fonda (Frank) on a hanging bed; according to Cardinale, Fonda's first-ever love scene, and the first scene shot for *Once Upon a Time in the West*.**
Above right: **Publicity still of Claudia Cardinale (Jill) and Charles Bronson (Harmonica), just after Harmonica rips the neckline off Jill's dress, *Once Upon a Time in the West***

playing out of the choreography of the shots synchronized to the music, and the time he took to play up certain moments – the intercutting back and forth between a face and a fly, and the hat and the water dripping on the hat, and all these images in the precredits sequence of *Once Upon a Time in the West*. And the extraordinary shootout at the end – between Henry Fonda and Charles Bronson – the choreography of the camera as they circle each other. This became something that found its way into *Raging Bull* and *Color of Money* and pictures like that – there's no doubt about it. And the amount of time he took to do it, too, was quite extraordinary.

What do you think was Sergio Leone's main movie legacy?
Leone's movie legacy is extraordinary: He created a new genre. He created the Italian Westerns. What they call the "spaghetti Western" – which I think is a put-down of it – I don't like that term. But he created a new genre. It really was a major departure for Italian cinema. But it was just as poetic and epic, because of this evolution into cinema as opera.

You got to know Sergio Leone well. What sort of personality was he?
The last time I saw Sergio Leone alive was in 1988, when he was very thin and it was at the showing of *The Last Temptation of Christ* at the Venice Film Festival, and he asked after my mother and father: "They're really sweet people, how are they?"

And then the first day of shooting *GoodFellas* was the day we got the news that he had died. In the early 1980s, when I was married to Isabella Rossellini, I would sometimes have dinner at his house in Rome. I spent a New Year's Eve at his place, and at a lunch I had with him, there were maybe twenty people, one of whom was Dante Ferretti – whom I was later to work with on my *Age of Innocence*, *Casino*, and *Kundun* [and *Gangs of New York*].

In 1977, I moved my mother and father out of the Lower East Side to an apartment on Eighteenth Street and Third Avenue, near Gramercy Park, where they would have the ability to use an elevator and a doorman – because it was getting very hard for them to walk up and down the stairs – and I hadn't visited them yet. And Marian Billings, my public-relations person, said, "Sergio Leone's in town, would you like to see him?" I said yes, and he had the director Elio Petri with him, and she said, "Why don't we go over to your mother's for some food," and so that's what we did. And as we were walking in, he said, "This is the first time you've entered your mother and father's apartment?" and I said yes. He said, "Well, this is an historic occasion." So he came in with Elio Petri – who has now also gone – and we all had quite a meal together. And my mother really liked Sergio because, she said, "He is a good eater – he really ate very well." And he preferred the different dishes that were traditional Italian – not the obvious ones, but special kinds of lamb stews and white sauce, that sort of thing – the kinds of things my mother and father had made from Sicilian recipes; and certain dishes she was making him taste, he said, "Oh, I haven't had this in years." And so we had quite a nice time.

And from that point on, from 1977, we became friends. I spent some time in Rome in the early eighties and would see him at his house there. And there was always talk about him doing *Once Upon a Time in America* – but it never seemed that he was going to get around to it. And then I remember Arnon Milchan talking to me about it, and I said, "This is a man you must work with; you must make this film; you really should support this filmmaker." And Arnon talked to Robert De Niro about it, and I remember De Niro asking if he could run my print of *Once Upon a Time in the West* because he didn't know . . . he hadn't seen any of Leone's films, and this was one of the few times I screened the print. I try to keep the print perfect.

Anyway, I remember that on the door of Sergio's house in Rome he had a door knocker in the form of a lion. For *Leone*. And lunch would consist of several different types of macaroni and pasta, not just one kind. He was a great enjoyer of life, a wonderful storyteller, and [he had] a great sense of humor. So he'd put people together in his house to let them get to know each other, and that sort of thing. I met a lot of wonderful people there, especially people in the Italian film industry.

The first time I had met Sergio was at the Cannes Film Festival in 1976. I was at Cannes with him in 1982 and also in Venice a few times. But in 1976, I was there for three days to promote *Taxi Driver*. And the head of the jury of the festival was Tennessee Williams. And Marian Billings told us – myself and De Niro and Schrader and Jodie Foster and the Phillipses, who produced the film – that Costa Gavras and Sergio Leone were on the jury and they really loved the picture. They wanted to take us to dinner. And they took us to a restaurant called *L'Oasis* – a long table, all of us there, at which they were very cordial, and Paul Schrader made a toast to Sergio Leone for making one of the greatest films ever made: *Once Upon a Time in the West* . . . Sergio and Costa Gavras told us how much they admired the film [*Taxi Driver*]. And the next day, the head of the jury, Tennessee Williams, came out in public and said how much he hated the film because it was so violent. And so we finished our work and went home. And a few days later, I got a call with the news that we had won the Grand Prix. And that was due to Sergio and Costa Gavras.

The first time I really heard anyone *talk* about Sergio Leone as a movie god, in a way, was a movie talk that Rod Steiger gave in a loft down on Great Jones Street in New York in the late 1960s. And he had us held rapturous. We watched him with rapt attention, as he spoke about Hollywood and his work and that sort of thing – he felt that one of the greatest people he ever worked with was Leone, *because of his love of actors*. And the way he photographed actors and the way he let actors move along at such a pace that you can get such incredible detail from their eyes, and their facial structure, and that sort of thing, and . . . it was the first time I had ever really understood what Leone was about. It was after I'd seen *Once Upon a Time in the West*; it must have been around

1969 that this happened. Also, Rod Steiger brought up the point – it was the first time I began to realize it – that there is no classical theatrical tradition in Italy; the theatrical tradition they do have is opera. And so maybe that was planted in my mind, when after a few years later – I'd seen *Once Upon a Time in the West* on television so many times – the music mixed with images, and that suggestion by Rod Steiger, together made me begin to understand that I was not to judge the Leone films with the same criteria as American Westerns. This was a very, very different thing.

Leone always said his films were like "fairy tales for grown-ups" – a modern version of the old myths. Each film could begin with the magic words, "Once upon a time . . ."
A major part of Leone as far as I was concerned was his interest in mythology, in the old myths. Even before he completed *The Last Days of Pompeii*, the 1959 film, or made *The Colossus of Rhodes*, he had worked as an assistant director on a number of American epics in Rome, and he said that his ultimate inspiration was Homer. And he transferred his interest in myth to his interest in America; I think he was interested in myth, and interested in the myth of America. For him, as for a lot of us actually, American history was history told by John Ford or D. W. Griffith. And their films, for him, were like textbooks of American history. Leone possibly saw the recurrence of classical mythology in John Ford's films. The Western myth is now seen, of course, with cynicism. In fact, the spaghetti Westerns are in many ways unconscious predictions of the violent use of political turmoil and terrorism that Italy was to live through in the 1970s, and when I was there, actually, in the late 1970s. In a funny way, they were a precursor of that time or a prediction of that time.

Another thought I have is about the Man With No Name being almost like a relative of Shane. The violence is very exaggerated in his films, so it always keeps the spectator off-center – the expectations of the spectator

are always being violated, in a way. The characters in his films, the protagonists, struggle for survival, and that struggle for survival is based on irony, as well as on the power of their guns and how intimate they are with death. But, particularly, that sense of irony is important. And I guess if you look at *Once Upon a Time in the West* – my favorite of his pictures; I eventually saw all the others – it is the most John Ford of his movies. In a funny way, Leone's pessimism is the pessimism one finds in the late pictures of John Ford – *Two Rode Together*, *The Man Who Shot Liberty Valance*, and pictures like that. And when you get to *Once Upon a Time in America*, the Chinese box idea is very interesting – it's a dream within a series of dreams. Once again, what ties them all together is death. Death is almost like the protagonist

Above: **Claudia Cardinale and Leone, on the set of *Once Upon a Time in the West***

of the picture; it's a film about memory, obsession, and friendship – or loyalty in friendship. Ultimately, this may have been for him a conscious act of love for what he felt was American cinema. And I remember him telling me – well, he said this a number of times – he used to say that the title should really have been *There Was Once a Certain Type of Cinema* rather than *Once Upon a Time in America*.

The bottom line, though, is that in his films you can see a real love for movies, for cinema, for spectacle. And there's no doubt that he created his own genre, and there's no doubt that he created his own special body of work, which is almost like the reinvention of film language. People try to imitate him, but he was the one, the original. And we look at Leone's films now, or over the past twenty or thirty years, for the inspiration they give us. Because, ultimately, I think he was a romantic who loved what he did and certainly believed in it.

LEONE IN AMERICA: A SCRAPBOOK

In the mid- to late 1960s, three young brothers – Bill (fifteen), Bob (thirteen), and Glen (eight) Grant – started compiling movie scrapbooks, and it became something of a shared hobby among friends in suburban Chicago. Glen recalls, "The impetus was to keep the memories of our favorite movies alive in our imaginations. In those days, before home video and the opportunity to watch a film whenever you want, you could see a movie in the theater and you'd be moved by it, but after it was over you were left with only the memory, a dim hope that it might show up on network television in a year or two and, if you could afford it, the soundtrack album. At some point, my brother Bill hit upon the idea to cut out the ads in the newspapers and save those; this way, you were preserving not only a memento of the movie, but also the time you saw it, since the theater's name was on the ad. So while it may seem an insignificant, even silly way of keeping the experience of the movie alive, it actually became a profound measure of the impact of film-going on our childhood."

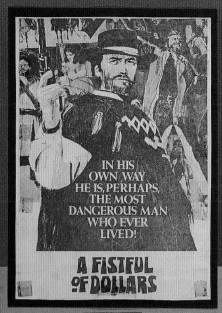

IN HIS
OWN WAY
HE IS, PERHAPS,
THE MOST
DANGEROUS MAN
WHO EVER
LIVED!

A FISTFUL
OF DOLLARS

This is the man with no name. Danger fits him like a tight black glove!

He triggers trouble –wherever he goes!

He makes no friends–a few enemies a few dollars–and none of them last!

The stranger and the woman he rescues — for another man.

FOR A FEW DOLLARS MORE

Clint Eastwood

When Marisol (Marianne Koch) rides into town, all traffic stops, except for bootlegging and gun-running.

Ramon Rojo (John Wels), a gang leader, serves on welcoming committee.

The Rojos throw a party; the stranger shoots it up.

FO-(25)-3.

"FOR A FEW DOLLARS MORE"—Clint Eastwood continues his role as "The Man with No Name" of "A Fistful of Dollars" in this western drama.

FDM-13

THE MAN WITH NO NAME IS BACK...
...THE MAN IN BLACK IS WAITING!
As if one wasn't enough...as if death needed a double!

"FOR A FEW DOLLARS MORE"

FDM-7

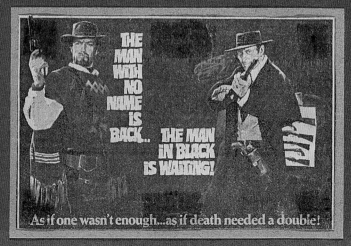

THE MAN WITH NO NAME IS BACK... THE MAN IN BLACK IS WAITING!

As if one wasn't enough...as if death needed a double!

"For a Few Dollars More," Clint Eastwood returns as The Man with No Name, a professional gunslinger, who this time competes with another bountyhunter [Lee Van Cleef] as they try to track down a Mexican bandit [Gian Maria Volonte] with a price on his head.

Clint Eastwood

For Three Men ... The Civil War Wasn't Hell. It Was Practice!

CLINT EASTWOOD in "THE GOOD, THE BAD AND THE UGLY"

co-starring
LEE VAN CLEEF

ALDO GIUFFRE | AND WITH MARIO BREGA

also starring
ELI WALLACH
in the role of Tuco

SCREENPLAY BY
AGE-SCARPELLI, LUCIANO VINCENZONI and SERGIO LEONE
MUSIC BY
ENNIO MORRICONE · ALBERTO GRIMALDI for P.E.A.–Produzioni Europee Associate, Rome

DIRECTED BY
SERGIO LEONE

Lee Van Cleef

DISGUISED AS Confederate soldiers, Eli Wallach and Clint Eastwood are captured by Union army in "The Good, the Bad and the Ugly," action-packed western in Oriental.

"THE GOOD, THE BAD, AND THE UGLY"— Clint Eastwood (The Man with No Name) is threatened by a grim Eli Wallach seeking a hidden treasure in this western drama in color

GUB-30

GUB-25

Eli Wallach is a Mexican bandit in "The Good, the Bad and the Ugly."

The Man with No Name Returns !

CLINT EASTWOOD
THE GOOD, THE BAD AND THE UGLY"

TECHNISCOPE' TECHNICOLOR

co-starring
LEE VAN CLEEF
also starring
ELI WALLACH
in the role of Tuco

BAD MAN

Lee Van Cleef is a sadistic killer seeking stolen gold in "The Good, the Bad and the Ugly," at the Oriental Theater. The Civil War Western co-stars Eli Wallach and Clint Eastwood.

ORIENTAL—Clint Eastwood and Eli Wallach in "The Good, the Bad, and the Ugly."

• BACK AGAIN as a toughie is Lee Van Cleef in "The Good, the Bad, and the Ugly"

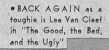

The Man with No Name Returns !
"THE GOOD, THE BAD AND THE UGLY"

TECHNISCOPE®
TECHNICOLOR®

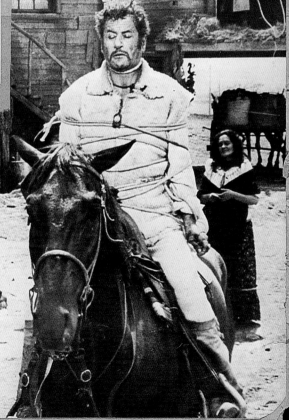

GUB-9

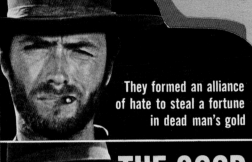

They formed an alliance
of hate to steal a fortune
in dead man's gold

THE GOOD
THE BAD
THE UGLY

The Man with No Name is back,
spreading carnage in "The Good, the
Bad and the Ugly," opening Dec. 20
at the Oriental. Eli Wallach (left) and
Clint Eastwood star in the sequel to
"Fistful of Dollars" and "For a Few
Dollars More."

Mostly Ugly and Bad
CLINT EASTWOOD is deadly Man with No Name in
"The Good, the Bad, and the Ugly," Oriental theater's
film. Lee Van Cleef and Eli Wallach co-star.

"THE GOOD, THE BAD, AND THE UGLY"— Clint Eastwood (The Man with No Name) returns — to face a hangman's noose — in this grim western melodrama.

CLINT EASTWOOD

Clint Eastwood ponders his predicament in "The Good, the Bad and the Ugly."

Esteban (S. Rupp) and Benito Rojo (Antonio Prieto) share the family appetite—for blood.

"THE GOOD,
THE BAD AND
THE UGLY"

ELI WALLACH
in the role of Tuco

A FILMOGRAPHY OF LEONE'S WESTERNS

AS DIRECTOR

A Fistful of Dollars/
Per un Pugno di Dollari   **1964   It/Sp/Ger**

DIRECTED BY: Bob Robertson [aka Sergio Leone]
CAST: Clint Eastwood [dubbed by Enrico Maria Salerno]
(the Stranger), Marianne Koch (Marisol), Johnny Wells
[aka Gian Maria Volonté] [dubbed by Nando Gazzolo]
(Ramón Rojo), Wolfgang Lukschy (John Baxter, the
sheriff), Sieghardt Rupp (Esteban Rojo), Joe Edger
[aka Josef Egger] (Piripero, the undertaker), Antonio
Prieto (Don Miguel Rojo; "Benito" in Italian print), José
"Pepe" Calvo (Silvanito, the cantina owner), Margherita
Lozano (Consuela Baxter), Daniel Martin (Julián), Benny
Reeves [aka Benito Stefanelli] (Rubio), Richard Stuyvesant
[aka Mario Brega] (Chico), Carol Brown [aka Bruno
Carotenuto] (Antonio Baxter), Aldo Sanbrell (Manolo);
Uncredited: Fredy Arco (Jesús), José Riesgo (Mexican
cavalry captain), Antonio Vica, Raf Baldassarre, Umberto
Spadaro (Miguel), José Orjas, Antonio Molino Rojo,
Antonio Pico, and Lorenzo Robledo (Baxter gunmen), José
Halufi, Nazzareno Natale and Fernando Sanchez Polack
(Rojo gunmen), Bill Thomkins, Joe Kamel, Luis Barboo,
Julio Perez Taberno, Francisco Braña, Mañuel Peña, Juan
Cortes, and Antonio Moreno
SCRIPT: (uncredited) (Duccio Tessari, Victor Catena,
Sergio Leone, Fernando Di Leo; from the screenplay
"Yojimbo" by Ryuzo Kikushima and Akira Kurosawa)
STORY: (uncredited) (Sergio Leone, after Kurosawa)
DIALOGUE: Mark Lowell (and Clint Eastwood, uncredited)
INTERIORS: Cinecittà, Rome
EXTERIORS: Almería; Colmenar Viejo, near Madrid
ART DIRECTOR, SET DECORATOR, AND COSTUMES:
Charles Simons [aka Carlo Simi]
MAKEUP: Sam Watkins [aka ?]
SPECIAL EFFECTS: John Speed [aka Giovanni Corridori]
STUNTS: W.R. Thompkins [aka Bill Tompkins],
Benito Stefanelli
PHOTOGRAPHY: Jack Dalmas [aka Massimo Dallamano],
assisted by Federico Larraya
PROCESS AND COLOR: Techniscope and Technicolor
CAMERA OPERATOR: Steve Rock [aka Stelvio Massi]
SOUND: Edy Simson
CONTINUITY: Tilde Watson

UNIT MANAGER: Fred Ross [aka ?]
PRODUCTION MANAGERS: Frank Palance
[aka Franco Palaggi], Günter Raguse
SECOND-UNIT DIRECTOR: Frank Prestland
[aka Franco Giraldi]
NEGATIVE: Eastmancolor
EDITOR: Bob Quintle [aka Roberto Cinquini]
MUSIC: Dan Savio/Leo Nichols [aka Ennio Morricone]
TRUMPET PLAYER: Michele Lacerenza
GUITAR, WHISTLE, AND CHORAL ARRANGEMENT:
Alessandro Alessandroni
CHOIR: I Cantori Moderni di Alessandroni, soprano
Edda Dell'Orso
DUBBING FACILITIES: Titanus, CDC
MUSIC PUBLISHERS: RCA Italiana
TITLES: Luigi Lardani
PRODUCERS: Harry Columbo [aka Arrigo Colombo],
George Papi [aka Giorgio Papi]
PRODUCTION COMPANIES: Jolly Film (Rome), Ocean Film
(Madrid), and Constantin Film (Munich/Monaco)
DISTRIBUTED IN USA BY: United Artists (1967)

For a Few Dollars More/
Per Qualche Dollaro in Più/
La Muerte Tenia un Precio

1965   It/Sp/Ger

DIRECTED BY: Sergio Leone
CAST: Clint Eastwood (Manco, the bounty hunter),
Lee Van Cleef (Colonel Douglas Mortimer), Gian Maria
Volonté (El Indio), Mara Krup (hotelier's wife), Kurt
Zipps (hotelier), Luigi Pistilli (Groggy), Klaus Kinski
(Wild, the hunchback), Josef Egger (the Old Prophet),
Panos Papadopoulos (Sancho Perez), Benito Stefanelli
(Huey, a member of Indio's gang), Aldo Sanbrell
(Cuchillo), Roberto Camardiel (station clerk), Luís
Rodríguez (Guy Callaway), Tomás Blanco (Santa Cruz
telegrapher), Lorenzo Robledo (Tomaso, the betrayer),
Sergio Mendizabal (Tucumcari banker), Dante Maggio
(Indio's cellmate), Diana Rabito (girl in tub), Giovanni
Tarallo (El Paso guard), Mario Meniconi (train
conductor), Mario Brega (Niño); Uncredited: Carlo Simi
(bank manager), Rosemary Dexter (Mortimer's sister),
Peter Lee Lawrence [aka Karl Hirenbach] (Mortimer's
brother-in-law), Diana Faenza (Tomaso's wife), Aldo
Ricci, Ricardo Palacios (saloonkeeper), José Marco Davo
(Red "Baby" Cavanagh), Guillermo Mendez (Sheriff
of White Rocks), Jesus Guzman (salesman on train),
Enrique Navarro (sheriff of Tucumcari), Werner Abrolat
(Slim), Frank Braña (Blacky), Antonio Molino Rojo
(Frisco), Antonio Ruiz (child in El Paso), Francesca
Leone (baby)
SCRIPT: Luciano Vincenzoni, Sergio Leone (and Sergio
Donati, uncredited)
STORY: Sergio Leone, Fulvio Morsella
DIALOGUE: Luciano Vincenzoni
INTERIORS: Cinecittà (Rome)
EXTERIORS: Almería; Guadix; Colmenar Viejo
ART DIRECTOR, SET DECORATOR, AND COSTUMES:
Carlo Simi
ASSISTANT ART DIRECTORS: Carlo Leva, Raphael
Ferri [Jorda]
HEAD MAKEUP ARTIST: Rino Carboni
MAKEUP: Amedeo Alessi
SPECIAL EFFECTS: Giovanni Corridori
STUNTS: Benito Stefanelli
DIRECTOR OF PHOTOGRAPHY: Massimo Dallamano

PROCESS AND COLOR: Techniscope and Technicolor
CAMERA OPERATORS: Eduardo Noé, Aldo Ricci
ASSISTANT CAMERA OPERATOR: Mario Lommi
SOUND: Oscar De Arcangelis, Guido Ortenzi
CONTINUITY: Maria Luisa Rosen
ASSISTANT DIRECTOR: Tonino Valerii
DIRECTOR'S ASSISTANTS: Fernando Di Leo, Julio Samperez
PRODUCTION MANAGER: Ottavio Oppo
PRODUCTION SUPERVISORS: Norberto Soliño,
Manuel Castedo
PRODUCTION SECRETARY: Antonio Palombi
SUPERVISING EDITOR: Adriana Novelli
EDITORS: Eugenio Alabiso, Giorgio Serralonga
MUSIC: Ennio Morricone, conducted by Bruno Nicolai
MUSIC PUBLISHERS: Eureka Edizioni Musicali
WHISTLE AND CHORAL ARRANGEMENT:
Alessandro Alessandroni
CHOIR: I Cantori Moderni di Alessandroni
GUITAR: Bruno D'Amario Battisti
RECORDED AT: RCA Italiana studios
SYNCHRONIZATION: International Recording
DUBBING STUDIO: CDS
MIXING: Renato Cadueri
TITLES: Luigi Lardani
PRODUCER: Alberto Grimaldi
PRODUCTION COMPANIES: PEA [Produzioni Europee
Associate] (Rome), Arturo Gonzales (Madrid),
Constantin Film (Munich/Monaco)
DISTRIBUTED IN USA BY: United Artists (1967)

The Good, the Bad and the Ugly/
Il Buono, il Bruto, il Cattivo

1966   It/USA

DIRECTED BY: Sergio Leone
CAST: Clint Eastwood (Blondie), Eli Wallach (Tuco [Benedicto Pacifico Juan Maria] Ramírez), Lee Van Cleef (Angel Eyes; "Sentenza" in Italian print), Aldo Giuffrè (Captain Clinton), Luigi Pistilli (Padré Pablo Ramirez), Rada Rassimov (Maria, the prostitute), Enzo Petito (storekeeper robbed by Tuco), John Bartha (sheriff), Livio Lorenzon (Baker), Antonio Casale (Jackson, alias "Bill Carson"), Claudio Scarchilli and Frank Braña (gunmen in ghost town), Benito Stefanelli (member of Angel Eyes' gang), Angelo Novi (monk), Antonio Casas (Stevens), Aldo Sanbrell (member of Angel Eyes' gang), Al Mulock (one-armed bounty hunter), Sergio Mendizabal (blond bounty hunter), Antonio Molino Rojo (camp commandant), Lorenzo Robledo (Clem, a member of Angel Eyes' gang), Mario Brega (Corporal Wallace); Uncredited: Chelo Alonso (Stevens's wife), Antonio Ruiz (Stevens's youngest son), Silvana Bacci (prostitute), Nazzareno Natale (Mexican bounty hunter), Janos Bartha (sheriff), Sandro Scarchilli (deputy), Jesus Guzman (hotelier), Enzo Petito (gunsmith), Victor Israel (Confederate sergeant), Romano Puppo (Slim), Luigi Ciavarro (member of Angel Eyes' gang)
SCRIPT: Age [aka Agenore Incrocci], [Furio] Scarpelli, Luciano Vincenzoni, Sergio Leone, (and Sergio Donati, uncredited)
STORY: Luciano Vincenzoni, Sergio Leone
ENGLISH DIALOGUE: Mickey Knox
INTERIORS: Elios Film (Rome)
EXTERIORS: Almería; Colmenar Viejo, Covarrubias, south of Burgos; Guadix; La Pedriza Manzanares el Real
ART DIRECTOR, SET DECORATOR, AND COSTUMES: Carlo Simi
ASSISTANT ART DIRECTOR: Carlo Leva
MAKEUP: Rino Carboni
HAIRDRESSER: Rino Todero
EQUIPMENT SUPPLIERS: Tani
COSTUME SUPPLIERS: Western Costume, Antonelli
SPECIAL EFFECTS: Eros Bacciucchi
STUNTS: Benito Stefanelli

DIRECTOR OF PHOTOGRAPHY: Tonino Delli Colli
PROCESS AND COLOR: Techniscope and Technicolor
CAMERA OPERATOR: Franco Di Giacomo
ASSISTANT CAMERA OPERATOR: Sergio Salvati
SOUND: Elio Pacella, Vittorio De Sisti
CONTINUITY: Serena Canevari
ASSISTANT DIRECTOR: Giancarlo Santi
DIRECTOR'S ASSISTANT: Fabrizio Gianni
PRODUCTION SUPERVISOR: Aldo Pomilia
PRODUCTION MANAGER: Fernando Cinquini
PRODUCTION ASSISTANTS: Carlo Bartolini, Federico Tofi
PRODUCTION SECRETARIES: Antonio Palombi, Luigi Corbo
EDITORS: Nino Baragli, Eugenio Alabiso
TITLES: Luigi Lardani
MUSIC: Ennio Morricone, conducted by Bruno Nicolai;
LYRICS OF THE SONG "THE SOLDIER'S STORY" BY: Tommie Connor
ORCHESTRA: Orchestra Cinefonico Italiana
SOLO PERFORMERS: Bruno D'Amario Battisti (guitar), E. Wolf Ferrari, I. Cammarota, F. Catania, Michele Lacerenza (trumpet), N. Samale, Franco De Gemini (harmonica), F. Traverso
CHOIR: I Cantori Moderni di Alessandroni
WHISTLE: Alessandro Alessandroni
VOCALS: Alessandro Alessandroni, E. Gioieni, F. Cosacchi, G. Spagnolo, Edda Dell'Orso
RECORDED AT THE STUDIOS OF INTERNATIONAL RECORDING BY: Giuseppe Mastroianni
MUSIC PUBLISHERS: Eureka Edizioni Musicali
SOUND MIXING: Fausto Ancillai
SOUND DUBBING: Goffredo Potier
DUBBING STUDIO: CDS
SYNCHRONIZATION: NIS Film
PRODUCER: Alberto Grimaldi
PRODUCTION COMPANY: PEA [Produzioni Europee Associate] (Rome)
DISTRIBUTED IN USA BY: United Artists (1968)

Once Upon a Time in the West/
C'era una Volta il West/
Hasta Que Llego Su Hora

1968   It/USA

DIRECTED BY: Sergio Leone
CAST: Claudia Cardinale (Jill McBain), Henry Fonda (Frank), Jason Robards (Manuel "Cheyenne" Gutierrez), Charles Bronson (Harmonica), Gabriele Ferzetti (Mr. Morton), Paolo Stoppa (Sam), Woody Strode (Stony), Jack Elam (Snaky), Marco Zuanelli (Wobbles), Benito Stefanelli (member of Frank's gang), Keenan Wynn (sheriff of Flagstone), Frank Wolff (Brett McBain), Lionel Stander (trading post owner and barman), Livio Andronico, Salvo Basile, Aldo Berti, Marilù Carteny, Luigi Ciavarro, Spartaco Conversi (member of Frank's gang shot through Cheyene's boot), Bruno Corazzari, Paolo Figlia, Stefano Imparato, Frank Leslie, Luigi Magnani, Claudio Mancini (Harmonica's elder brother), Umberto Marsella, Enrico Morsella, Tullio Palmieri, Renato Pinciroli, Conrado Sanmartin, Enzo Santaniello (Timmy McBain), Simonetta Santaniello (Maureen McBain), Sandra Salvatori, Claudio Scarchilli, Ivan Scratuglia, Fabio Testi (member of Frank's gang), Dino Zamboni; Uncredited: Al Mulock (Knuckles), John Frederick (member of Frank's gang), Dino Mele (young Harmonica), Aldo Sanbrell (member of Cheyenne's gang), Michael Harvey (Frank's aide), Raffaela and Francesca Leone (girls at Flagstone station), Luana Strode (Indian woman)
SCRIPT: Sergio Donati, Sergio Leone
STORY: Dario Argento, Bernardo Bertolucci, Sergio Leone
ENGLISH DIALOGUE: Mickey Knox
INTERIORS: Cinecittà and Luce (Rome)
EXTERIORS: Almería; Guadix; Arizona; Utah
ART DIRECTOR, SETS, AND COSTUMES: Carlo Simi
ASSISTANT SET BUILDER: Enrico Simi
FURNITURE SUPPLIERS: Cimino, Ellis Mercantile, Matheos
SET DRESSERS: Carlo Leva, Raphael Ferri
ASSISTANT SET DRESSER: Tonino Palombi
KEY GRIP: Franco Tocci
GAFFER: Alberto Ridolfi
WARDROBE: Marilù Carteny
HEAD DRESSMAKER: Valeria Sponsali
COSTUME AND FOOTWEAR SUPPLIERS: Safas, Western Costume, Antonelli, Pompei

MAKEUP SUPERVISOR: Alberto De Rossi
MAKEUP: Giannetto De Rossi
MAKEUP ASSISTANT: Feliziani Ciriaci
HAIRDRESSER: Grazia De Rossi
ASSISTANT HAIRDRESSER: Antonietta Caputo
WIGS: Rocchetti
SPECIAL EFFECTS: Eros Bacciucchi, Giovanni Corridori
STUNTS: Benito Stefanelli
DIRECTOR OF PHOTOGRAPHY: Tonino Delli Colli
PROCESS AND COLOR: Techniscope and Technicolor
CAMERA OPERATOR: Franco Di Giacomo
ASSISTANT CAMERA OPERATOR: Giuseppe Lanci
SOUND: Claudio Maielli, Elio Pacella, Fausto Ancillai
CONTINUITY: Serena Canevari
STILLS: Angelo Novi
FIRST ASSISTANT DIRECTOR: Giancarlo Santi
DIRECTOR'S ASSISTANT: Salvo Basile
PRODUCTION MANAGER: Claudio Mancini
PRODUCTION SUPERVISOR: Ugo Tucci
PRODUCTION ASSISTANTS: Camillo Teti, Manolo Amigo
PRODUCTION SECRETARY: Glauco Teti
PRODUCTION ACCOUNTANT: Raffaello Forti
NEGATIVE: Eastmancolor
EDITOR: Nino Baragli
ASSISTANT EDITORS: Andreina Casini, Carlo Reali
SOUND EFFECTS: Luciano Anzilotti
SOUND EFFECTS EDITORS: Italo Cameracanna, Roberto Arcangeli
EDITING, MIXING , AND SYNCHRONIZATION: NIS, with the participation of CDC
MUSIC: Ennio Morricone, conducted by Ennio Morricone
MUSIC EDITED AND RECORDED: RCA Italiana, S.p.A.
HARMONICA: Franco De Gemini
VOCALS: Edda Dell'Orso
WHISTLING: Alessandro Alessandrini
EXECUTIVE PRODUCER: Fulvio Morsella
PRODUCER: Bino Cicogna
PRODUCTION COMPANIES: Rafran; San Marco
DISTRIBUTED IN USA BY: Paramount (1968)

Duck, You Sucker/
A Fistful of Dynamite/
Giù La Testa/
Il était une fois la révolution/
Todesmelodie/
Agachate, Maldito!

1971   It/USA

DIRECTED BY: Sergio Leone
CAST: Rod Steiger (Juan Miranda), James Coburn (Seán Mallory), Romolo Valli (Dr. Villega), Antonio Domingo [billed as Jean Michel Antoine in English-language print] (Col. Günther Reza/Gutiérrez), David Warbeck (Seán's friend Nolan, in flashback), Maria Monti (Adelita, the woman on the coach) Rick Battaglia (Santerna), Franco Graziosi (Don Jaime, the governor) Giulio Battiferri, Poldo Bendandi (executed revolutionary), Omar Bonaro, Roy Bosier (landowner), Vivienne Chandler (Colleen), John Frederick (the American), Amato Garbini, Michael Harvey (a Yankee), Biagio La Rocca (Benito), Furio Meniconi (stage driver), Nazzareno Natale, Vincenzo Novese (Pancho), Stefano Oppedisano. Amelio [Meme] Perlini (a peon), Goffredo Pistoni (Niño), Renato Pontecchi (Pepe), Jean Rougeul (monsignor on coach), Corrado Solari (Sebastian), Benito Stefanelli, Franco Tocci, Rosito Torosh, Anthony Vernon (coach passenger); Uncredited: Antonio Casale (the notary), Franco Collace (Napoleone)
SCRIPT: Luciano Vincenzoni, Sergio Donati, Sergio Leone
ADDITIONAL DIALOGUE: Roberto De Leonardis, Carlo Tritto
STORY: Sergio Leone, Sergio Donati
INTERIORS: De Laurentiis Studios
EXTERIORS: Almería; Dublin, Howth; Wicklow; Gergal; Guadix Medinaceli
ART DIRECTOR: Andrea Crisanti
SET DECORATOR: Dario Micheli
ASSISTANT SET DECORATORS: Franco Velchi, Ezio Di Monte
FURNITURE SUPPLIERS: Cimino, Rancati
KEY GRIP: Franco Tocci
GAFFER: Massimo Massimi
COSTUMES: Franco Carretti, Tirelli, Pompei, Nathan, Western Costume
WARDROBE SUPERVISOR: Luisa Buratti
JEWELS: Nino Lembo
MAKEUP SUPERVISOR: Amato Carbini
HAIRDRESSER: Paolo Borselli
WIGS: Rochetti
ARMS AND EXPLOSIONS: Eros Baciucchi

ARMORERS: Giovanni Corridori, Tonino Palombi
SPECIAL EFFECTS: Antonio Margheriti
STUNTS: Benito Stefanelli
DIRECTOR OF PHOTOGRAPHY: Giuseppe Ruzzolini
CAMERA OPERATOR: Idelmo Simonelli
ASSISTANT CAMERA OPERATORS: Alessandro Ruzzolini, Roberto Forges Davanzati
PROCESS AND COLOR: Techniscope and Technicolor
SECOND-UNIT DIRECTORS: Giancarlo Santi, Martin Herbert [aka Alberto De Martino]
SECOND-UNIT DIRECTOR OF PHOTOGRAPHY: Franco Delli Colli
CONTINUITY: Serena Canevari
STILLS: Angelo Novi
ASSISTANT DIRECTOR: Tony Brandt
PRODUCTION MANAGER: Camillo Teti
PRODUCTION SUPERVISOR: Claudio Mancini
PRODUCTION SECRETARY: Vasco Mafera
PRODUCTION ACCOUNTANT: Raffaello Forti
NEGATIVE: Eastmancolor
EDITOR: Nino Baragli
FIRST ASSISTANT EDITOR: Rossana Maiuri
ASSISTANT EDITORS: Gino Bartolini, Olga Sarra
SYNCHRONIZATION: NIS Films, and CD
MUSIC: Ennio Morricone, conducted by Ennio Morricone
MUSIC RECORDED BY FEDERICO SAVINO AT INTERNATIONAL RECORDING STUDIOS BY: Unione Musicisti di Roma Symphony Orchestra
MUSIC PUBLISHERS: Bixio – Sam (Milan)
MIXER: Fausto Ancillai
DUBBING DIRECTOR: Giuseppe Rinaldi
SOUND EDITOR: Michael Billingsley
ASSOCIATE PRODUCERS: Claudio Mancini, Ugo Tucci
PRODUCER: Fulvio Morsella
PRODUCTION COMPANIES: Rafran Cinematografica, San Marco Films, Miura, Euro International Films
DISTRIBUTED IN USA BY: United Artists (1971)

AS PRODUCER

My Name Is Nobody/
Il Mio Nome è Nessuno   **1968   It/USA**

DIRECTED BY: Tonino Valerii
SOME SEQUENCES DIRECTED BY: Sergio Leone
CAST: Henry Fonda (Jack Beauregard), Terence Hill
(Nobody), Jean Martin (Sullivan), Leo (V.) Gordon
(Red), Neil Summers (Squirrel), R.G. Armstrong
(Honest John), Steve Kanaly (first false barber), Geoffrey
Lewis (Wild Bunch leader), Piero Lulli (sheriff), Mario
Brega (Pedro), Marc Mazzacurati (Don John), Benito
Stefanelli (Porteley of the Wild Bunch); Uncredited:
Alexander Allerson (Rex of the Wild Bunch), Franco
Angrisano (train driver), Emile Feist (real barber),
Antonio Luigi Guerra (official), Carla Mancini (mother),
Humbert Mittendorf (carnival barker), Ulrich Muller,
Angelo Novi (barman), Antonio Palombi, Remus Peets
(Big Gun), Tommy Polgar (Juan), Antoine Saint Jean/
Domingo Antoine (Scape), Antonio Molino Rojo (U.S.
army officer), Antonio De Martino (dwarf on stilts),
Claus Schmidt
SCRIPT: Ernesto Gastaldi
STORY: Fulvio Morsella, Ernesto Gastaldi, from an idea
by Sergio Leone
INTERIORS: De Paolis, Rome
EXTERIORS: Almería; New Mexico; New Orleans
ART DIRECTOR: Gianni Polidori
ASSISTANT ART DIRECTOR: Dino Leonetti
SET DRESSER: Massimo Tavazzi
KEY GRIP: Gilberto Carbonaro
COSTUMES: Vera Marzot
COSTUME SUPPLIERS: Tirelli, Western Costume
FOOTWEAR SUPPLIERS: Pompei
EQUIPMENT: Gianni Fiumi
MAKEUP: Nilo Jacoponi
HAIRDRESSER: Grazia De Rossi
WIGS: Rochetti-Carboni
SPECIAL EFFECTS AND FIREARMS: Eros Baciucchi,
Giovanni Corridori
STUNTS: Benito Stefanelli
DIRECTOR OF PHOTOGRAPHY: Giuseppe Ruzzolini
(Italy, Spain), Armando Nannuzzi (USA)
PROCESS AND COLOR: Technicolor and Panavision

CAMERA OPERATORS: Elio Polacchi, Giuseppe Berardini,
Federico Del Zoppo
CONTINUITY: Rita Agostini
STILLS: Angelo Novi
SOUND: Fernando Pescetelli
ASSISTANT DIRECTOR: Stefano Rolla
PRODUCTION SUPERVISOR: Piero Lazzari
UNIT MANAGERS: Franco Coduti, Paolo Gargano
EDITOR: Nino Baragli
ASSISTANT EDITOR: Rosanna Maiuri
SOUND EFFECTS: Roberto Arcangeli
SOUND MIXING: Fausto Ancillai
MUSIC: Ennio Morricone, conducted by Ennio Morricone
GUITAR SOLOS: Bruno Battisti D'Amario
MUSIC EDITING: General Music (Rome)
MUSIC PUBLISHER: Nazionalmusic
EXECUTIVE PRODUCER: Fulvio Morsella
PRODUCER: Claudio Mancini
PRODUCTION COMPANIES: Rafran Cinematografica
S.p.A. (Rome), Les Films Jacques Leitienne s.r.l. (Paris),
La Société Imp. Ex. Ci. (Nice), La Société Alcinter
s.r.l. (Paris), Rialto Film Preben Philipsen GMB &
Co. KG. (Berlin)
DISTRIBUTED IN USA BY: Universal (1973)

ACKNOWLEDGMENTS

At the Autry National Center, warm thanks to Marva Felchlin, project manager of the Leone exhibition project, as well as to the whole exhibition team. To John Gray, the Center's president and CEO, who believed in the project from the outset. And above all to Estella Chung, my cocurator, for her patience, level-headedness, and persistence. Thanks also to former Autry staffer Kevin Mulroy, who championed this project in its early stages.

Thanks to the many colleagues and friends of Sergio Leone who have – over the years – agreed to talk with me about his life and work, and especially Clint Eastwood, Eli Wallach, Carlo Simi, Tonino Delli Colli, Luciano Vincenzoni, Sergio Donati, Bernardo Bertolucci, Alessandro Alessandroni, and Martin Scorsese. Ennio Morricone was interviewed as part of my BBC television documentary *Viva Leone!*, directed by Nick Freand Jones; and Lee Van Cleef was interviewed by filmmaker Alex Cox. Thanks, too, to Nick and Alex, Philip Priestley, Howard Hill, Hubert Corbin, and Louise Swan, who kindly gave me various segments of unpublished interview material; to John Exshaw who helped with the filmography; to Howard Hughes who generously shared his ideas; to Maurizio Graziosi, who drew us the map; and, in Rome, to Anna-Maria Mecchia, Luca Morsella, and Elisabetta Simi and the Associazione Ricordando Carlo Simi. But most of all, the warmest possible thanks to Carla and Sergio Leone. Carla made me welcome, over many visits to the Leone family home; and Sergio not only made great films but talked with me at length about them. In the early 1980s, he was still touched and slightly amused that this particular writer was taking his work so seriously. I like to think he'd have loved this exhibition and book.

CHRISTOPHER FRAYLING
SEPTEMBER 2004

Ten gallon hats off to the Sergio Leone exhibition and book team at the Autry National Center, particularly Stephen Aron, Estella Chung, Marva Felchlin, John Gray, Marlene Head, and their colleagues. Thanks are also due to Glen Grant, Susan Van deVeyvre, Bill Grant, and Glenn Erikson, whose expertise on and enthusiasm for Leone benefited the editing of this book greatly. In addition, much appreciation to those at Harry N. Abrams who went above and beyond on behalf of *Once Upon a Time in Italy*: Eric Himmel, Deborah Aaronson, Maria Pia Gramaglia, and also the designers Prem Krishnamurthy and Adam Michaels. In addition, Sarah Lazin, Ellen Nygaard, Robert Warren, Joe Ciardiello, and Gillian Plummer offered invaluable assistance.

HOLLY GEORGE-WARREN
OCTOBER 2004

ILLUSTRATION CREDITS

Courtesy the Frayling Archive:
Pages 2, 6–7, 8, 11, 12–13, 21
(photographed by Susan Einstein,
Los Angeles, CA), 22–23, 25, 26, 28,
29, 30, 31, 32, 35, 36, 37, 39, 40–41, 42,
43 (photographed by Susan Einstein,
Los Angeles, CA), 44–45, 46, 47, 48,
50, 52–53, 54, 56, 58, 65, 66, 67, 68, 69,
72–73, 74, 75, 76, 79, 80, 87, 89, 90, 91,
92, 93, 94, 95, 96, 97, 98, 99, 100, 104,
105, 108 (left), 109, 110, 111, 112, 114,
116 (photographed by Susan Einstein,
Los Angeles, CA), 118 (photographed
by Susan Einstein, Los Angeles,
CA), 137, 138, 141, 146, 149, 150, 153,
154, 159, 163, 164–165, 167, 169, 171
(photographed by Susan Einstein, Los
Angeles, CA), 172, 173, 175, 176, 179,
181, 187, 188, 191, 193, 194 (bottom),
197, 198–199, 205, 206–207, 226–227

Courtesy the Leone Family Archive:
Pages 14, 15, 16, 20, 133, 166

Courtesy Sandro Simeoni:
cover poster illustration, pages 8, 47

Courtesy MGM Studios:
Pages 17, 18, 49, 51, 64, 99, 102, 106,
117, 140, 145, 170, 180, 183

Courtesy Warner Bros.
Entertainment, Inc.: Page 24

Courtesy Renato Casaro and
General Music: Pages 70, 71

Courtesy Paramount Pictures
(ONCE UPON A TIME IN THE
WEST © Paramount Pictures.

All Rights Reserved): Pages 11, 29,
32, 37, 55, 56, 57, 58, 118, 160, 163, 194
(bottom), 200, 202

Courtesy RCA/BMG:
Pages 92 (left), 93, 94, 98 (left)

Courtesy the Autry National Center,
Los Angeles, CA:
Pages 27, 84, 108 (right)

Courtesy United Artists:
Pages 91, 92 (right), 95, 96 (right),
98 (right)

Courtesy Ariola Records:
Page 96 (left)

Illustration courtesy Sandro Simeoni
(photographed by Susan Einstein,
Los Angeles, CA): Page 121

Courtesy the Associazione Ricordando
Carlo Simi: Pages 122, 124, 131

Courtesy Patio de Luces de la
Diputacion de Almeria; Diputacion
de Almeria; Departamento de Cultura
(photographed by Susan Einstein,
Los Angeles, CA): Pages 125, 126,
129, 142

Courtesy Carlo Leva: Pages 125, 126,
129, 142

Courtesy Motion Picture *Yojimbo*:
© 1961 Toho Co., Ltd. All Rights
Reserved/courtesy of Toshiro Mifune
Productions (photographed by Susan
Einstein, Los Angeles, CA): Page 132

Courtesy Howard Fridkin
(photographed by Susan Einstein,
Los Angeles, CA): Page 145

Courtesy Sergio Leone Productions:
Page 194 (top)

Courtesy Glen and Bill Grant
(photographed by Susan Einstein,
Los Angeles, CA): Pages 209–225

INDEX